the inside story of Australia's special forces The

Amazing

SAS

Ian McPhedran

HarperCollins*Publishers*

HarperCollins_Publishers_

First published in Australia in 2005
by HarperCollins_Publishers_ Pty Limited
ABN 36 009 913 517
A member of the HarperCollins_Publishers_ (Australia) Pty Limited Group
www.harpercollins.com.au

HarperCollins_Publishers_
25 Ryde Road, Pymble, Sydney NSW 2073, Australia
31 View Road, Glenfield, Auckland 10, New Zealand
77–85 Fulham Palace Road, London W6 8JB, United Kingdom
2 Bloor Street East, 20th Floor, Toronto, Ontario M4W 1A8, Canada
10 East 53rd Street, New York NY 10022, United States of America

National Library of Australia Cataloguing-in-Publication data:

McPhedran, Ian.
  The amazing SAS: the inside story of Australia's special forces.
  ISBN 0 7322 7981 X.
  1. Australia. Army. Special Air Service Regiment. 2. Australia.
  Army - Commando troops. I. Title. II. Title : Amazing Special
  Air Service.
358.41310994

Cover design by Stuart Horton-Stephens, Geeza Design
Cover pic of soldier: photograph by John Feder, courtesy News Limited
Map courtesy of SAS soldiers
Back cover photograph courtesy of SAS soldiers
Internal design by Katy Wright, HarperCollins Design Studio
Typeset in 11.5 on 16.5pt Bembo by Helen Beard, ECJ Australia Pty Ltd
Printed and bound in Australia by Griffin Press on 79 gsm Bulky White

5 4   05 06 07 08

For Verona and Lucy

Acknowledgments

This book would not have been written without the hard yakka, support, tolerance, professionalism and love of my wife, Verona Burgess. She not only transcribed and organised some 350 000 words of interviews, but she was my in-house editor, critic, sounding board and the brains of the outfit. The fact that we barely had a cross word throughout the twelve-month process is a tribute to her sunny disposition.

My daughter, Lucy, took the absences and lack of attention from her dad in her stride, and my stepchildren, Daniel and Jenna Cave, cheered the project on.

Convincing the powers–that–be of the value of the book was a challenge. After extensive lobbying, I finally wore down the then head of Special Operations Command, Major General Duncan Lewis. He accepted my argument that the profile of the SAS was so high that a book was inevitable and best done cooperatively. I thank him.

Former Chief of the Defence Force General Peter Cosgrove supported the concept and encouraged me.

Army chief Lieutenant General Peter Leahy was 100 per cent behind the project from day one. It was his decision to give the go-ahead and I am grateful for his enthusiasm.

Ex-SAS veteran Major Terry O'Farrell, then SAS Executive Officer, was given the unenviable task of smoothing my path into the regiment. Terry passed on valuable insights into the workings of the SASR. His terrific book *Behind Enemy Lines* was an inspiration and a handy research tool.

Another former SAS Executive Officer, Major Grant, was also extremely helpful. His knowledge and diplomatic skills opened a lot of doors.

The head of Special Operations Command, Major General Mike Hindmarsh, made it plain that he would prefer that this book not be written. Despite this, he honoured the commitment. His liaison team of Jason Logue, Gabby Turnbull, Sean Burton and Tony Park was very helpful.

Three former SAS commanding officers — Tim McOwan, Gus Gilmore and Lieutenant Colonel Rick — gave generously of their time and opened their souls to some surgical examination.

I thank Pete Tinley, Jim Truscott and Ken Webb for their wise counsel and enthusiasm, and the Army intelligence officers ('int pests') for their assistance.

David Horner's book *SAS Phantoms of War* was a fine reference work. Also useful were *Shadow Wars* by David Pugliese and *Special Operations in Iraq* by Mike Ryan.

Others who provided great support were News Limited photographer and good mate John Feder, who worked with me in East Timor, Afghanistan and Iraq and gave generously of his wonderful images, as did News Limited. Thanks to my sister Lynne, her husband Alan and my younger sister Jane, who looked after me in Perth, and my father Colin, sister Cheryl and brother-in-law Michael, and my brother Shaun.

My boss, Bruce Loudon, and my employer, News Limited, were strong supporters from the start, as were fellow journalists Mark Dodd, Lindsay Murdoch, Michelle Grattan, Ray Brindal and Paul Daley and former journos Tony Melville and Tony Hill.

The late Australian war correspondent Ron McKie inspired me to follow the craft.

Special thanks to Taur Matan Ruak, Pedro, Phil McNamara and Dr Graeme Hammond. I am grateful to Susan Crystal from the US Embassy in Canberra for facilitating my interview with US special tactics airmen. To Shona Martyn, Sophie Hamley, Alison Urquhart, Christine Farmer and the rest of the team at HarperCollins, many thanks.

Finally I offer heartfelt gratitude to all the SAS soldiers, and their families, whose names we cannot publish but who gave generously of their time and whose extraordinary deeds inspired this book.

Opinions expressed, unless otherwise stated, are mine and do not reflect the policies of the Australian government, the Australian Defence Force or individuals within them.

Ian McPhedran
Canberra, May 2005

Contents

Making the Cut

East Timor

At Home

Afghanistan

Iraq

GLOSSARY

1 SAS	1 SAS Squadron
2IC	Second in command
2RAR	2nd Battalion Royal Australian Regiment
2 SAS	2 SAS Squadron
3RAR	3rd Battalion Royal Australian Regiment
3 SAS	3 SAS Squadron
ADF	Australian Defence Force
AO	Area of operation
ASLAV	Australian Light Armoured Vehicle
Cams	Camouflage gear
Cantonment	Base area for troops or fighters
CBR	Chemical, biological or nuclear weapons
CDF	Chief of the Defence Force
Civpol	Civilian police
CLU	Command launch unit
CNRT	National Council of Timorese Resistance
CT	Counterterrorism
DS	Directing Staff of SAS selection
DSD	Defence Signals Directorate
Falintil	Army for the National Liberation of East Timor
FOB	Forward operating base
GPS	Global positioning system
Helo	helicopter
Hide	Another term for observation post (OP)
Humint	Human intelligence
IDP	Internally displaced person
IED	Improvised explosive device
INTERFET	UN International Force for East Timor
IRF	Immediate Reaction Force
JDAM	Joint direct attack munitions
JIRU	Joint Incident Response Unit
KIA	Killed in action
Kopassus	Indonesian special forces
LO	Liaison officer
LRPV	Long Range Patrol Vehicles
LUP	Lying up position

Medevac	Medical evacuation
Medkit	Medical kit
MEI	Mission essential items
MREs	Meals Ready to Eat
NCO	Non-commissioned officer
NVG	Night-vision gear
OP	Observation post
Picquet	Guard duty
POW	Prisoner of war
RAAF	Royal Australian Air Force
RAEME	Royal Australian Electrical and Mechanical Engineers
RHIB	Rigid Hull Inflatable Boat
RMC	Royal Military College, Duntroon
RPG	Rocket-propelled grenade
RSM	Regimental Sergeant Major
RV	Rendezvous point
SASR	Special Air Service Regiment
SBS	Special Boat Service (UK)
SEK	Survivability enhancement kit
SF	Special forces
Sigint	Electronic signals intelligence
Sitrep	Situation report
SOC	Special Operations Command
SR	Surveillance and reconnaissance
STS	Special tactics squadron (US)
SUV	Sports utility vehicle
TAG	Tactical assault group
TNI	Indonesian Armed Forces
Troop-plus	Troop plus one or more extra members
UBA	Unauthorised Boat Arrival
UN	United Nations
UNAMET	United Nations Mission in East Timor
Unimog	All-wheel drive truck
UNTAET	UN Transitional Authority in East Timor
USAF	US Air Force
WMD	Weapons of mass destruction

Preface

My first close encounter with the men of the SAS was in 1996, when fifteen perished, along with three Army aviators, after two Black Hawk helicopters crashed during a night training exercise.

Reporting on the story, I came to admire these mysterious soldiers and the dangerous work they do. The fuse for this book was lit.

Late in 1999, photographer John Feder and I were in Bobonaro in the mountains of East Timor, close to the West Timor border, on patrol with an Infantry section. We found ourselves in what looked like an office in the main street of the town. Inside, two Australian soldiers were armed with unusual, nonstandard-issue weapons and we guessed they were SAS men, but they disappeared out a back door without a word.

Some time later at SAS headquarters at Campbell Barracks in Swanbourne, Perth, I met one of the soldiers and, recognising him, reminded him of the encounter. He gave me a knowing grin, but didn't want to talk about it. We would meet again in 2002 on a charter jet carrying SAS reinforcements and gear to the war in Afghanistan. Again, conversation was minimal.

During that same Afghanistan trip, John and I were eating in a huge United States mess hall at Bagram air base, north of Kabul. At another table sat a bunch of bearded, long-haired men, some dressed in shorts, chatting and laughing. They were Australian SAS troops enjoying some time off in between patrols in the mountains of eastern Afghanistan.

It was the shorts that gave the game away again, this time in Iraq in April 2003, when the vehicle I was sharing with an ABC TV crew approached an SAS checkpoint on Highway One to the west of the Euphrates River. The Aussie accents were a welcome break on the hazardous road trip from Jordan to Baghdad. We tried to talk to them, but they refused and sent us packing.

I discovered later that concealed SAS troops had, eleven days earlier, watched my car speed down the same highway in the opposite direction, after another journalist and I were expelled from Iraq by the dying regime of Saddam Hussein.

The theme running through these encounters was the mystery of these men. What were they up to in these obscure corners of the world?

Some of the soldiers I have encountered in faraway places are featured in this book. Every quote is genuine, chosen from dozens of interviews conducted during 2004. The soldiers and commanders of the SAS Regiment have made it clear to me that they do not consider themselves heroes, nor do they think of their actions as particularly outstanding or amazing.

Their humour, intelligence and professionalism shone through in all our conversations and, I hope, also shine through these pages, which span the regiment's operations from East Timor to Iraq, 1999 to 2003.

This is their story.

COUNCIL OF WAR

Nerves were taut as two American helicopters descended through pale moonlight into the ancient city of Kandahar for a historic council of war.

Australia's top special forces soldier, Lieutenant Colonel Peter 'Gus' Gilmore, the commanding officer of the Special Air Service Regiment, was one of a select group of men on board. For an hour they had flown low and fast across the barren landscape of southern Afghanistan, away from the coalition forces' forward operating base, 'Rhino', towards Kandahar, the country's second biggest city.

The modified Chinook special-operations helicopters had just reached the outskirts of the city when Gilmore heard a loud bang and saw sparks spewing from the back of the machine. He thought they had been hit by ground fire.

'It took me a couple of seconds to realise we were still flying, so of course we weren't hit,' Gilmore says now.

It was only a backfire, but it frightened the living daylights out of him and the others on board the blacked-out chopper. Machine gunners at the rear ramp and side doors anxiously scanned the eerie, softly lit land below.

United States Marine commander Brigadier General James Mattis — the commanding officer of Task Force 58, the task group formed to secure southern Afghanistan — had invited Gilmore along for his first meeting with anti-Taliban leader Hamid Karzai.

'I'm going to go up tonight to speak with Hamid Karzai in Kandahar about how we will prosecute the plan that we've been putting in place,' Mattis had said to Gilmore. 'And I'd like you to come with me.'

The general had been contemplating how he would occupy Kandahar when a message came through from a US special forces team accompanying Karzai, saying that he would be in town on this night. Earlier in the campaign the same American team had narrowly escaped annihilation when a misdirected bomb had landed. A number of Americans had been killed and the commander, a lieutenant colonel, was still deaf in both ears when he met the general's delegation.

'He had seen his sergeant, five feet in front of him, just disappear in a puff of smoke because the bomb had literally landed 20 metres in front and they'd lost half the team, just like that,' says Gilmore.

Mattis, a straight-talking officer in the Marine Corps tradition, had already decided he wanted to enter Kandahar peacefully and be welcomed by the long-suffering locals, rather than going in all guns blazing and risking further civilian losses.

'He knew that they would have to live there and therefore that how you occupy would be critical to the ongoing success of the forward operating base, and, in turn, operations in the south.'

The helicopters touched down at one o'clock in the morning in what appeared to be a park on the outskirts of town.

It was early December 2001, not quite three months since Osama bin Laden's al Qaeda terrorist group had flown two planes into the World Trade Center in New York and a third into the Pentagon, while a fourth, probably on its way to the White House, had crashed in Pennsylvania. More than 3000 people died in the worst terrorist attack in history on that day, 11 September 2001.

On 20 September, US President George W Bush addressed both houses of Congress and declared the so-called War on Terror. America then unleashed her military might against the Taliban regime of Afghanistan, which was harbouring bin Laden and his al Qaeda fighters.

As the helicopters flew into Kandahar, a city which had been in the hands of allied Northern Alliance forces for just 36 hours, the area around the international airport was still being contested by pockets of Taliban resistance. Two four-wheel-drive vehicles manned by the special forces operators waited to take the Marine commander and his Australian offsider into the city.

Kandahar, Afghanistan's major trading centre, was founded by Alexander the Great in the fourth century BC. The Pashtun city has been fought over every few centuries ever since. It fell to the Islamic fundamentalist Taliban in 1992.

As the vehicles drove quietly through the city's narrow and deserted streets towards the former palace of Taliban leader Mullah Omar, Gilmore thought it was like a scene from a movie. But this was not a Hollywood production, and he knew that down any one of the narrow alleys could be someone willing to kill him.

Gus Gilmore had been commanding officer of the SAS since January 2001. An intense and quite formal officer, the father of three is regarded as one of the finest strategic thinkers ever to have worn the sand-coloured beret and winged-dagger badge of the SAS Regiment.

For this mission he was heavily armed, clad in body armour and ready to fight. 'There were shady figures in the middle of the night, wearing their black garb, standing around street corners and down little alleys. You're always conscious of the fact that there's a vulnerability, but you get on with it,' he says.

Once they reached the palace compound, Gilmore, General Mattis and the other American officer on the trip, a US special forces commander, were given a guided tour by a member of Karzai's staff. In the moonlight the bomb damage was obvious.

They finally entered a gaslit room. There was Karzai with about eight advisers and bodyguards. Also present was Karzai's appointed governor for the region, Sharzai. The floor was covered with beautiful Afghan rugs and cushions, and as they settled down in the traditional surroundings, the modern-day chiefs of war were served pistachio nuts and black tea.

'There was nothing particularly formal about it. It was almost, "Well, we're here", and the meeting began,' Gilmore recalls.

Karzai welcomed them, telling Mattis that the reputation alone of the US Marines was worth 10 000 men. The cultured and well-educated

Afghan then told the group the story of the offensive from the north and the capture of Kandahar.

'He was genuinely pleased to lift the scourge of the Taliban, who had persecuted his people for so long. He was very bitter against the Taliban and clearly optimistic and hopeful of a better life for Afghanis. It was incredibly interesting hearing Hamid Karzai talk as a military commander about how they had just taken Kandahar — his elation, I suppose, plus the fact that things were turning out well for him at the time.'

After a while the conversation became less formal and the others began telling their stories. Gilmore was fascinated by the tales of this ragtag army sweeping down from the fabled northwest frontier, using taxis and whatever else they could get hold of to carry their fighters. He was seated next to a bearded warrior aged about forty-five who had skin like leather, a battered face and the toughest hand he had ever shaken. The man, who didn't speak much English, had been liberated from a Taliban prison a few weeks earlier after years in custody and his tales of torture sent a chill down Gilmore's spine.

'Their favourite was to tie them up essentially on a crucifix so that their arms were outstretched and they were standing up,' he says. 'Then the guards would stand behind them and just push them forwards so they'd land flat on their face on the ground. They'd do this over and over again.'

Women prisoners were tied up and placed in containers, then their feet were beaten with sticks.

'He told me he couldn't get the sound of their screams out of his head.'

After about three hours in Kandahar it was time for General Mattis and Colonel Gilmore to leave the historic meeting and fly back to Rhino.

'In some ways it was quite surreal. Here we were in the middle of the night in Afghanistan, in this town that had been overtaken, sitting in this environment with a gaslit lantern. It was, I suppose, one of the privileges of command to have that exposure early on,' Gilmore states.

They left before dawn and arrived at Rhino just as the sun was rising. Gilmore rang Canberra on a satellite phone to report the meeting and to outline plans for his SAS task group to move into Kandahar.

A small advance element was sent to Kandahar International Airport the next day. When Gilmore arrived at the airport terminal to establish his headquarters, he chose a room just two doors away from Mattis.

The squadron moved into a wing of the Kandahar hospital, a shell structure with no doors and few windows which, like so many buildings in the struggling country, had no water, no power and no sewerage. The soldiers set about connecting a few luxuries, including hot showers and a 'choofa' or water boiler. The twelve rooms would be the squadron's home for the next two months, until they moved north to the old Russian air base at Bagram, near Kabul.

In the meantime, General Mattis and, subsequently, the head of the Combined Task Force, Major General John Vines, would use the Australian SAS to conduct very complex tasks. The regiment never faltered, despite working in a situation of extreme mortal danger.

As one seasoned SAS soldier, Warrant Officer Steve, puts it, 'We knew for a fact that if you got caught by al Qaeda there, you were toast.'

Over that year in Afghanistan, the SAS patrols provided the highest levels of military leadership with some of the most vital intelligence on the movements of al Qaeda and Taliban forces. They discovered detailed terrorist training manuals, the location of former al Qaeda training camps, weapons caches and strategic routes. They also engaged in some of the most deadly encounters and cunning manoeuvres of the War on Terror.

As Mattis himself would write later, 'We Marines would happily storm Hell itself with your troops on our right flank.'

An American general had dared — and Australia's hand-picked, best-trained diggers would win.

MAKING THE CUT

Chapter 1

A LUCKY DIP

The young soldier could not sit still.

His eyes darted skywards and then downwards as he shuffled his feet around, pushing back in his chair and then leaning forward.

It was September 2004. Private Bruce had just completed the most gruelling weeks of his life and the moment of truth was at hand.

This is where it all starts for the elite members of Australia's Special Air Service Regiment: the pain and hardship of the infamous SAS selection course.

As Private Bruce waited to find out whether or not he had passed, his small, skinny frame as tight as a spring, he looked more like a naughty schoolboy waiting to see the headmaster than one of Australia's best soldiers-to-be. The SAS selection process does this to men.

'Most people fail through lack of self belief and the mind bit,' says SAS veteran Major Terry O'Farrell. 'All sorts of mind games go on during selection. They self select out. We sack very few people; they sack themselves.'

Since 1968, thousands of men have attempted the selection course; just 36 per cent have made it into the regiment. For days on end, the course supervisors deprive the participants of some of life's basic necessities — food, sleep and recognition. They march hundreds of kilometres through rough country, carrying almost unbearable loads. They are called upon to make snap decisions and solve problems, and are pushed harder and further than they ever thought possible — and then pushed some more.

All the while they come under the eagle eyes of experienced SAS members — the Directing Staff (DS), as they are called — who do not provide even the smallest amount of feedback, not one hint as to how the men are faring. Attempts to wheedle comments out of the DS are met with an impassive, neutral response — the DS merely repeat their instructions or ignore the question. They keep watch day and night, observing everything, making notes in their small field notebooks, marking up what are called 'speeding tickets' with red and black ink (red is not good).

Even before being admitted to the selection course, though, would-be SAS soldiers have to pass two hurdles after they apply.

The first is the Special Forces Paper Board, the initial screening of candidates to ensure that they are psychologically and medically fit to join the SAS, and that they demonstrate potential for service in Australia's special forces.

About 80 per cent of applicants then go on to the second hurdle: the Special Forces Entry Test (previously called the 'barrier test'). This is a series of physical and psychological tests involving 60 push-ups; 100 sit-ups; 10 heaves; a 2.4-kilometre run in uniform with 7 kilograms of webbing plus a rifle in 12 minutes or less; a run; a dodge; a jump test in uniform in under 50 seconds; and a 400-metre swim in uniform and runners in under 18 minutes after treading water for 2 minutes. There is also a navigation theory test and a 15-kilometre endurance march carrying a 20-kilogram pack, 7 kilograms of webbing and a rifle, which has to be completed in under 2 hours and 40 minutes.

About 80 to 85 per cent of the men pass this test. From there they go on to the SAS selection course itself, which has only a 25 to 30 per cent pass rate and is designed to emulate actual combat stresses as best as can be done during peacetime.

'I think for years a lot of people saw the selection as physical stuff,' says course convenor Captain Gary. 'But with the deprivation of food, deprivation of sleep, people react differently under those circumstances, you know, and all those sort of things start to play and they play on people's minds. That's when we see the person who may have a temper, for instance, and because things aren't quite going his way he'll actually snap. And we pick that sort of thing up, where we've got to remember we're training, or selecting, SAS soldiers to do stuff that the rest of the army, the conventional forces, aren't able to — we need those people who can continually handle those sorts of pressures.'

The selectors start with the body, then reach into the soul to get to the nitty-gritty of the man.

Terry O'Farrell served in the SAS for thirty-eight years on and off, including two gruelling tours of duty to Vietnam, and he knows a thing or two about the sort of bloke who will make the grade. He believes the physical aspect is overplayed. Rather, he rates mental toughness and an ability to work in a small team as the crucial attributes for an SAS soldier or officer.

O'Farrell, who retired from the regiment in September 2004, says most candidates fail through a lack of self belief: 'There is no program issued, you have to be ready to go all the time and do whatever is thrown at you. People can't cope with that because they are living in a chaotic world, they like things to be neat and tidy. No feedback, for example — everyone wants a pat on the back. The only communications with staff are directions. Do this or do that, there is no debrief, just get on with it.

'This builds up in a bloke's mind. He will say, "I don't know how I am going, I have no idea." All of a sudden things get a bit tough, he won't know how much further he has got to go and he will say to himself, "I am not doing any good in this, fuck it, I am out."'

The selection course replicates conditions on a mission, where the men don't know what is going to happen next. Of those who quit, many do so within metres or minutes of their goal — not knowing that they are so close to the end.

So how does a soldier cope under strains that would break most men? Can he make a rational or even creative decision under severe duress? Can he see the funny side of even the darkest situation? These are the vital tests that are applied to the candidates who believe they have what it takes.

Once they make it through selection, most survive the following months of intense reinforcement training — known as 'Reo' — before they join an active squadron. The few who do not make it through the reinforcement training are usually lacking situational awareness, says O'Farrell. For example, during a team live-fire exercise they tend to suffer from tunnel vision, seeing what is in front but not what is going on around them. 'That makes them dangerous,' he says.

'Who Dares Wins' is the SAS motto, and in the rough scrub of the Bindoon army base northeast of Perth, a group of young Australian men are coming to the end of the biggest dare of their lives.

The Bindoon camp includes live-fire ranges, training areas and the SAS mock-up area which is, in effect, a small town, with a large 'embassy' building and two multi-storey sniper towers. Here, numerous hostage dramas and other scenarios are played out and resolved by the crack troops as they train for just about any situation.

Adding to the sense of the absurd — a vital ingredient for an SAS soldier — are the names of the exercises that candidates are forced to endure: 'Lone Warrior', 'Happy Wanderer' and 'Lucky Dip'. For the last few days of every SAS selection course, Bindoon hosts the notorious Lucky Dip.

On the second-last day of the course, one patrol of exhausted, hungry and unwashed diggers plods into a 'guerrilla' camp, to be greeted by the so-called 'chief' of the local militia (in reality, a senior SAS soldier). A no-nonsense character speaking in a strange accent, carrying a hessian bag and a large timber staff, the chief gives the exhausted soldiers their next orders.

To reach this point the small patrols of would-be recruits have already endured weeks of physical and emotional duress. On this course they have been whittled down to just 30 per cent of the original candidates. These men have been on the go for weeks and for the last two days have not slept or eaten a hot meal. Now, under the watchful eye of the chief, they are ordered to carry a difficult, heavy load to a position some kilometres away, through the bush.

These soldiers are the cream of the crop, but they are having difficulty coming up with a rational plan to move the heavy load. It isn't easy to divide. What's more, the chief has said that the sentries — the guards positioned in front of and behind the patrol — must keep their arms free to be able to use their weapons.

The patrol starts planning how to tackle the tricky task but they are given only a couple of minutes. 'Let's move!' the chief says suddenly.

The patrol commander (one of the candidates) issues his orders. Several men will carry part of the load, the sentries will carry none and they will move in stages. The men are humping a massive all-up load of up to 80 kilograms per soldier. One man thinks he has discovered a clever shortcut, which he keeps secret from his fellow patrol members, hoping to use it for his benefit alone. But unbeknownst to him, he has been set up. His act of selfishness will earn him a red mark and count against him in his final assessment.

To cap it off, this patrol fails to solve the brain-teaser — a closely guarded regimental secret — and therefore takes much longer and expends much more energy than is necessary. They have already been on the go solidly for 48 hours, lifting and carrying various loads.

This Lucky Dip is a 'silent running' exercise, so two 'guerrillas' control the activity and the two SAS observers, watching the soldiers' every move, are banned from communicating with them at all.

About a kilometre into the task the open scrub is replaced by dense 'parrot' bush, a yellow wildflower native to Western Australia whose sharp serrated leaves add to the torture of carrying the 80-kilogram load.

It takes the patrol three and a half hours to cover the 3 kilometres and arrive at the edge of a muddy dam. Here they are presented with empty oil drums, timber poles and long ropes, and told to make a raft on which to float their loads to the other side.

The Lucky Dippers confer. Several minutes later they set about wrapping their packs in waterproof shelters, or 'hoochies' as they are called in the army. Several men are selected to ferry their packs across the dam. The packs themselves float, but the exhausted troops, still wearing clothes and boots, have to wade and swim their way across, steering the packs to the far side. They squelch ashore through the mud and unwrap the gear while they wait to help pull the makeshift raft across.

The rest of the patrol gets on with lashing the poles to the drums to make the craft. They load the precious cargo, then plunge in to push the raft across the dam. Some appear to find the muddy dip a relief, clothes and all, after days without washing, while others cast weary glances at the sinking sun and contemplate the long, cold night ahead lying up in the bush soaked to the skin.

Just when they think they have finished, a voice booms across the dam: 'What about me?'

It is the chief, still sitting propped up with his wooden staff on the far bank; the patrol has forgotten its human cargo. Their faces fall — more red marks. They do not have to go back for him, though — he hitches a ride across on the safety boat — but as soon as he steps ashore, dry, comfortable and swaggering, he announces, 'You have two minutes before we move.'

As they shoulder their loads once more and stagger back towards the bush, the chief approaches the regimental doctor, who is standing by in case of injury, and tells him that one of the men has been cadging painkillers off his mates — each soldier carries painkillers. The soldier has crushed his thumb at some stage but is enduring the pain for fear of another red mark.

The doctor calls the digger over and examines his thumb.

'You can either have more painkillers or I can puncture the nail to relieve the build-up of blood,' he says.

'Just do it, doc!' comes the reply.

The minor surgery takes about 30 seconds, bringing the soldier instant relief. 'Aaah, that's great, doc, thanks,' he says and rejoins his patrol.

One of the candidates, Signaller Brendan, has been on sentry duty as part of the patrol. As a signaller — or 'chook', as they are called — and a member of the 152 Signal Squadron, a part of the SAS Regiment at Swanbourne, he knew better than most candidates what to expect from the gruelling selection course. But the soaked and exhausted digger admits that he is starting to feel the strain.

'The last couple of days have been the hardest. I mean, it has been a hard course overall, but the last couple of days have been really challenging after being worn down over the last few weeks,' he says. Yet despite his condition, the super-fit thirty year old remains focused: 'My first goal is the challenge of trying to finish the course, and the second goal is to move on, further my career and do all the courses. I really want to move on, I don't want to go back and say that I failed this course. I want to put in my best effort and know that in myself I did everything I possibly could, 100 per cent every time.'

Moving on means being able to wear the regiment's sand-coloured beret and winged-dagger badge and proceed to the following months of intensive training, before qualifying to join one of the three SAS 'sabre', or operational, squadrons.

However, Brendan is not thinking of that just now. In the final stages of the selection course, food fantasies are dominating any spare thoughts.

'I just said to the boys before, I want to go to a coffee shop and get a latte and just have a big cream cake, chocolate and just eat absolutely everything. The way to a man's fuckin' heart is through his stomach,' Brendan says. 'I am trying to block it out because it would just drive me crazy at the moment. Last night, before we zoned, passed out and slept, we were just thinking about food.'

The single digger from Melbourne is under no illusions about what is at stake: 'It's the best thing you can do in the Army. If you want to aim for the top, I mean, this is it. All the courses you can get to do. It is a challenge to yourself. There is a money incentive, but that is not the major factor.'

If he is selected? 'We will be out for some champagne — or, in my case, coffee and cake.' And if not? 'You will get the psych debrief and be pretty shattered.'

Later that evening the Lucky Dip patrols are given their first square — and, more importantly, hot — meal in more than two days. The steaming stew of pig's head, lambs' brains, tripe, red and green eggs, and a variety of unidentified vegetable matter has been prepared by gleeful and imaginative cooks back at the headquarters kitchen. This meal, designed to look as unappetising as possible, is an important test for the candidates, as any reluctance to bog into the hideous-looking but sweet-smelling creation will be frowned upon. At least this brew does not include whole chickens (feathers and all) which have featured on other selection courses.

As soon as the 'hot box', which stores the surprise dish, is opened the air around it becomes black with bush flies, but the men don't care. They almost dive in head first, each scooping up a serve of the brew and slicing off pieces of the pig's head with their field knives.

'This rubbery stuff tastes like soft crackling,' one of the diggers mumbles in ecstasy, the offal hanging out of his mouth as he gobbles it up. What he is chewing on is a lump of slimy tripe, but it may as well be a gourmet delicacy.

After ten minutes of ravenous consumption the feast is over, the twilight silence broken only by the buzz of flies and the loud burps of some very satisfied young men. Never has a hot meal tasted so good or had such an uplifting impact on morale. As Brendan recalls, 'It was just so soothing to sit there and have a hot meal. You take those things for granted. It's not until you do an activity like that that you appreciate little comforts like a hot meal.'

Two days later the final group of candidates is back at SAS headquarters at Swanbourne, near Perth, for the last hurdle in their quest for selection — the final Board of Studies. The soldiers' fate is decided in the headquarters conference room, where a group of SAS officers and senior soldiers have gathered to mull over each man's performance and to pass judgment on the borderline cases.

The board is run by the commander of the Special Forces Training Centre at Singleton in New South Wales, SAS veteran Lieutenant

Colonel Mark Smethurst. His father, Major General Neville Smethurst, was commanding officer of the SAS Regiment from 1973 to 1976 and pioneered the officer selection course (there are separate courses for officers and soldiers).

The training centre is independent of the regiment; it is subcontracted by the regiment to monitor the selection process and is basically there to keep the SAS honest. The final decision about whether or not a borderline case is in or out rests squarely with the SAS commanding officer, Lieutenant Colonel Rick.

In the conference room, they deal with the soldiers first. Each candidate's file flashes up on a screen, with a photograph, his name, age, regiment (all are serving members of the Australian Defence Force) and a detailed spreadsheet covering his performance. Each facet of the course as undertaken by the candidate is presented on screen and colour-coded. Green means pass, yellow just failed, and red a clear fail.

The course tests a range of attributes, with key requirements focused on self-discipline, confidence and teamwork. Individual performance is graded at either 'well below standard', 'below standard', 'at the standard required', 'above standard' or 'excellent'.

Each attribute is carefully defined and linked with a set of associated behaviours.

'Self-discipline', for example, is defined as 'the ability to control and direct one's activities to achieve a desired outcome'. Its associated behaviours are 'controlled aggression, patience, tolerance, calm/anger, ethical options and immoral options'. An excellent candidate in terms of self-discipline, for example, is 'able to use humour to lift morale, aggressive when required, calm, patient and persevering, and able to develop and maintain rapport with all team members'.

The performance of each candidate on all phases of the course is assessed and marked in detail. Soldiers can get through with some yellow on their sheets, but for officers it is either red or green — pass or fail — and they have had to endure an extra 'officer's module' to boot. An SAS officer is required to function at a much higher level than a soldier, so the extra module assesses additional leadership characteristics plus offensive operations skills. The assessors are particularly interested in how officer candidates might respond to dynamic situations.

All the men in the room for the final Board of Studies, including the regimental psychologist, can have their say. This is Rick's last turn in the judge's chair, as he has finished his two years as commander and is about to be promoted from the regiment to a job in Canberra.

A deep thinker, Rick weighs up all the information before him and the comments from those around him as he makes the Caesar-like call on several 'yellow' candidates who could go either way. In most cases his thumb points up. He is prepared to give them a go because he regards them as 'trainable'. But some of the assessors make highly critical comments about these candidates. Rick listens for a while, then turns around and says to the whole room, 'Think back to how you went on selection.'

There is a moment of reflection as each man remembers his individual hell and his own shortcomings. The loudest of the critics fall silent. Others laugh nervously at the memory: 'Bloody good point, it was terrible.' From then on, they see what Rick is getting at when he assesses a candidate as a 'pass with strong counselling and further assessment' or 'after selection we still don't know this guy'. Thus, each candidate is given every opportunity to be selected by a rigorous and fair process, overseen by a compassionate man.

'It is always tough to make the big calls,' Rick says afterwards. 'No one can say they have been dealt with unfairly. We owe them a good and fair assessment.'

Former SAS operations officer Pete Tinley passed selection twice, first as a soldier in 1983 and again as an officer in 1992, and says, 'The SAS selection course — there's a whole lot of myth and crap about it. [It's] often seen as purely a hurdle which people jump over. What people miss is, having been on them and run them — I used to run them as a senior instructor in the reinforcement wing — it is also the launching point from which personal growth is built within an individual to allow them to undertake the next level of excellence.'

He says the foundation block for the SAS is the individual. 'A lot of people say, "Oh, it's meant to be all about teamwork." Yeah, but if you . . . enhance the qualities that pre-exist, and give them the skills, then they will join a team. They commit themselves to teamwork because they will not want to [let] anybody else down, not least of which is themselves. So you work on the individual to understand how can they continually contribute and participate.'

The new recruits' commitment to operating in small teams with specialist skills will come under the microscope for the duration of SAS basic training, which focuses on the jungle environment, with a growing emphasis on the high-technology equipment carried by the modern special forces soldier. Surveillance and reconnaissance patrolling remains the core skill of an SAS soldier. They must be able to work alone or in small groups for long periods of time, feeding vital information back to commanders. The ability to operate in an urban environment and in a counter terrorist capacity comes when they are appointed to one of the three 'sabre' squadrons.

Most of the applicants are in their mid to late twenties, although on this course there was one forty-one year old who lasted a week before his body let him down.

'You could say it's probably a young man's game, realistically. When I say "young man", I mean up to thirty-five,' says course convenor Captain Gary.

Tinley says there is a moment of truth for every individual on the selection course.

'It might be three o'clock in the morning or five o'clock in the afternoon, bashing your shins through the bush, that you'll — and most blokes do this — you put your pack on the ground and you sit on it and you just cry — "Fucking can't handle this". And there's that cathartic point or that watershed point where you just go, "No. They're going to have to take me off this course on a stretcher — I'm not giving up. I can do this." That is, then, the single point of commitment to this concept of SAS . . . that individual commitment to the organisation, and that builds people forever.'

He believes it is just not possible to pick the winners, those who will dig deep and find that inner strength, before the course starts.

'It's mental, it's purely mental. I've seen 170 people line up in a road at the start of a selection course and even the oldest, gnarliest warrant officer cannot tell you with any guarantee who's going to get in. And you have guys who are porky, skinny, absolutely peak of physical conditioning — Army PTI [physical training instructor] or something like that — and all sorts of shapes and sizes, and you just can't pick it. Because the one thing you can't pick — there's no pen and paper test for desire, other than just putting the torch to it and seeing if it's really keen.'

The best analogy he can think of is elite athletes.

'The professional sportsman or Olympian, they just live and breathe their sport, it's such an intense period of [their lives]. You say, "This is the only single focus in my life and everything else is secondary, including [my] family, till I achieve this goal." And then you train, eat, sleep, think nothing else but this.'

After two and a half hours of deliberation, the final judgments on the diggers are made and it is time to notify the worn-out candidates of the outcome. On this course the success rate has been below the overall average of 26 to 27 per cent.

For those who are not selected it is a world of pain; the look of disappointment and despair on their pale, drawn faces is a moving sight, and for the moment they are inconsolable.

'We warn them [up] front, survival is not enough,' Captain Gary says. 'You've still got to show us. And throughout this week we can pick the guys who are [just] surviving, usually pretty accurately. They're the ones who aren't actually doing a lot of the physical work, who'll never contribute to the team, they're just there and hopefully at the end they think they'll get through. But we can usually pick those people out.'

One soldier who does not make it is thirty years old and on his third attempt. The SAS is not for him and he is told not to apply again. But a consolation prize awaits: he is invited to join the army's other special forces unit, the Commandos.

Some are told that they may reapply. Others who 'failed to show initiative' or who were 'ineffective leaders' have their files marked 'Not to Reapply'.

By contrast, the successful candidates will take days to wipe the smiles off their faces.

Soon after eating his lunch — the best feed he reckons he ever had — Signaller Brendan marches into Captain Gary's office braced for the worst.

'Take a seat. How do you reckon you went?' the officer teases.

'I think I went okay,' the soldier says, but he is clearly not confident.

'Well, congratulations. You have passed selection.' Captain Gary extends a large hand to the regiment's newest recruit.

The soldier skips out of the office. Flying high on the good news, the thirty year old says he doesn't know whether to laugh or cry.

'I feel just like laughing and cheering and almost crying. It is an awesome feeling, especially after Lucky Dip. It exceeded every boundary I have ever done before, it was harder and I exceeded the point of no return. It was through group effort, because there were a lot of times where you really feel like giving up and you look at the other guys and they are just as buggered as you, and you know that they won't be able to complete that exercise if you drop out. It helps you go on.'

Even when the course was virtually over, he says, there was no let-up.

'We carried an extremely heavy stretcher through the bush and down a road. Your legs are wobbly, breathing hyperventilating almost, your heart's just doing crazy things, starting to get dizzy. Just had three minutes' rest and a truck rocked up. He said there was a whole heap of stores in the back and, "I want you to carry them a long distance to get to the hospital." Your heart just sort of drops through your boots and we went around to the back of the truck reluctantly to get these stores and there were the other guys in the truck! That is another point where emotions just blow over you and you think, "Holy shit, that's the end and we are getting in the truck."'

Even during the two-hour bus ride from Bindoon back to Swanbourne, none of the candidates had put on a confident face. At first they were all simply happy that the ordeal was over, but then one by one they fell silent, thinking of the final challenge ahead with the Board of Studies. They bumped along in the truck, mulling over how they had gone and what the final decision would be. Occasionally someone spoke up.

'I think I stuffed up here.'

'I don't think I did the right thing. I argued too much.'

Then they stopped talking again.

Brendan knows that the way ahead as an SAS trooper will be difficult and dangerous, and he is under no illusions about what will be required.

'When you join the Army you have to prepare for the fact that your job is going to be going into action. I am not 100 per cent keen on it, but I won't shy away when the time comes. It is my job, I am a professional soldier, and I am prepared to do whatever has to be done.'

For now, though, his mood is one of sheer joy: 'I am over the moon, the world is my oyster at the moment and all I can see is sunshine ahead.' He plans to share his good news with his dad, an engineer who hasn't been thrilled by his son's career choice, and then it will be back to the grindstone. Brendan's immediate goal is to put back on the 10 kilograms of bodyweight that he has shed during the course before he enters the reinforcement cycle so he can qualify for the sand-coloured SAS beret and winged-dagger badge.

While Brendan is looking happily to his future, Private Bruce is still twitching nervously in his seat. Then he is called into the room for the verdict. The skinny, nerve-racked young Chinese-Australian, who speaks five languages, turns out to have been the most outstanding candidate of the course. He will become the first Australian of Asian parentage to join the SAS Regiment. A new era has begun.

EAST TIMOR

Chapter 2

SPITFIRE

On 26 August 1999, Lieutenant Colonel Tim McOwan was driving up a freeway to Lopburi, a Thai special forces training camp north of Bangkok.

McOwan, the commanding officer of the SAS at that time, was booked to give a lecture to the Thai National Security Command on emerging forms of terrorism. Beside him sat his boss, Brigadier Phil McNamara, the then head of Australia's Special Forces.

Suddenly their mobile phones started ringing. On the other end of McOwan's was Gus Gilmore, calling from headquarters in Sydney. The top brass wanted both men back in Australia pronto. McOwan was to go straight to Swanbourne, the home of the SAS regiment in Perth. He did not have to guess why.

East Timor had been a thorn in the side of Australia's relationship with Indonesia since the latter invaded the former Portuguese colony in December 1975. Successive Australian governments under Gough Whitlam, Malcolm Fraser, Bob Hawke and Paul Keating had supported the Indonesian occupation of the province in order to prevent what was described, in official policy documents, as the 'Balkanisation' of the world's largest Muslim country. They feared the island nation could fracture into non-viable mini-states. But it was an uneasy situation: Australians had fought alongside the Timorese against the Japanese during World War II, and many war veterans and ordinary Australian people were opposed to the occupation.

Matters had come to a head in May 1999, when the then Indonesian president, BJ Habibie, agreed to a plan mooted by the Prime

Minister of Australia, John Howard, to allow the East Timorese to vote on their future. Howard had hoped that the move towards autonomy would travel at a slow pace, and he was surprised when Habibie proposed an immediate 'independence' ballot. It was to be held on 30 August. But the situation in East Timor deteriorated throughout 1999, and by August militia mobs, backed by Indonesian troops, were rampaging throughout the province, murdering and terrorising people opposed to Indonesian rule.

As early as February 1999 the militia groups began a recruitment campaign, paying poor villagers to join unruly mobs such as Thorn or Aitarak, Besah Merah Putih and Mahidi, to intimidate, assault and ultimately murder supporters of the independence movement. On 6 April a large militia force, supported directly by Indonesian troops, attacked the coastal village of Liquica, about 20 kilometres east of Dili, killing more than twenty-five people. Up to that point their tactics had mainly involved burning houses and bashing people; now it was mass murder.

The possibility of an uprising in East Timor was already on the SAS Regiment's radar.

Crystal-ball gazing might seem an odd skill for a soldier, but the ability to study the future and plan for a range of contingencies are crucial traits for SAS officers. They must be able to think strategically and outside the square, with an eye to the big picture, leaving the practical side of soldiering to the senior noncommissioned officers. Officers of the SAS constantly monitor the media looking for probable 'jobs'.

'We were clearly watching what was going on in East Timor in the build-up in early '99,' says McOwan, 'in anticipation of something potentially going wrong there, well before there was any sort of inkling or suggestion that the ADF [Australian Defence Force] might be involved in it.'

Lieutenant Colonel McOwan was to lead the regiment in its first major operational deployment since the Vietnam War.

Born near Ararat in rural Victoria in 1957, and a graduate of the Royal Military College (RMC), Duntroon, McOwan, a thoughtful man, joined the SAS in 1981. A tall, highly intelligent officer with an engaging smile and sincere nature, he is one of the most popular and well-respected men in the tight-knit special forces community. He has served as a patrol, troop and squadron commander, spent two years with the British SAS and was adjutant of the Australian regiment. He is married to Dominica and they have a daughter and a son.

When McOwan called his operations officer, Major Jim Truscott, in February 1999, asking whether he had heard that some United Nations (UN) staff had been forced out of East Timor, Truscott began to draw up a plan.

'I might have been the first person in the ADF to start writing a contingency plan for Timor,' Truscott recalls. 'We built that plan over the next month and we were ready for East Timor six months before we went in. You could see the writing was on the wall.'

In early 1999 the SAS Regiment comprised three squadrons, each with about 100 men. McOwan and Truscott knew that 3 SAS Squadron, which was in line for the possible East Timor job, had a language deficiency. It had several Bahasa Indonesia speakers, but not one knew a word of Tetum, the bastardised Portuguese dialect spoken by the East Timorese. So McOwan put a group of men through a Tetum language course, which would be vital if they were to communicate with the local people.

The government had moved an infantry brigade to Darwin in the early 1990s under its Defence of the North strategy, and that force now stood ready to tackle any trouble in Indonesia, especially in East Timor. In June, it was placed on twenty-eight days' notice to move.

The 3 SAS Squadron's non-combat regime continued as usual, with high-intensity training and planning. They honed skills such as long-range patrolling, classic helicopter raiding, mixing and working with indigenous guerrilla forces, intelligence-gathering through extended observation, personal escorting duties and humanitarian 'hearts-and-minds' work.

'It was the full spectrum of tasks, from active soldiering and destroying things through to medical help,' says Truscott. All of these would come into play in Timor.

Jim 'Taipan' Truscott, who retired from the Army after the 2000 Olympic Games in Sydney, is a wiry figure with thick glasses. He exudes energy and passion for the craft of special forces soldiering and has little time for fools. A lively character, he thinks and talks at a hundred miles an hour. A mountaineer in his spare time, Truscott was born in Brisbane in 1956 and wanted to be a soldier from the age of fifteen.

His father was not convinced, so young Jim had to wait until he was eighteen to follow his dream and enrol at the nation's top military school, the Royal Military College (RMC), Duntroon, in Canberra. Truscott studied civil engineering so, despite his wish to join the infantry, he was commissioned into the Corps of Engineers. Two years later he moved on to the SAS, becoming just the second or third officer accepted into the regiment from outside the Infantry Corps.

For Truscott, as for many Duntroon graduates, it was some of the RMC instructors — senior and battle-hardened SAS soldiers — who inspired him to make his career in special forces. They were men of the calibre of Major Terry O'Farrell, a Vietnam veteran, the regiment's longest-serving member and author of *Behind Enemy Lines*, a no-holds-barred account of his adventures with the SAS; and Clem Dwyer, another tough, no-nonsense Vietnam veteran.

'They were very professional soldiers and they showed me that if you wanted to be in the Army, the SAS was *the* place to be. Why join the B team?' Truscott says now.

Because demolitions is such a vital string to the SAS bow, Truscott's engineering skills stood him in good stead. He admits to having destroyed more things than he has ever built, but is proud that he could bring a 'degree of technical expertise' to blowing things up.

After a hectic dash from Bangkok, McOwan arrived back in Perth the next morning to find that Truscott had preparations well advanced.

The commander of 3 SAS Squadron, James McMahon, was also away from home at the time. He was in Brisbane completing an operations course at the Army Promotion Training Centre at Canungra when he, too, received orders to return home immediately.

A new-generation Army officer, Major McMahon was the son of a Perth pharmacist and studied accountancy before being bitten by the warrior bug. A sports fanatic, he was inspired to join the Army when he saw a poster in a Perth shop front showing an infantry section running up a hill.

'I thought, "I'll do this for a couple of years", and it just seemed like a good thing to do.'

He soon found his way to officer school and, after that, to the SAS, where he specialised in water operations. He served in the regiment for five years before taking on other jobs, including a stint with 22 SAS in Britain, the sister regiment of the Australian outfit. A cheerful, intelligent and good-humoured officer, McMahon returned to the Australian regiment in 1998 and became commander of 3 SAS Squadron in January 1999. His focus, too, was on the brewing situation in East Timor.

McMahon arrived back at Swanbourne the next morning but had no time to go home. He had a brief reunion with his three-months'-pregnant wife, a Perth woman, in the officers' mess. They had just half an hour together before he was on his way with the squadron group heading north. As with most operational SAS deployments, McMahon was not allowed to tell his wife where he was going or what he would be doing, let alone when he might be home.

'This is probably a no-notice activity, where we're going,' he told her. He knew slightly more than that, but just said goodbye with the words SAS wives hear with increasing regularity: 'I'll see you when I see you.'

The 'when' turned out to be three months down the track.

'I wanted to say goodbye to my wife,' says McMahon, 'as I think that's important, and that gives me a bit of stability inside, I'll be frank about that, that's a thing that I have to do and she was amazingly supportive. In fact she said, "Do what you've got to do and be safe."'

Later that day McOwan, Truscott, McMahon and elements of the squadron group arrived at Pearce RAAF base north of Perth. They loaded the squadron group, some vital equipment and themselves on board two RAAF C-130 Hercules transport aircraft for the five-hour flight to the Northern Territory.

Things were moving at a blistering pace, and by the next morning McOwan had been appointed commander of Joint Task Force 504, in direct command of seven C-130s, fifteen Black Hawk helicopters, a rifle company and up to 600 individuals.

He also had access to high-level intelligence.

Although it is never officially declared by the government, it is well known (and has been widely written) that Australia has sophisticated intelligence assets such as electronic signals intelligence (Sigint) provided by the electronic eavesdropping agency, the Defence Signals Directorate (DSD). The DSD picks up radio and phone traffic across Southeast Asia and the Pacific via powerful listening stations in Western Australia and near Darwin. That material is supplemented by other high-tech listening equipment on board Air Force planes and Navy ships, including one of the most effective of all: the Collins Class submarine, which can sit quietly off a target for days on end, simply listening.

The intelligence feed to ADF officers in East Timor would become the subject of national controversy when one of the databases was deliberately turned off for twenty-six hours by someone in the Defence Intelligence Organisation in Canberra.

James McMahon and his squadron hit the ground running at Tindal air base near Darwin, moving into an intense rehearsal phase. The squadron was made up of three elements, each specialising in a different insertion skill. (This term refers to how troops arrive on the job — by either air, water or land.) Each element has a number of smaller teams. The squadron group would be supplemented by elements from the British Special Boat Service (SBS) and the New Zealand SAS, making it effectively a two-squadron force.

There were four five-man patrols in each troop and each one came under the command of a captain. The patrols practised every aspect of the operation, including the evacuation of Australian and United Nations personnel from East Timor, with or without Indonesian help.

Just three days after flicking the green light, the government had its rescue capability in place.

'It was a very busy period,' McMahon recalls. 'There was a lot of planning going on, we were doing a whole lot of training for a lot of different scenarios the government would potentially want us to do, so we were training very heavily. They were busy, long days.'

A typical 18-hour day began early with an intense physical training regime followed by up to eight hours of planning sessions, then practising and completing an exercise by day or night. The drills included tactics for a so-called 'special recovery' operation for rescuing people — in this case, from the UN compound in Dili — against an opposing force, and also for what are known as 'services-assisted' and 'services-protected' evacuations. 'Services-assisted' means soldiers helping people to move with the support of local forces. 'Services-protected' means possibly having to fight their way out. A plan for a full-scale 'protected' rescue mission would also have involved the Townsville-based 3rd Brigade, the army's high-readiness brigade.

As voting day in East Timor approached and the violence escalated, McOwan and his task force began rehearsing detailed scenarios for the evacuation.

Despite the intimidation campaign, on 30 August almost 80 per cent of East Timorese voters opted to cut ties with Indonesia after twenty-four years of brutal occupation.

When the result was announced on 4 September, a ferocious orgy of Indonesian-backed militia violence erupted; it would cost hundreds of lives, displace tens of thousands of people and destroy most of East Timor's already limited infrastructure.

By this time the UN boss in Dili, Ian Martin, had recalled most of his staff to the capital, where the UN had a walled compound, because there had been a number of serious attacks by heavily armed militia units against unarmed UN staff in remote areas. Many thought it was just a matter of time before there would be fatalities among the blue berets of the unarmed UN civilian police.

The debate about armed versus unarmed personnel had raged during the deployment of Australian Federal Police officers to act as civilian police (Civpol) for the UN operation. The police had deployed without firearms and had been given a rough time by local militia, who knew they could not shoot back. Many saw that decision as a serious mistake, and while no Australian police were killed or badly wounded, quite a few were seriously traumatised.

Attacks against civilians also intensified and several foreign journalists were singled out. One, BBC reporter Jonathan Head, received a broken arm and another, Keith Richburg from the *Washington Post*, was hit across the back with the flat side of a machete. Others were shot at and forced to shelter inside hotel rooms and the UN compound, and all the while Indonesian troops just stood by and watched.

Several Australian reporters barricaded themselves inside the bathroom of *Age* journalist Lindsay Murdoch's room when armed militiamen stormed the journos' favoured accommodation in Dili, the Tourismo Hotel, looking for the media. The Australians' only weapon was a stainless steel water jug. In a separate incident, one unfortunate Canadian aid worker was mistaken for a reporter and bashed in the hotel's leafy tropical garden. These attacks were designed to intimidate the media — and they worked. About seventy journalists and other staff left the next day on a charter flight to Bali.

The journalists still on the ground in East Timor were witnessing atrocities daily. Despite what the Australian government was saying publicly at the time about 'rogue elements', there was no doubt in the minds of those eyewitnesses that the militia were being guided and directed by Indonesian Armed Forces (TNI) at the highest levels, with elements of Kopassus, the Indonesian Special Forces, also playing a role.

The UN compound was the final safe haven in Dili, and its population grew to bursting in the days that followed as desperate men, women and children climbed through razor wire to seek shelter from the mobs.

As the results of the UN supervised ballot were announced, McOwan received a direct order from the Chief of the Australian Defence Force, Admiral Chris Barrie, to be ready to launch a special recovery operation (rescuing Australians while battling opposing forces) within twenty minutes of receiving the 'go' order.

'I had given [Admiral Barrie] a full risk appraisal of what might occur if we had to launch in to recover personnel from within the [UN] compound,' says McOwan. 'I expected that in those circumstances we would have lost soldiers. I gave him honest advice as I saw it: "Yes, we can do it, but be aware that it's very likely that we will lose soldiers, potentially major equipment, helicopters, things like that." It was not surreal but it was very, very sobering.'

Also sobering was the fact even a tiny slip-up could escalate into all-out war between Australia and Indonesia.

When Jim Truscott's original planning document for East Timor had been presented to a contingency planning meeting at the Headquarters Australian Theatre in Sydney, it had revolved around two warring factions, Falintil (the Timorese resistance force) and the militia, with a neutral force in the middle. It was modelled closely on the British special forces plan used in the former Yugoslavia, but fortunately it didn't pan out that way because the militia abandoned the war. Truscott regards this as a massive strategic error on the militia's part.

'If they'd stayed in location we would have had a devil of a time,' he says. 'They misjudged it. If they had gone into cantonments [designated base areas where troops or fighters live], such as Falintil had, we would still be there now. It would be a nightmare.'

After talking to one of Falintil's key Australian contacts, the late Dr Andrew McNaughton, at a clandestine meeting in Katherine, McOwan was confident Falintil would cooperate with his force.

As 3 SAS Squadron worked up its 'full mission profile' for the evacuation of Australians, UN staff and other nationals from Dili, McOwan was under growing pressure from his commanders regarding his capabilities. He got a call from Major General Peter Cosgrove, the Commander Deployable Joint Force Headquarters in Brisbane, who had been earmarked to head any future international force in East Timor. Cosgrove wanted to know whether McOwan was confident that he could hold a special-recovery capability while conducting a services-assisted or services-protected evacuation from Dili.

'I said yes, I did have that capacity, depending on the way they wanted it done, and they came back and said, "Well, you tell us how you think you could do it",' McOwan recalls. 'It was a recovery capability which was achievable inside 24 hours easily.'

Initially the special-recovery capability was designed solely to rescue personnel from the UN compound, which housed most UN staff — including the Australian civilian police — and hundreds of displaced East Timorese who had scrambled in. The compound was under constant attack and threat from the militia.

The whole strategy was to defuse the situation and avoid any conflict: 'SAS soldiers are taught to do that, under certain circumstances to de-escalate, and suppress aggression, and they'll do that through their demeanour,' says McOwan. 'It's a conscious element of our training. If you mean business and it is required, you have the capacity to escalate.'

At the strategic and political levels, intense negotiations with the Indonesians were under way, to gain their permission to fly into East Timor to rescue Australian and UN personnel. Such an evacuation would involve RAAF C-130 Hercules transport aircraft landing at Dili, loading their human cargo and returning to Darwin. The Indonesians granted permission on 5 September. The next morning McOwan and a group of his soldiers began eight days of hard work that would deliver 2700 people from Dili to Darwin.

Under the agreement the Indonesians were responsible for bringing evacuees to two airports, one in Dili and the other at Baucau to the east. The Australians would not leave the airport perimeter and no RAAF aircraft would be allowed to stay on the ground overnight.

McOwan arrived in Dili on the first Hercules. 'Because of the strategic consequences of what we were doing, I remember it being made quite clear to me that yes, I needed to be there on the ground,' he says.

Lieutenant Colonel McOwan was met by Brigadier Jim Molan, the Australian defence attaché in Jakarta, and Colonel Ken Brownrigg, the Army attaché. McOwan had spoken with the pair a number of times and they were liaising closely with the Indonesian military and with Ian Martin and his staff at the UN compound. He was also introduced to an Indonesian Air Force special forces captain who briefed him on security arrangements at Komoro airport in Dili. The young officer took his new Australian comrade for a drive around the airport perimeter to show off his gun positions and his security positions. Most of the guns were pointed towards the airfield — the soldiers were obviously more focused on what was happening within the perimeter than on any threat from outside the fence.

Says McOwan, 'They were there to make sure that we did not go beyond the boundary of Komoro airfield. And that was made quite clear to me, in the disposition of the soldiers and the security positions. And they told us what we could and couldn't do around the airfield.'

The situation was very delicate. McOwan had brought several linguists who spoke Bahasa Indonesia to help defuse the situation. The atmosphere was very tense when they arrived and there was a lot of automatic gunfire. McOwan had no doubt that the aim was to frighten or intimidate his men and the internally displaced people who were at the airport.

On one occasion two goats wandered across the small car park out the front of the airport and two TNI guards shot the animals in full view of the SAS men.

'Clearly they had never met guys who weren't readily intimidated, and on those first couple of days you could see they were meeting professional soldiers that they had never met before, people with a level of professionalism and competence that they had never previously witnessed,' McOwan recounts.

He and his troops set up a small emergency evacuation handling centre which involved quarantine, health and immigration checks, and mustering and passenger manifests for the Hercules flights into Darwin. At the behest of Ken Brownrigg, the Indonesians transported the UN evacuees from the compound to the airport in trucks. Many were suffering from severe stress.

McOwan recalls: 'I remember one of the Australian police [who had been in the compound] saying, "Yep, we know who you guys are. For God's sake, when you're unleashed on these guys, give it back to them!" And some of them were in tears, they were deeply traumatised. All of the individuals there who provided the evacuation handling centre, the immediate security of the area, were SAS blokes.' They escorted the passengers out to the aircraft as well as providing physical security for them.

By the time the first couple of aircraft had departed, the SAS troops had established contact with TNI soldiers right around the airfield. McOwan frequently saw his men and the Indonesians deep in conversation in Bahasa Indonesia. That, and the fact the men had been briefed to be in 'benign' mode, did a lot to reduce the tension of the situation.

'It was interesting to see a little bit of a relationship developing between [the] TNI and our guys over the period of the evacuations,' he says. Those personal relationships were to come in very handy in the days and weeks ahead.

Each time they landed at Komoro there was gunfire, at first close by and then off in the distance. And every day, once the day's evacuations had finished, the troops would fly home and return to East Timor the following morning.

While UN staff were living in the compound prior to evacuation, the Indonesians had locked local internally displaced people (IDPs) and other potential evacuees inside the Komoro airport terminal under inhumane conditions. They included people who had been working as locally engaged staff for the UN, and they were terrified. By the second day the Australians were confronted with more than 300 people sleeping and defecating in the same room.

'They [the Indonesians] clearly did not allow them to even leave the building overnight. The second morning that we came back, there was shit everywhere, literally, they had clearly just locked them into the terminal and under pain of death they were not allowed to leave. There was a stench you could not believe.'

Just a few days later, McOwan received quite a shock when he returned with advance elements of General Cosgrove's International Force for East Timor (INTERFET) to find the terminal spotless. The Indonesians had cleaned it up after the evacuation and were clearly keen to be seen in a better light by the international media.

Upholding the status of the SAS soldiers as strategic troops at the front end of a major national operation which could lead to all-out war, was a mantra for every SAS officer. Suddenly, at an airfield in a poor third-world country less than one hour's flying time from Darwin, the mantra had become manifest: one false move from any of the troops and the consequence could have been war between Australia and Indonesia.

'If we had done something really stupid there it would have had strategic consequences, it would have had enormous consequences for Australia, and we were acutely conscious of that all the while,' McOwan says now. 'It had been made quite clear to me by the likes of Peter Cosgrove and Chris Barrie: "Be aware, this cannot go wrong." I spoke to the guys individually before we boarded the aircraft ... I'd given deliberate orders to James [McMahon] for the evacuation and every day we'd give those orders again. Before we'd board the aircraft I'd get the guys together and explain to them the gravity of what we were doing, the fact that it could not go wrong and that there could be no escalation.'

The evacuation was conducted entirely from Komoro airport with one exception — when McOwan sent a detachment up to Baucau, East Timor's second biggest town, where a particularly tense situation had developed.

Accompanied by Brigadier Jim Molan and eight SAS soldiers, James McMahon flew into Baucau to negotiate directly with local militia over the evacuation of UN staff and East Timor's high-profile religious leader, Bishop Carlos Belo. The negotiations were successful. However, when Belo was being escorted to the aircraft by an SAS patrol, the group was surrounded by thirty militia and a group of TNI soldiers. During the tense standoff, McMahon held major concerns for the welfare of his men and the aircraft. Eventually the aircraft departed for Darwin, but other soldiers waiting to board the second aircraft saw shots being fired at the Herc as it carried Belo away to safety.

By the end of Operation Spitfire on 14 September, some members of 3 SAS Squadron had made six flights in and out of Komoro airport.

'East Timor was in many ways a lot more complex than movement in and out of Iraq and movement in and out of Afghanistan, which I also had something to do with [later],' McOwan says. East Timor was strategically vital for Australia, so '[it was] an extremely sensitive period for the government. A really sensitive period.'

At the end of Operation Spitfire virtually every squadron member had been into Dili at least once. The intelligence they gathered would prove vital in the weeks ahead.

By the time the evacuation was complete, McOwan had made seven flights into Dili, and he could see that the place was still extremely volatile. 'As you flew into Dili every day the place was still burning and they were still clearly burning other quarters. Every day that I flew in you could see, particularly in the first couple of days, a stream of trucks going west down to the border, literally convoys and convoys of them, and they were full of people and full of loot, I suppose, or personal belongings,' he said.

The final group of UN staff left the compound that day with heavy hearts. They knew they were leaving hundreds of thousands of East Timorese at the mercy of the militia and their humiliated Indonesian masters.

For Tim McOwan and his men, the hard yards had only just begun.

Chapter 3

TIMOR BURNING

It was a vivid scene, like something from Dante's inferno — Dili was burning and the sky was a malevolent red. A pall of smoke hung in the atmosphere as Tim McOwan made his way down to the port with some SAS troops.

It was the evening of 20 September 1999 and the end of the first exhausting day of Operation Stabilise. Australia's General Peter Cosgrove was Commander of INTERFET and he had named McOwan as his Special Operations Commander.

As he entered the port McOwan was amazed to see crowds of people crammed into the area. He could see that they were being corralled there to be taken away from East Timor by the Indonesians.

Just outside the immediate port area he could see an Indonesian landing craft of the type that had already been used to forcibly remove many East Timorese to West Timor.

There were piles of burning rubbish amongst all the people. At first McOwan thought there was just refuse everywhere, but then he realised that the piles that weren't burning were the people's meagre possessions. 'These poor devils were obviously taking what few belongings they had because they knew they were being lifted out of Dili to go God knows where. You could tell they were terrified.'

The fear was apparent in their eyes. They didn't know who the Australians were or what they were doing there, and there was no dialogue, just silent looks.

'They didn't willingly approach us, so we took from that, that amongst the crowd there were militia elements, although that wasn't evident. A lot of individuals were carrying machetes.'

Speed had been of the essence throughout that first day.

Just eight days earlier, on 12 September, then Indonesian President BJ Habibie had agreed to allow an international peacekeeping force into East Timor. The brilliant but unpredictable new Indonesian leader was known to many Australians as 'Dr Strangelove' because of his occasionally bizarre behaviour and manic laugh, and his decision in May to allow an early independence vote in the province had caught Australia and the international community completely by surprise. Few had imagined he would defy his generals a second time and open Indonesia's borders to an international force, especially one led by Australia. Such humiliation would be difficult to swallow for military men used to absolute power under the iron thirty-year rule of General Suharto. But defy them he had.

During Indonesia's 24-year occupation of East Timor, Suharto's regime had spent a great deal of money trying to improve what had been largely neglected by the former colonial master, Portugal. Many Indonesian businessmen and army officers had profited and now East Timor was burning. It was obvious to journalists and other eyewitnesses that the militia groups and some of their Indonesian masters were intent upon destroying what they now realised they had lost.

Before the evacuation Australia had drawn up a detailed military plan, codenamed Operation Warden, to go into East Timor to quell the militia and provide security. Like a lot of good plans, it didn't last long. On 14 September, as the last rescue flight left Dili, the plan was junked when the Howard government agreed to a request from UN Secretary-General Kofi Annan to lead an international force into Timor.

3 SAS Squadron, which had successfully undertaken the evacuation operation, became the INTERFET Response Force. The force would include a troop from the New Zealand SAS and a troop-plus from the British Royal Marines special forces unit, the Special Boat Service. Their

orders included preventing or reducing cross-border incursions and stopping the militia from bullying IDPs, as well as supporting the return of those people to their homes. INTERFET's mandate, approved by the UN, was to restore peace and stability to East Timor, to protect and support the UN authorities and, within force capabilities, to facilitate humanitarian assistance.

On 12 September Tim McOwan and Jim Truscott flew to Brisbane to brief Major General Cosgrove and to hear the good news that, if they got the go-ahead, the SAS would lead INTERFET into East Timor. Suddenly, after twenty years in the shadows, the regiment was about to emerge into bright light at the head of Australia's biggest overseas military deployment since the Vietnam War.

Two things about that meeting stood out to McOwan. The first was that Cosgrove said to him, 'This is likely to be the last thing that I do in the military, Tim — I've been told essentially that this will be my last posting in the military.' In fact, Cosgrove went on to become Chief of the Army and then Chief of the Defence Force.

The second was that McOwan became thoroughly alarmed when the logisticians around the table said they did not have the capacity to support the operation, even though it was so close to Darwin.

'They were worried, dreadfully worried, about their capacity to logistically support and sustain it. The professional logisticians, unlike the warrior-class guys, were lost, that's the best way to describe it. We did get around it, so there was clearly an element of inexperience too, or lack of experience in a logistics sense. It wasn't through any lack of competence or professionalism.'

As well as the problems with logistics, McOwan was concerned about the apparent lack of a defined concept for how the operation would progress once the force arrived. He wanted to know how they would overcome the supply problem, re-establish order and support the establishment of the United Nations Transitional Authority in East Timor (UNTAET).

He discussed it with Cosgrove, who said, 'Well, firstly we'll concern ourselves with the lodgment and then we'll address issues as they require addressing on an individual basis.'

The general's 'oil spot' philosophy was indeed the way the operation unfolded.

And McOwan knew he had Cosgrove's support. 'General Cosgrove is an excellent commander, and I'm not just saying that because he's got to the level that he's got, but he really reassures you, he is honest and he's absolutely decisive. You can take a problem to him, or an issue to him, and say, "What is your guidance on this?" and you'll unequivocally get guidance. From the military point of view he's a very good commander, and is prepared to support you as well.'

In Timor, Cosgrove was confronting an array of problems, acutely aware that every day that passed was a day of disaster for the people of the province. He wanted his force to move in fast and he insisted it be led by troops with the 'most sensitive antennae' of any soldiers in the Australian Defence Force — the SAS.

'They would have to behave in a way which was competent, professional, but not in any way provocative or disturbing to Indonesian troops, who understandably would be on edge themselves,' Cosgrove says. 'So the special forces were a natural pick. They had already been there, knew what it looked like on the ground, and had even probably met some of the Indonesian troops responsible for general airfield security. So, on return, the first task for the SAS was to lead INTERFET onto the ground and establish a professional climate of military presence by a new force, acting in a mature way, which reduced to the minimum the possibility of provocation. We gave them that job and they did it very well.'

Cosgrove had long been both a fan and a supporter of the SAS. During his time as an infantry platoon commander in Vietnam (where he won the Military Cross), his men deployed and recovered SAS patrols and several of his Duntroon classmates had become SAS officers, or 'chicken stranglers' as they are affectionately known for their ability to live off the land. On his journey up the ranks, Cosgrove had also been Director of Infantry.

'There is such a kindred nature that the Director of Infantry has always had them [the SAS] in the fraternity. The fact is that most SAS come from infantry backgrounds. The Director of Infantry to a large degree helps to career-manage a lot of SAS officers.'

So Cosgrove was well aware of the squadron's capabilities and had watched them perform Operation Spitfire virtually without a hitch. He was also keenly aware of the hostility which some in the wider Army harboured towards the SAS.

'I had this professional relationship with them. It would be wrong to say, "Oh well, you know chicken strangler, be suspicious." That exists today, but it is a superficial attitude, which is mostly on the non-SF [special forces] side, but sometimes on the SF side, and it never survives the urgency of operational deployment. It can't.

'The real thing is: give the SAS tasks, monitor the tasks, and the tasks will always be a stretch ... you wouldn't give them trivial tasks. Give them a task, make sure they have got the wherewithal, monitor what they are doing and they will always produce wonderful outcomes.'

Meanwhile, back in Australia, Tim McOwan was grappling with revised plans that left him without several Hercules aircraft.

His new plan involved inserting his force ahead of the main push, using Black Hawk helicopters with extended-range fuel tanks and the minimum number of C-130s. That would give him mobility on the ground and allow the SAS to secure the Dili port area so that the Infantry's 2nd Battalion and 3rd Battalion could land there.

'Having been in there through Op Spitfire,' says McOwan, 'and knowing what Dili itself was like and the environs around Komoro [airport], and knowing that the Indonesians were pulling back to the port area, I was concerned that we went in with a posture that provided us with maximum security.'

He reorganised everything so that troops could fly in on a combination of Black Hawks and C-130s but in an 'unthreatening but secure posture', so they could respond if required.

At the embassy in Dili, meanwhile, the small SAS reconnaissance team that had been left behind after escorting Cosgrove for his first visit on 19 September, was working frantically with Ken Brownrigg and a liaison officer from Cosgrove's headquarters, Lieutenant Colonel Roger Joy. They were also providing intelligence support to Jim Molan and Ian Martin.

After extensive discussions with the Indonesians, Brownrigg and Joy reached the view that the advance SAS deployment should not, under any circumstances, arrive in Dili in a threatening manner.

So at 8 p.m. on the night before the SAS was due to move, McOwan received fresh orders that his force was to deploy in a 'benign manner'. They would have to travel in C-130s with the Black Hawks following behind the huge transport planes. He felt extremely uncomfortable about the plan as it would leave his men exposed.

'Imagine this: us flying in, an SAS squadron, in a series of C-130s, in a benign manner into Komoro airfield and getting the shit shot out of us there,' he says. 'It wouldn't be just fifty, sixty, seventy, eighty Australian SAS servicemen losing their lives — it would mean strategic defeat. It would have been strategic defeat. I made this representation to General Cosgrove, I felt so strongly about it.'

McOwan felt betrayed by the men in the embassy from Cosgrove's headquarters. He believed they had been swayed by the Indonesians, with whom they were working daily. He realised that his own perspective was a soldier's perspective, but he also strongly felt that it was an unwise move: 'We should have gone in there looking like we meant business rather than going in as though we were just flying into an exercise. Now, keeping in mind that we had been in and out of this airfield on seven different occasions, it wasn't as though we were going to go in there with guns blazing or whatever.'

His own intention had been to arrive in a secure manner but in a benign disposition to avoid what he saw as an unnecessary risk. 'I still believe it to have been a strategically risky deployment. It need not have been done in that way.'

Cosgrove's instinct, however, was to trust the Indonesians, whom he knew well, and McOwan lost the argument. He had to rewrite all his orders, reissue them and reconfigure all the aircraft loads in order to meet the takeoff time. The entire joint task force worked through the night. No one slept, and they went into East Timor the following day at first light absolutely exhausted.

The date was 20 September 1999, incredibly only six days after the UN request. A brigade-sized force of several thousand soldiers would be lodged in a foreign country in just over seven days' time; it had taken six months to land the nation's last expeditionary task force, in South Vietnam in 1964.

Cosgrove identifies the close links between Australian and Indonesian armed forces, developed over many years, as crucial to the early success of Operation Stabilise.

'It turned out we had a number of different officers who recognised Indonesian counterparts,' he says.

By good fortune, the senior Indonesian ground commander in the Dili area was an officer called Colonel Girhan, whom Cosgrove had met earlier in the year.

'Hello, Colonel Girhan,' was the first thing Cosgrove said when he saw him in Dili on 19 September.

The SAS also had links with the UN Mission in East Timor (UNAMET), via a couple of military observers and the UN security officer, Ian Young. These links were only informal, however, because the UN is not involved in intelligence-gathering.

Jim Truscott was standing next to Tim McOwan in the cockpit of the first of three Hercules carrying SAS troops to land at Komoro.

The plan called for a combat unload, so the aircraft's engines would stay on full power, ready to make a rapid exit if they were attacked. The aim was to unload a lot of ammunition as quickly as possible so that the force could be sustained for a very long time, if necessary. As soon as the plane landed, pallets of ammunition in the back of its cargo bay would be secured to a forklift (pre-positioned on the tarmac by the advance SAS troops who had accompanied Cosgrove on the 19th) and yanked out as the aircraft taxied off.

'We had asked the patrol that spent the night to try and find the forklift we knew was at the airport,' says Truscott.

Because he spoke Indonesian, Truscott was the first person off, carrying his weapon in an inoffensive fashion as he made his way to the Indonesian officer wearing the most braid. 'I saluted him and started talking to him.' Truscott asked the Indonesian officer who he was and where his people were, and told him it was crucial to avoid 'friendly fire'. It was soon apparent that there would be no attack on the aircraft.

As Truscott recounts: 'We wanted to get to the high ground, so I asked him to tell his people we were coming. He gave us a liaison person and our patrols moved out to the perimeter. It was very hard to talk with the C–130 burning and churning 100 metres away!'

At the same time McOwan was met by Molan and Brownrigg, who briefed him and confirmed that the heliport, which was closer to town, was available for them to occupy. McOwan had told Brownrigg the night before that he intended to secure first the airfield, then the port. He would then be relieved by the 2nd and 3rd Battalions Royal Australian Regiment (2RAR and 3RAR) at both locations before going on to secure the heliport.

Much to Truscott's surprise, at the airport he encountered another Australian defence attaché to Jakarta, Brian Millen, who had flown in the day before. 'It was reassuring, because we knew it wasn't going to be guns blazing. I had to yell to talk to the Indonesian general to tell him that very soon there would be a lot of our troops moving around the airport.'

One of the first tasks was to secure the place so that the advance elements from 2RAR could land. Says Truscott, 'We established that things were going to be okay and were able to send those critical code words so the mission could continue as planned.'

A media contingent was also there to record the arrival and Truscott was surprised when a journalist approached him and offered him $5000 for his name and an interview.

'He said "You will be famous!" And I said I would love to but it was not appropriate.'

Dili is built on a narrow strip of land between the sea and a mountain range that rises steeply just to the south of the built-up area. Its borders are the airport to the west and a mountain to the east of the town, with a 30-metre statue of Jesus (a gift from former Indonesian president, Suharto) built on top of it. Komoro airport is about 10 kilometres from the Dili town centre. The port is in the centre of the town, roughly 5 kilometres east of the heliport which would become McOwan's Response Force headquarters and home to 3 SAS Squadron.

Truscott's job was to establish the headquarters and find road transport to carry the troops into town so they could secure the heliport and the port. James McMahon's job was to secure the port — but they had no vehicles to get them there.

Before leaving for Dili, many of the senior SAS soldiers thought they should take their specialised Long Range Patrol Vehicles (LRPVs) into East Timor. Tim McOwan had disagreed because he thought the distinctive six-wheel cars could become sought-after ambush targets. Given the terrain of East Timor, they would have had to drive on the roads, and this visibility was too risky. So he decided they would use helicopters for tactical mobility and go everywhere else on foot, unless they could reach a region safely by vehicle. 'Cleanskin' (unmarked and not equipped for military operations) four-wheel-drive vehicles were brought in later for exactly that task, but in the meantime they had to make do with what they could get.

McOwan had a plan up his sleeve, though. During the evacuation he had met a UN security officer who told him there were UN vehicles parked in a fenced paddock opposite the compound. 'He said we could take what we needed if they weren't wrecked by the militia.'

So McOwan asked James McMahon to send a troop over to the UN compound to hot-wire the vehicles. McOwan had commanded that very troop years before and knew they could hot-wire anything; sure enough, 'They returned to the Komoro airfield with about eighteen vehicles.'

The Aussies also 'borrowed' several Indonesian military trucks under a deal struck by Ken Brownrigg. Meanwhile, the advance elements of 2RAR had arrived and established headquarters in the airport terminal, the same building that had been filled with human excreta during the evacuation just over a week before.

Truscott and his headquarters staff jumped onto the Indonesian trucks when they arrived and drove into town without stopping to think about the effect that might have on the terrified locals.

'That was pretty dumb of us, given that the local people must have wondered what was going on. I was on the first truck to the heliport. There were very few people around, a stench of destruction, smoke palls, utter destruction,' Truscott recalls.

3 SAS Squadron took over the heliport, occupied several big hangars and established an operating base with the Black Hawk crews from 5 Aviation Regiment. The SAS squadron regrouped that night and, in the words of Jim Truscott, 'We were fucked. We were just so whacked, people were wandering around like zombies.'

By the end of day one they had handed the airport over to 2RAR and the seaport to 3RAR, who had arrived on the fast catamaran HMAS *Jervis Bay*. Later that night Peter Cosgrove and his advance element would arrive.

Towards last light, Tim McOwan went to the port to check on James McMahon's progress. With the burning town behind him, he saw for himself the throng of misery huddled at the seaside.

James McMahon had been determined to create the illusion, at least in the minds of the militia, that there were a lot more INTERFET troops around than the thirty or so men he had with him.

'People knew we were there so we wanted to keep that rolling and give a presence of "Jeez, there's a lot of people here!" Because I think it was important from a militia perspective to realise that "Oh, they're here and there, now they're in town."'

His main priority as they approached the port area in their beaten-up trucks was the safety of his men. It was vital to avoid an ambush, as he explains: 'My view is that that would have been a significant blow to INTERFET if you'd had fifteen blokes wounded, three shot dead on day one. So although being bold in our move down there, once you're open and you're on the ground and people can see you, my number one priority was not losing people.'

There were, however, several standoffs: 'People were about to raise weapons but then decided otherwise, because it was that aggressive stance and people realised, "Oh well, there's no point in me shooting at these people, because they're going to clean me up."'

McMahon knew that if he had lost men there, the situation could become very bloody, and, 'the potential was there. We would have been cut off. Numbers wise it would have been a bit of OK Corral stuff.'

The SAS soldiers could see heavily armed militia driving past in vehicles, and there was shooting in the distance. But none of the militia was prepared to take them on, so the bluff seemed to be working.

'We had a couple of Kiwi patrols with us,' says McMahon, 'and I remember there was one incident when we first got into the area and somebody was pulling a weapon. A big hairy [Kiwi] fellow grabbed it from the side and the militia fellow turned around and went, "Oh shit, I think I'll leave!" It just sent a good message.'

There were about 400 people at the port and amongst the prisoners were some armed militiamen who also made the wise decision to depart.

'We did not initially open fire on those people,' McMahon says. 'If we had, again, strategically, that would not have suited our purpose, because there were a lot of trucks with guns. At the end of the day you can be as good as you want to be, but you've got to pick the fight that you can win.'

The controlled use of force was a vital tactic that had been emphasised during briefings back in Australia. McOwan had insisted on formal training in the rules of engagement and detailed 'what if' scenarios. McMahon had been very careful with this training and it paid a handsome dividend on the stinking and volatile Dili dock area. Flexibility was the key in this incendiary situation where a lot of civilians could have been killed.

So the first day of INTERFET was over. The force had landed and established a firm foothold and the SAS squadron group was safely bedded down in its new headquarters. Only two shots had been fired by an Australian soldier — a nervous military policeman attached to 3 Brigade headquarters (3 Brigade is the larger force that includes 3RAR). Against his rules of engagement he fired two rounds at an escaping militiaman who had jumped through a glass window at the airport terminal and was running across the car park.

'Thankfully both of them missed this militia guy, who was desperate to get away,' remembers Tim McOwan. 'They ran after him into the scrub, into the banana plantation opposite the Komoro airport there, but they didn't get him. He got away.'

In the days that followed, the SAS consolidated its position in Dili and mounted a humanitarian patrol to Dare, in the hills just above the capital. The patrol also extended the force's presence beyond Dili and tentative arrangements had been made by Andrew McNaughton for a meeting with Falintil representatives in Dare. As it turned out, the troops only made contact with a representative from the rival faction from the National Council of Timorese Resistance (known as CNRT).

The next step would be to establish formal links with the Falintil guerrillas, who had fought a 24-year war against the Indonesians and were crucial to the fledgling nation's future.

Before that, however, Tim McOwan was to find himself face to face with his own mortality and that of his troops.

Chapter 4

DATE WITH DESTINY

'Switch to auto!'

Tim McOwan gave the order with the clear intent of taking out as many of the enemy as he could if a firefight broke out.

He was reassured by the curt, no-nonsense response from his SAS Regimental Sergeant Major (RSM), Warrant Officer Greg: 'What the fuck do you think we are on?'

McOwan thought that was a typical digger's response and was able to laugh about it later.

It was 25 September 1999, just five days into the INTERFET deployment in East Timor, and a potential worst-case scenario was being played out. The commanding officer of the Australian SAS Regiment, arguably one of the nation's most important soldiers, and his senior noncommissioned officer were literally staring down the barrel of a gun.

'Oh shit,' thought McOwan, 'I've got these young blokes killed.'

The Tibar incident, as it became known, started as a simple graves registration operation to verify information that bodies had been dumped off the side of a road up the hill from the village of Tibar, 5 kilometres west of Dili. The militia had buried many bodies in makeshift graves during their ethnic cleansing operations and revenge attacks in the days after the independence ballot at the end of August.

McOwan had ordered an eight-person graves registration team to follow up the Tibar information. Led by Greg, with the Regimental Medical Officer, Major Carol, and a sergeant from the British SBS, the team had exhumed four bodies separated by about 600 metres. They had photographed them, tried to find papers or other identifying information, and then re-interred them, prior to getting a reliable fix on their global positioning system (GPS).

Along with SAS intelligence officer Major Andrew and an SAS trooper, McOwan drove out to see how the team was getting on. As they drove through the village they were surprised to see locals holding up a banner that read *Viva INTERFET*. He felt amazed that the villagers already knew who they were, and realised that they had prepared the banner for the registration team, who were working up on the high ground 1500 metres south of the village. There were twenty or so local men looking on and taking a great interest in the exhumations.

When McOwan and his companions arrived, the graves registration team was just finishing up. McOwan was leaving the bush at the side of the road to set off back to the Dili heliport — by now the SAS HQ — when he heard a burst of gunfire, followed by screaming, coming from the village.

From the team's position they could see the bitumen road that ran directly through Tibar. Looking down, they saw thirty or forty people rushing away from the village in a southeasterly direction, across the road and into the scrub. They were clearly terrified and running as fast as they could. The group comprised mostly women, old men and children, because the majority of the village's men were already up on the hill watching the graves registration process.

McOwan could not see any militia, but he could see smoke rising from the northern side of the village. He glanced at the Tibar men, who were looking at him as if to say, 'Well, you INTERFET have come here to help, what are you waiting for?'

Despite the lack of numbers and lack of preparation, McOwan decided they had little option but to try to clear the village — to secure it and ensure that all militia had been removed. In his judgment, INTERFET had to be seen to be doing something and, apart from one troop's move into Dare, no troops had yet left Dili. He felt a moral responsibility that the forces should do what they could for the people of East Timor. In addition, the only way back to Dili was through Tibar.

It was just a tiny hamlet, but Greg reminded him that the only SAS-qualified soldiers in the party were the two of them and the trooper. McOwan was conscious of how small his force was, and of the fact that they did not have the equipment to conduct a tactical operation.

As the residents streamed out of the village, McOwan ordered Major Carol and the SBS sergeant to remain where they were, and he began the clearance operation.

The six soldiers drove back to Tibar in their commandeered UN Land Rover before splitting into two groups to clear the huts on both sides of the road. They had gone about 100 metres and cleared several huts when they heard a vehicle approaching.

'I'm going to stop it. Can you give me covering fire?' McOwan asked Greg.

He waited behind a large palm tree until the car, a small sedan which was travelling very slowly, came around the bend directly towards them. The occupants were obviously looking for someone or something in the scrub and the coffee warehouse on the right-hand side of the road, where McOwan was.

McOwan stepped out into the path of the car, yelling, '*Berhenti! Berhenti!*' ('Stop! Stop!') while aiming his M4 carbine at the occupants. It was the only Bahasa Indonesia that he could remember from his days as a young platoon commander in Malaysia.

McOwan did not know whether the men understood what he was saying, but they certainly understood his intent. They slammed on the brakes and the Australians surrounded the car with their weapons trained on the occupants.

The driver was a man with long black hair. There was a second man in the passenger seat and a third in the right-hand rear passenger seat.

As the vehicle slowed, the rear-seat passenger, dressed in Indonesian military kit, jumped out and bolted into the bush.

The Australians relieved the remaining militiamen of an SKS carbine and several grenades, put them face down on the ground and restrained them with plastic handcuffs. The long-haired man became very agitated about being detained. McOwan ordered a soldier to guard the pair as the clearing operation resumed, with McOwan and two soldiers on one side of the road, and Greg and another soldier clearing the other side.

Shortly they heard trucks approaching from the west.

'We had no time to react,' McOwan recalls. 'The trucks began to slow down as they saw the detainees on the side of the road ahead. I moved back towards them and onto the side of the road, and motioned for the trucks to slow down. I expected the trucks to be East Timorese, but to my horror I realised they were full of militia. I could see them all standing in the rear of the trucks, and as they drew up just short of the detainees, but abreast of us, I could see they were all well armed. The weapons were SS1s, very similar to the M16. I was immediately aware that there were only six of us but three truckloads of them.'

As the trucks groaned to a stop, every one of the forty or so occupants of the first two vehicles had their weapons trained on the three diggers. McOwan, cut off from Greg on the other side of the trucks, was now totally exposed with two other soldiers up against a 2-metre-high concrete wall with dozens of assault rifles pointed at them.

He fully expected to be shot at any second, hoped he would still be able to fire his own weapons if it happened. 'I don't remember being afraid,' he recalls, 'but I do remember being really pissed off that we had no cover and that we were so exposed.'

Intending to spray automatic fire into the lead truck, he said to the two diggers, 'Cover the second and rear trucks, but don't fire unless we're fired on.'

In the meantime a young, well-armed man had jumped down from the lead vehicle and was talking with the long-haired prisoner as he cut him free.

'I remember how violent and angry this character [the long-haired man] was as he went to the back of the first truck and tried to grab a weapon,' McOwan says now. 'He clearly wanted to start shooting at us. He yelled at us and again tried to get a weapon from the men in the trucks. I said to the two blokes with me that I'd take him if he were given a weapon, as I would not wait for him to fire on us.'

After the second prisoner was cut free, the young leader retrieved the SKS and some rounds and climbed back into the truck. The long-haired man mounted the first truck and was still trying to get a weapon from the militants as the vehicles disappeared around a bend about 70 metres up the road.

After contacting Response Force headquarters in Dili to request that the Immediate Response Force (IRF) be deployed to Tibar, Tim McOwan realised that the militants in the trucks would probably destroy the village. Indeed, they simply went further down the road, dismounted and began to burn the houses on the far side. It was only the arrival of the two IRF Black Hawk helicopters that saved Tibar from total destruction.

After the incident, McOwan, an eighteen-year veteran of the SAS and commanding officer since January that year, was hit by a mixture of relief that everyone was all right and anger that events had turned sour so quickly. He knew that it was only the obvious willingness of his men to use close-range automatic fire while the militia were standing bunched together in the back of trucks that prevented what could have been the firefight that triggered an all-out war between Australia and Indonesia.

'I have no doubt that had anyone opened fire, we would have been killed. We could never have adequately defended ourselves, as we had been caught in the open against a concrete wall only about 10 metres from sixty to seventy militia, all of whom were armed with automatic weapons.'

The incident had a profound impact on the SAS commander and was a defining moment in his career: he was emotionally bruised for a considerable time and had great difficulty adjusting to the fact that he had not had full control over the situation.

'I had been trained by the best regiment in the world and was disturbed that I had little control over what had occurred,' he says. 'This was at odds with my training and what I had become, unrealistically, accustomed to expect. I was deeply disturbed that someone else could have such absolute power over whether those with me or I were going to live or die. I was upset that I had nearly got others killed and that the situation could change from one of relative security to absolute powerlessness in seconds. I felt pretty battered by the experience and, I suppose, some of the other stresses and experiences I had.'

McOwan had never felt the burden of command so heavily. He experienced an acute sense of loneliness and of having to make difficult decisions with little support.

'I was very conscious of the imperative to prevent any escalation,' he explains. 'This was not like other operations where we were with the US forces. We were on our own. Command of men in such uncertainty is a huge weight.'

It took Tim McOwan some six months before the vivid flashbacks and nightmares faded. He told no one about them except his wife, who was very aware of the issue from the day he arrived home.

'I don't regret having decided to clear the village,' McOwan insists. 'We all recognised that we had been sent there to assist the people of East Timor. However, if I had to do it again, I would certainly do it differently.'

About a year later he read the patrol report that he had written about the incident, and was dismayed to find that it didn't register as a significant event in the squadron diaries and reports. McOwan realised that he had simply been too busy to properly express the gravity of the encounter. While sparsely accurate, he felt his account did not really reflect the intensity of the situation and the emotions he had experienced that afternoon — but he also realised that it was unreasonable to expect that it should. On the lighter side: 'I'm now able to laugh with Greg at how we must hold an SAS record for holding detainees for the shortest time!'

The RSM, Greg, would later become embroiled in public controversy when he was investigated and, eventually, completely exonerated for allegedly abusing the dead body of a militia fighter following a firefight on another occasion. After a drawn-out process, the charges were dropped and Greg received a full apology from the Chief of Army, Lieutenant General Peter Leahy. The matter left a sour taste in the mouths of the men of the SAS regiment, who are well aware that the secret nature of their work makes them vulnerable to false allegations.

The incident at Tibar took place just three days after another dangerous encounter on the road near Bekora, a hotbed of militia activity on the far eastern outskirts of Dili.

Tim McOwan, Jim Truscott and some troopers had just driven through Bekora on their way to check out a small port town over the rise beyond the Jesus statue. Driving up the winding mountain road, they ran headlong into what subsequently turned out to be troops from the Indonesian 745 Battalion.

'We came round one bend in the road and there was a truck full of TNI territorial soldiers, and they were as alarmed as we were at seeing them,' says McOwan. 'Then we rounded the next bend and that truck had already dismounted, and they were clearly going to move into Bekora on foot at this point, back into their battalion barracks area.'

As the SAS men came around the corner, all the Indonesians pointed their weapons at them. 'Fuck off Australia, fuck off Australia!' they said in English.

It happened so quickly that the Aussies were already moving off around the corner; when they got to the top of the rise they saw another three truckloads coming up. Truscott wanted to drive back down the hill past the troops, but his suggestion alarmed the three troopers in the back of the 'borrowed' four-wheel drive.

'No, let's not go back down there,' the three soldiers said, quite unsettled.

McOwan agreed. 'No, no, we're not going back down through there.'

Instead, the Australians weaved their way back through little dirt roads and came out behind the battalion garrison area in Bekora.

That afternoon, Dutch journalist Sander Thoenes, who had only just arrived from Jakarta to cover the story, was murdered probably by those same troops, and about a week later an Australian patrol found six or seven bodies in the same area.

McOwan felt his men were operating under restricted rules of engagement, but he recognised the strategic imperatives at stake. 'I remember being unsettled at this ambiguous direction [asking men to confront an armed enemy but to restrict their use of force],' he said. He also felt there was a lack of coherent objectives from higher command. 'I felt very pressured to arrive at a sound strategy in the absence of any direction.' McOwan found this alarming and disconcerting when added to what he thought was frequently gratuitous advice coming from the strategic and political levels.

Compounding the pressure was the very sudden nature of the deployment. 'None of us had time to say goodbye to our families. We went to work, were "called out" and flew out that afternoon. This created significant family and personal stresses.'

McOwan was learning some hard lessons about the true nature of leadership and the loneliness of command. 'The imperative to send men into harm's way is a terrible responsibility. One does not sleep easily. This is made more difficult as casualties commence.'

In the first six weeks of Operation Stabilise, his men would use deadly force on thirteen occasions and would conduct more than fifty separate tasks.

The first two months in East Timor marked the start of four years of high-intensity operations for the SAS, which was on its steepest learning curve since Vietnam. Every lesson learnt would be incorporated into the planning for future operations.

Twenty-two members of the SAS would receive awards and decorations for their service in East Timor. Lieutenant Colonel Tim

McOwan was awarded the Distinguished Service Cross and Major James McMahon received the Distinguished Service Medal. Both would move on to higher roles.

Despite his self-criticism and doubts, the time McOwan spent on the ground in East Timor as commanding officer of the SAS was pivotal to the growth of the regiment's self-confidence.

'In retrospect, I felt that I led the way in many aspects of what was to come for the SAS Regiment,' he says now. 'Thereafter, there was a sense that they knew they could achieve excellent results in almost any situation.'

Chapter 5

THE GUERRILLA CAMP

The Australian Black Hawk helicopters circled above the village, the pilots checking and double-checking their landing zone. The clearing was just big enough for two of the large, loud, turbine-driven choppers to land side by side. It was not ideal, but it would have to do.

The Falintil guerrillas watching the machines descend had spent days perched in their mountain hideouts, observing the war birds hovering and darting above Dili, flying up and down the coast and out to Navy ships moored off the port.

Now two of the noisy, windy machines were landing on their parade ground at the guerrillas' headquarters cantonment at Uamori in the centre of the island, inland from Los Palos to the east of Dili.

Falintil is the military wing of Fretilin, the revolutionary front for independence in East Timor. The name Falintil is a Portuguese acronym for the Army for the National Liberation of East Timor, which was the dominant resistance force in East Timor, along with the CNRT.

Uamori was the mountain stronghold of Falintil's deputy commander and chief of staff, Taur Matan Ruak, and about 300 of his fighters. It was also home for another 700 or so family members and supporters. Ruak — whose name in East Timor's Tetum dialect means 'two eyes always open' — had taken over the leadership when his commander, Xanana Gusmao, was captured by the Indonesians in 1992.

No direct contact with Falintil had been made by INTERFET prior to the arrival of the force, although indirect links had been established through the Australian East Timor activist Andrew McNaughton and the United Nations office in Dili. Ruak was in contact with McNaughton's Darwin-based go-betweens via satellite phone, and McNaughton himself had been a regular visitor to the Falintil strongholds.

Tim McOwan and Jim Truscott had met with McNaughton in Katherine, in Australia's Northern Territory, prior to Operation Spitfire. Like most senior SAS officers, the pair had considerable experience in training and running guerrilla forces.

'Andrew McNaughton — who was quite helpful to us — gave us quite a bit of information, but it came to a certain point where I realised that his information didn't provide us with the fidelity that I needed,' says McOwan.

In fact, McNaughton's information was not particularly current; it had been gained through his considerable philanthropic work in East Timor, and thus he was not able to provide the detailed information about Falintil and the militia that INTERFET and Major General Cosgrove required.

McOwan knew that Falintil presented the best chance of obtaining such information, so, 'I was determined that we should make contact with them early to tap into this intelligence, while recognising the limitation.' Accordingly, he asked McNaughton to make contact with Falintil, which McNaughton did, through his East Timorese friends in Darwin.

Despite the contacts and assurances that Australian troops would be welcome at Uamori, McOwan felt quite uncertain as he and James McMahon touched down on the rebel parade ground just three days into the mission. The camp wasn't visible from the air and all they had to go on was a map reference. The only way they were able to find it, after flying up and down the watercourse for some time, was when they saw several women near a clearing, washing clothes in the river.

As McOwan recalls: 'The overpowering thing I remember is, as soon as we arrived on this parade ground, there was a wall of bamboo on one side and underneath the bamboo there would have been thirty or forty little huts, and there would have been about eighty or ninety

Falintil guerrillas, and they were all armed. My guys came out of the aircraft and we clearly meant business, not threatening, but in a professional posture. We knew that if these guys fired upon us — we didn't know how they'd treat us at this point — but if there was to be any firefight, these guys knew that they were up against thoroughly professional soldiers.'

McOwan walked up towards the high corner of the little parade ground and out from underneath the bamboo came a man. It was Taur Matan Ruak. McOwan's first thought was, 'Oh gosh, this man's a small man, he's tiny!'

They shook hands, and the Australian could see that Ruak was extremely nervous: 'He didn't know how to treat us, he couldn't smile, he was clearly very, very nervous.'

McOwan had been briefed that an Australian woman named Margharita Tracanelli would accompany Ruak to their meeting. She had been working with Jose Ramos Horta, a leader of the East Timorese resistance movement and 1996 Nobel Peace Prize winner, who had sent her in to make contact with Ruak. Tracanelli had also been working with the CNRT secretariat.

The SAS commander felt a little perplexed as to what she was doing at the meeting. She sat off to the side while Ruak invited the Australian officer to sit. The two men had a cup of coffee together while thirty of McOwan's men stood around.

It was clear to the Australians that they were in a reasonably benign environment — the Falintil guerrillas appeared quite fascinated by the SAS men and displayed great admiration for their M4 carbines and other kit. Through an interpreter, Ruak said, 'If we'd had these weapons we could have killed a lot more Indonesians!'

McOwan's abiding memory of that first encounter with the resistance fighter was the food: 'I remember vividly the first meal that I had with Ruak, and I subsequently had a lot more meals with him. In a little plastic bowl they gave us some Weet-Bix to eat, some dry Weet-Bix ... So we had coffee and Weet-Bix, Ruak and I.'

Ultimately SAS 'liaison and communication' teams were deployed with Falintil units, with the primary task of feeding intelligence back via McOwan into General Cosgrove's INTERFET intelligence mechanisms.

'Falintil fed us information, or we were able to get them to gather information,' McOwan explains, 'because they clearly had an active underground still, or were able to tap into the normal infrastructure, the normal support elements that they had right across East Timorese society, and tell us what was going on.'

The soldiers tested the veracity of the intelligence several times before they gained confidence in it. But it quickly became clear that human intelligence (Humint) of this sort was *the* intelligence currency in East Timor. Happily for McOwan, 'We were able to provide General Cosgrove with a lot of high-value intelligence very early in the piece.'

It took about two weeks for the response force to build enough trust with Ruak to enable it to react to Falintil intelligence. As well as Uamori, the resistance fighters had bases at Los Palos in the east and Ermera in the centre of the province, and near Bobonaro, close to the West Timor border. Once INTERFET became established and the situation stabilised, the Falintil headquarters and main cantonment shifted to Alieu, closer to Dili and more central within East Timor.

For SAS soldiers, guerrilla fighters are regarded almost as kindred spirits: warriors who are prepared to live rough, be patient, operate undeclared, fight hard and melt back into the shadows. These are many of the core skills of the special forces soldier.

In East Timor, men such as Ruak and his fighters and their extended families had been living rough, fighting hard and watching their comrades and loved ones die for twenty-four years. The opportunity to be alongside them at the hour of liberation was in many ways a dream assignment for soldiers like Jim Truscott.

Tim McOwan was also acutely aware of how guerrillas operated. He knew that a guerrilla army had both an auxiliary (a group of associated fighters) and an underground, and that was the case with both

Falintil and the militia. The trick for the SAS would be to plug into those mechanisms while keeping the two sides apart, avoiding favouritism, and staying out of local political arguments.

McOwan had gone into East Timor with a clear plan to access both sides. 'Both Falintil and the militia would have their underground elements, totally undeclared, providing them with support, and their auxiliaries, their people providing them with intelligence and direction and the like, in the classic guerrilla warfare model,' he says. 'My strategy had been to disrupt this by placing liaison and communication teams with both Falintil and the militia, so we [could] find out what's going on, try and separate the two, and at the same time we will attempt to sever them from their underground and auxiliary support. That was the aspiration. As it turned out, we weren't able to realise this strategy as effectively as we had hoped.'

The force made advances through the local Catholic nuns to try to contact the high-profile militia chief Eurico Guterres, but, not unexpectedly, he refused to cooperate.

Falintil, however, did work with them willingly and so the SAS was able, through Andrew McNaughton and UN chief Ian Martin's contacts, to establish contact with them and CNRT very early on in the mission.

As it turned out, all attempts to get in touch with the militia failed and they ultimately fled, so Falintil became the main game. McOwan was not surprised at the militia's negative response, but he was taken aback one day when he witnessed a phone call between Ruak and Guterres, who by this time was based in the militia stronghold of Atambua in West Timor. 'I still to this day do not understand how that transpired. I don't think they knew each other intimately, but Ruak definitely spoke to him on one occasion that I know of.'

Ruak explained to McOwan that Guterres had essentially been subverted, and in Ruak's view the Indonesians were totally responsible. Stories abounded about Guterres being adopted by the feared Indonesian special forces unit, Kopassus, when he was orphaned as a boy.

Interestingly, the SAS had in the past trained Kopassus troops in counterterrorism tactics.

'There was no ambiguity in [Ruak's] thinking at all,' says McOwan. 'This was not a home-grown effort. This was not some militia gone wrong. This was completely orchestrated. And you know, all our intelligence corroborated that.'

The man pulling Guterres's string was Indonesian General Zacky Anwar, who flew into Atambua in West Timor a number of times during the early days of INTERFET. Anwar was linked to Kopassus operations.

Tim McOwan sent Jim Truscott up to Uamori to spend some time with Ruak, because McOwan needed to know what Ruak was thinking and what his future plans were. He also knew that Truscott desperately wanted to spend time with the guerrillas. The SAS operations officer jumped at the chance.

McOwan was also very concerned that General Cosgrove would try to disarm Falintil, which he believed Ruak would never agree to, given the tragedies that had occurred on two occasions under Indonesian rule when Falintil and its predecessor, Fretilin, had agreed to disarm.

The two unconventional warriors hit it off straightaway, although on the first night Truscott became a bit worried when the guerrilla leader invited him to share his hut. Ruak insisted that he and his Portuguese-trained interpreter aide-de-camp, Pedro, would share a bed and that Truscott could have the other one. 'At first I thought they were homosexual and I might have to do it for my country like Lawrence [of Arabia]!' Truscott says now.

The SAS veteran was also surprised to see a 2 Commando Company plaque on the wall. The SAS's predecessor, the 2/2 Independent Company, had served in Timor during World War II, and the guerrilla fighters — and many East Timorese — had forged strong bonds with the earlier diggers.

In keeping with that tradition, Truscott worked hard at building a rapport with Ruak, who still did not trust INTERFET.

'He [Ruak] was testing us,' explains Truscott. 'Once he told us they had found a landmine at a Kopassus base. It wasn't a mine at all — it was a part from a washing machine!'

Truscott settled into life in the guerrilla camp, as happy as anything. He was fulfilling a lifelong ambition to study a guerrilla organisation at close quarters.

'We were fed buffalo milk and Timor coffee, which was narcotic,' he remembers. 'They would do their drills, flag raisings.'

Despite their nervous start, Ruak and his men were soon pleased to have their new comrade from the SAS around the camp. It allowed them to 'play' with some of the latest military hardware.

'They teach them how to use night-vision gear,' says Ruak. 'They see us at night. Maybe when you make love the soldiers see you with your girlfriend. We have never seen this before.'

One major problem with the arrival of the international community in Timor had been the UN-sponsored food drops. Not only were the falling parcels killing and maiming the locals, but the ration packs were incompatible with their tastebuds.

'The people say, "Even our pigs don't want this food",' Ruak says. 'I rang the UN and said, "Please send rice. The people don't want to eat this food. It provokes diarrhoea."'

The Timorese weren't the only ones having problems with the ration packs. The SAS troops attached to the Falintil camps would often try to barter their 'instant' tucker, chocolate bars and chewing gum for fresh food, especially fresh deer meat gathered by Falintil hunters.

'They have their own rations and if, for example, we are going hunting and get any deers or whatever, we just share with them and they happy to take any deers we gave to them,' says Ruak's translator, Pedro.

McOwan asked General Cosgrove if he would meet with Ruak. To his relief, Cosgrove said he would, but also said that his chief of staff, Colonel Mark Kelly, should meet Ruak first, the following day.

Things became tense at that meeting when Kelly suggested to Ruak that he would have to disarm his guerrillas.

'I was completely taken aback by this, and Taur Matan Ruak was visibly upset at the prospect,' says McOwan. 'I explained to Mark that I didn't think it was wise to seek disarmament so early.'

In any case, Ruak drew McOwan aside and said he would never ask his fighters to disarm. Back in Dili, McOwan told Cosgrove about Ruak's reaction. Cosgrove agreed that it was too early to ask him to disarm — and to Ruak's delight, the general told him so in person the very next day at Uamori.

Sitting at the table with formal translators, Ruak was at first cautious.

'I have spoken to lots of generals. Why should I believe you?'

'You are just going to have to take me at face value,' Cosgrove replied.

So they agreed with cantonment status and an element of trust was established. Cosgrove gave Ruak a pen and said, 'When the first East Timorese officer graduates from Duntroon, use this pen to sign his commission.'

As McOwan went to board the Black Hawk with Cosgrove after that meeting, Ruak grabbed his hand and hugged him around the neck. He had tears in his eyes.

'I think it was at that point that meeting, he realised that independence might just become a reality,' says McOwan.

One day not long after that meeting, Ruak and Pedro rode unannounced into the SAS headquarters at the Dili library on a motorcycle.

'I snuck him into the headquarters and took his bike down to get it fixed, and gave Ruak a UN car with the numbers painted out,' Truscott says. 'He refused to give it back to the UN because [Ruak assumed] it was a gift, and they eventually sent troops to try and retrieve the vehicle.' In Truscott's view that was an incredible thing to do, given that Ruak was a major stakeholder. 'Giving away a car is chicken shit. He needs mobility or we have to go to him all the time.'

For his part, Ruak described Jim Truscott and Tim McOwan and their men as his 'brothers'. Despite his twenty-four years as a freedom fighter, often existing on little more than berries or grass, he came to respect the SAS troops.

'To be a soldier is something that is very hard and when people decide to be a military, these people accept all challenges and sacrifice to give peace,' he says. 'It is not easy to leave your country, fight in another country — even sometimes you don't know why we need to do it. There are some things I admire a lot about them.'

Ruak even had a good word for the Indonesian invaders, with whom he had negotiated a ceasefire in 1983. 'We admire them even though they come here to fight for things that don't benefit them. That is their orders and many of them died here for nothing and we respect these people.'

And he has a simple explanation for Falintil's controversial decision not to respond to the militia rampage before INTERFET arrived: 'They [Indonesia] wanted to show the confrontation was not between Timorese and Indonesians, but between Timorese and Timorese. We always try our best to avoid this situation because we know that if we respond, maybe they say, "Yes, the confrontation is Timorese fighting each other and we Indonesians are here just to maintain the peace." That is what they would say and we say that is not true.'

The same situation existed during the period between the independence vote and the arrival of INTERFET. Indonesia had told the world it would guarantee the security of the East Timorese people when it had no such intention and was, in fact, doing the opposite.

Frustration levels mounted in the Falintil cantonments as the atrocities of the militia appeared on their satellite television sets. Ruak's translator, Pedro, said the fighters could see the burning, looting and killing, but discipline was largely maintained. The direct orders from Gusmao — still in Cipiang prison in Jakarta — not to respond were largely followed. There were occasional exceptions, as some commanders could not bear not responding as they saw on CNN their unguarded families being attacked. But according to Pedro, most fighters clearly understood the reason behind their commander's political decision to stay out of the fight.

Ruak had spent nine months in hiding in Dili between November 1998 and July 1999, and when the militia rampage began in earnest he returned to Uamori to concentrate his forces.

'I sent my soldiers to Portugal in 1998 and some to your country as well, but they were sent back by Immigration. I bought one boat for US$2500 and they were captured by the Australians. When they arrived in Darwin they asked, "Whose boat is this?" They said, "It is Ruak's boat." My Darwin contact called me and I said, "Deny it is my boat and help [them] to return."'

Ruak said one of Falintil's biggest problems had always been how to convince the world that their cause was just and that they weren't communist ogres who ate their children. He said the lack of assistance from Australia after the 1975 invasion was particularly difficult to understand for those East Timorese who had fought alongside Australian troops against the Japanese during World War II.

'One of our majors lost his three brothers,' recounts Ruak. 'His father died in 1983 in the jungle, and he was an Australian paratrooper in the Second World War. We know that our grandfathers and fathers say that the people of Australia are our friends.'

Despite this, Australia was the first country in the world to acknowledge Indonesia's occupation of East Timor in 1976. The Fraser government, and the Whitlam government before it, had strongly supported Indonesia's rule over the former Portuguese colony. This policy continued through the Hawke and Keating years, and it was not until 1999 that the Howard government was able to begin paying back the nation's World War II debt.

It was appropriate that special forces troops, the modern-day versions of the diggers from the famous 2/2 Independent Commando Company who fought in Timor during 1942, were back in the jungle helping to liberate East Timor.

'We are very happy when there is a change and you move your troops here,' Ruak said. 'The relationship with Australia and Indonesia is strategic, but even then Australia sacrificed the relationship in 1999 to help us. They are part of our history and nobody is going to forget them. It is important that this be written down for future generations. General Cosgrove we call Faohorai Lulik ["sacred python"] and Mark Webb we call Ramelau ["big mountain"].'

Webb is an ex-SAS captain who stands almost 2 metres tall.

The strong bonds continue, and Australia currently provides military trainers to the fledgling East Timor Defence Force, which is led by the now Brigadier General Taur Matan Ruak, and includes many of his former Falintil comrades.

According to Brigadier General Ruak, East Timor's independence rested on four pillars: 'First, we knew what we wanted, and second, we had one small group that was very strong. What they want is independence, freedom, democracy, and they will always fight for it. Third is how you involve your own people in the fighting. You must persuade them. Fourth, how you convince the international community that what you do is right so they increase their help.'

Speaking at his headquarters in a demountable building in a back street of Dili in mid-2004, Ruak said that the intervention of the international community in East Timor was a miracle. 'We always believed that we would win but not this early. We were thinking forty years, not in twenty-four years. This happened because we have many friends. Your country, the US, Europe, even some Indonesian people. You can't do it alone, you need help. Otherwise we would grow old in the jungle.'

During their guerrilla days, Ruak's right-hand man, Pedro, would monitor the progress of INTERFET via an email system set up at Uamori.

'We monitored all of the information from radio, from television and from the internet — we knew exactly that the decision to send the forces had been made and when INTERFET would arrive,' he remembers.

Pedro had been active with Falintil since 1997, after spending several years in Portugal being trained by the Portuguese Special Forces.

He then spent some time in Australia honing his English skills, before being summoned back to his homeland in 1997 to work for Ruak. His job was to conduct special operations and to facilitate communications between Falintil fighters, gather precise information for the headquarters and the leadership, and enhance their capability to fight the enemy.

So as a comrade in arms in the rarefied world of special forces, what did he think of the SAS soldiers?

'I must say that they are high-trained soldiers. They conduct a mission very well, they perform very professional, efficient, and I have no complaint about that,' he says. 'I could see that, I've done the same special forces training and they behaved as a special force, yes, well-orientated, objective and they know exactly what they were doing.'

While the SAS and Falintil never conducted joint offensive operations, they did work together a number of times. Pedro said Falintil fighters often travelled with SAS patrols to areas where the militia had murdered people. 'We went to the place showing them, they take all of the information, take pictures of dead bodies, and INTERFET has all of this kind of information.'

One Falintil fighter who had plenty of early contact with the SAS troops was a mysterious expatriate who had spent more than a year fighting with the guerrillas, and who was baptised in East Timor as Antony Nikimutin ('White Bat'). Pedro said Nikimutin became very excited when INTERFET arrived.

'He said to us, "They're my buggers, my mates." So some of the conversation is just between them because I was busy with some of the other things. They just talked between them,' Pedro said. He remembers Nikimutin as a brave soldier who experienced great hardships in the mountains.

Now living in Darwin, Nikimutin stayed with Falintil until the last boatload of Indonesian troops departed, then he left. According to Pedro, other volunteers helped in various ways, including with medical assistance, but Nikimutin was the only one who took up arms to join the fight against the Indonesians, 'especially having the direct communication and direct involvement with the fighters, living in the same conditions as the fighters,' he says. Sometimes that meant eating just grass or palms for days on end, and suffering severe hardship. The legend of Nikimutin will live on in East Timorese folklore for many years to come.

One of the great historic moments for Falintil came when their imprisoned leader, Xanana Gusmao, arrived back in East Timor.

The Falintil commander was released to the British embassy in Jakarta and was escorted to Darwin. He then flew into Baucau in a blacked-out C-130 Hercules, where he was met by Tim McOwan and transferred to Dili on a blacked-out Black Hawk.

'We had intelligence that suggested the militia would try to kill him upon arrival, and so we took some extraordinary precautions,' McOwan says.

Gusmao arrived at about nine o'clock at night and was taken to a safe house on the outskirts of Dili. He appeared to be very frightened. The next morning he was met by Ruak in the back of an Australian Bushmaster armoured vehicle. The comrades hugged, spoke softly in Tetum, and wept openly.

McOwan was sitting in the back of the Bushmaster with Falintil commander Lere, who was one level down from Ruak, when the reunion took place.

'It was an amazing meeting,' the Australian commander said. 'The thing that I remember most was the fact that both Xanana Gusmao and Taur Matan Ruak were crying. The tears flowed freely. I suppose it was the immense relief after so many years of fighting. Lere simply smiled. I think that was the only time I ever saw any emotion in him. He always struck me as being a pretty hard bastard.'

Gusmao put on his Falintil jacket and resumed duties as commander, and for the next three weeks the SAS provided close personal protection for East Timor's president-in-waiting.

Chapter 6

THE TURNING POINT

Late on 27 September 1999, Jim Truscott, who was still with Ruak at Uamori, heard some grim news.

A large militia force was raiding along the East Timor coast in the far east of the province. There had been a massacre of nuns and, reportedly, thousands of locals were being held at the old port town of Com, awaiting deportation to West Timor. Truscott reported what he had heard to Tim McOwan.

Com was built right on the ocean and its pier was a major distribution site for the isolated far eastern region of East Timor. It was also used for the militia ethnic cleansing operation, which had been going on since the results of the independence ballot were announced on 4 September.

Falintil forces had already responded to the raids, and without immediate INTERFET action there was a high risk of a major conflict between the guerrillas and the militia. This was the 'civil war' situation that Gusmao had been determined to avoid.

McOwan had proposed a number of raiding missions to Major General Cosgrove in the preceding days — drawing on Falintil-derived intelligence — but they had all been rejected.

McOwan realised that the latest situation was critical, and that there was a need for INTERFET to respond before it became general knowledge that Falintil were involved in gunfights against the militia outside the cantonments. He relayed the latest Falintil intelligence to Cosgrove, along with a plan for his force to respond.

To his amazement, this time the answer came back at once: 'Go, go, go.' And he was to keep Cosgrove fully informed at all times.

Cosgrove also agreed to reposition the amphibious ship HMAS *Kanimbla* off the coast of Com so that any casualties could be flown out to the ship's high-quality medical facility. McOwan was glad to hear it, because he thought it was very possible that they would need it.

Suddenly, with dusk approaching and a large distance to be covered, McOwan had the green light for a risky mission. He was relieved to get the go-ahead, but was also concerned.

'We really did go ... very, very quickly,' he explains, 'and upon reflection I would have liked to have done it more deliberately.'

The commanding officer of the Army's 5th Aviation Regiment, Lieutenant Colonel Mark Wheatly, was present at the Cosgrove briefing and McOwan told him to have three Black Hawks 'turning and burning' for an insertion before last light. He then issued very quick orders to James McMahon.

'I still, to this day, feel a bit guilty that I was only able to give James the most cursory of advice,' says McOwan. 'Nonetheless, both he and the soldiers under his command were so well trained that they understood my intent and what they had to achieve.'

Later, as McOwan was leaving East Timor, and in front of the entire 3 SAS Squadron, McMahon presented him with a field notebook containing the actual orders that he had been given. They covered just two pages.

'The only part of the orders that was clear was the rather open-ended mission statement, which I was careful to ensure James understood clearly. It was simply this: "3 SAS Sqn is to stop the killing at Com",' McOwan recalls.

At the SAS base at Dili heliport, frantic activity broke out. The three Black Hawks fired up their engines and McMahon and his headquarters group — a troop and three Kiwi SAS patrols, about fifty men in total — got their gear and climbed aboard.

McMahon reckoned it took about twelve minutes from when he received his orders until the machines lifted off. He had about two minutes to brief his commanders.

'General Cosgrove wanted it to happen because again it was a demonstration — for all the right reasons — of looking after people, but also it was a demonstration that we were here on the island and we were going to stop people indiscriminately killing,' says McMahon.

The briefings continued in-flight and, as he looked around in the gathering darkness, McMahon suddenly realised he had under his command two organisations that had not had the opportunity to work or train together prior to this operation: the Australian and New Zealand SAS forces.

Like their forebears at Gallipoli eighty-four years earlier, this Anzac force was venturing into the unknown. Fifty fully equipped special forces soldiers were heading into a night landing zone in an area where the pilots, who were frantically working their maps, had not even conducted reconnaissance, let alone landed before. It was also at the outer limit of their range and they had just five minutes' 'loiter' time to find a landing or roping zone (where troops rapel to the ground).

The plan was for the machines to drop the troops and then head out to sea to rendezvous with the frigate HMAS *Adelaide* in order to refuel before returning to Dili, leaving the ground mission without air support. James McMahon instructed the pilot to land short of Com to avoid any risk of ground fire and damage to the Black Hawks.

The soldiers were plugged into individual radio sets that allowed them to talk with each other throughout the 45-minute, 170-kilometre flight along the coast. So by the time they landed, the men had a clear idea of their commander's intent but little concept of what they might encounter on the ground.

'We got on the ground,' says McMahon, 'and we were shaking out and moving down to where we had to be, and it would have been an easy ambush, so we had to move tactically to get there, because people would have heard the helos.

'We didn't really know what to expect, but I was obviously very apprehensive. There was fighting going on, because you could hear the shots in the distance. This was probably going to be our first confrontation with the wrongdoers, and the problem was telling friend from foe. Someone could be shooting, defending themselves, and we didn't want to get into a position where we'd be shooting the wrong person.'

McMahon called McOwan back in Dili, seeking guidance. He described what was going on and said, 'Boss, I need some advice here. What do you want me to do? Do you want me to go in there armed?'

'James, I'm not in a position to be able to order you to do it,' McOwan replied. 'I would never order you to do it. You have been sent there with a mission, you know what the intent is. If you cannot achieve it, you need to come back and let me know. It's your call on the ground about how you want to go in and the depth you want to go in.'

McOwan says now, 'I think James initially thought that I wanted him to go in and conduct an assault through the compound, and that certainly wasn't my intent, but he needed to use some guile, which he did.'

McMahon was focused on securing the port without any loss of life. But he was determined that, if he had to fight to achieve his goal, then fight he would. The controlled use of force is an important part of SAS tactics and techniques, and had been a key priority in the pre-mission briefings before East Timor.

'There was a sense of, "Well, we've got to make sure that we choose the use of violence very carefully. It won't suit anyone very well if we start having a massacre." Com was all about stopping people being killed. That was the direction I had from the boss — get to Com and stop people being killed.'

For these highly skilled soldiers, the idea of killing anyone is regarded as the last resort. 'I think that's a standard that we work by, but in saying that, Com was all about stopping the civilians or anyone there killing each other.'

As his force approached the port from the west, McMahon was concerned that he might be lining his men up for the chopping block.

Back at INTERFET headquarters, Cosgrove was also feeling slightly apprehensive. Despite his supreme confidence in the group's abilities, he had until now resisted the temptation to employ the SAS in a situation where they couldn't be supported by a larger force. As he explains: 'I was anxious not to so employ them that I couldn't support them. I had great confidence in them. Everything I asked them to do they achieved to the highest degree. So there was a tendency to say, "They can do anything."'

As the soldiers approached the port area, which appeared green through their night-vision gear (NVG), the shooting stopped. On the port itself a lot of people were running around and a couple of fires were burning. McMahon could not see any dead bodies, so he felt relieved. But the whole situation was rather chaotic, with people dodging away and obviously wondering who the soldiers were. The gunshots stopped, however, and that was the aim.

McMahon led a small force forward in a 'robust' (ready to fight) formation. Some locals emerged from the shadows and told them that the bad guys had fled.

'That was tense in itself because again you're presenting yourself as a target,' he says. 'But to me it was the only logical way at the time, with the immediacy of the situation — who's good, who's bad ... we had to work that out.'

While looking after the locals was central to his mission, McMahon was acutely aware of the need to preserve his force unharmed. 'To lose one person there would have sent the wrong message, because potentially the militia would be saying, "Oh, these Australians, of course we can shoot them, look, they die!"'

Once he realised that the locals had been telling the truth about what was going on in Com, McMahon felt relieved. His first objective — to stop the killing — had been achieved. The soldiers then announced that they were leaving. Despite protests from the locals, they withdrew to the hills behind the port, whence they sent out scouts and established an ambush position overlooking what appeared to be the main street. The ruse had the desired effect: armed militiamen reappeared on the street. The Anzacs trained their weapons on them and they surrendered. The group, which included one man who had been shot (not by the SAS but probably by Falintil), was detained and later transferred to Dili for interrogation.

It became clear that the reports of 'thousands' of people waiting to be deported from Com had been slightly exaggerated. A message was sent to the remaining militia that they had until midnight to surrender or they would be arrested. A group of about eight men — who were clearly not militia — were sent out with their *parangs* (local knives), but from his earlier discussions McMahon knew there were more heavily armed people inside the port area.

He approached the entrance and, through an interpreter, presented an ultimatum: 'We know that you're in there. We know you have automatic weapons. You must come out by midnight, otherwise we're coming in.'

At about 11.30 p.m., through the night-vision gear, they saw twenty-four people come out and board a truck. They were detained, along with about twelve SKS carbines, without a single shot being fired. Despite this, James McMahon describes the Com operation as 'tense' and says he was amazed that there hadn't been a confrontation.

McMahon had seen only about 100 or so people gathered on the wharf area when he arrived. Others had been collected nearby. According to Cosgrove, the operation had allowed about 600 East Timorese, who were in imminent danger of being shipped out, to return to their homes.

In Tim McOwan's view the Com raid was pivotal, not only for the regiment but for the wider INTERFET mission. He said it was an exemplary SAS mission, led by a fine officer in James McMahon.

'General Cosgrove's confidence grew then; he knew that he had a force that was disciplined, that was able to capture these individuals without firing one shot,' the SAS commander says. 'We launched without adequate preparation, contrary to the way we would normally launch, but I guess we were poised. We were the only element in General Cosgrove's entire force that could have done it in that time frame. Upon reflection, I would have liked to have done it a little more deliberately, but it was timely because I think they probably would have taken the IDPs that night or at first light the following morning.'

The Com operation also showed Falintil that the SAS and INTERFET meant business: 'Falintil saw us react to their information, their intelligence, and they saw us moving efficiently against the militia elements. So it was about building their confidence and the confidence of the population as much as anything.'

Cosgrove thought the operation was well executed and tremendously well led, saying, 'I was very proud of the small group of SAS who did that. From that point on my advice to myself was, "But don't expose them too much." By that I mean, "Yeah, good, I can get them to do anything; no, I have to support them every time." They led the way and continued to do their classic small patrol framework operations to dominate an area and give me very reliable eyes on the ground. They were working very hard.'

The next morning the Black Hawks returned to Com from Dili. Twenty-four prisoners and a dozen captured weapons were loaded on board, and the force made a speedy withdrawal. The mission had achieved Cosgrove's intentions, which were to stop the fighting and forced deportations, and to demonstrate that INTERFET could react at short notice and achieve results without a blood bath.

For James McMahon, too, the Com job marked a turning point. He describes his entire three-month tour of East Timor as an incredibly rewarding, but testing professional experience: 'There wasn't a lot of loss of life, which is most probably the good thing, and it was a good thing for the locals, which was amazingly satisfying,' he said. 'You didn't have any problem getting out of bed in the morning because every day you'd do good. You could feel that. I might be a bit bold here, but I felt that the squadron and the people that we had work with us, I think we contributed a lot to the success of the mission.'

That contribution was recognised with the award of a Unit Citation to 3 SAS Squadron when it returned to Australia.

McMahon thought it was important for the Australian people to see that their defence forces could do the job they were paid to do. East Timor also provided the young major with some deeper insights into the character of the men who serve in the SAS.

'I think we are particularly lucky in the special forces community because of the character of the bloke we get. He's a reasonably robust character anyway. I remember travelling down to the [Oecussi] enclave [the western part of East Timor surrounded by Indonesian territory] during the night in the back of the helo and the doors were open and I was thinking, "We're a long way from support." And I looked around and some people have just got their eyes closed and you think, this could be very nasty in a whole lot of ways. But the fact you're there together sort of drives you on.'

McMahon said it was also crucial to maintain a sense of perspective when working constantly in nasty and tragic situations. 'We spoke to people in the enclave about pregnant women getting killed, and on the humanity side you wonder who you are dealing with.'

His wife was expecting their first child while he was in East Timor, and she sent him a tape of the Italian tenor Andrea Bocelli, with a message: 'Play that at night. It will remind you of the good things in life.' And he played it many times, lying on his bunk with earphones on, reflecting on what she had said.

'It was bloody good advice, because there are some very bad things in the world, but equally we're trying to fix that so we can get these very good things. But I just used to feel, well, it was easy for me because I was going home eventually, but you couldn't help thinking there's been a lot of horror for these people.'

McMahon's daughter was born soon after he returned home to Perth and that altered his perspective even more.

'A friend of ours sent a Persian rug to us from overseas. And my little girl — we were teaching her to come out of nappies — comes in, wees on the carpet, the brand-new rug. And my wife said, "Oh, it hasn't been a good day!" and I replied, "Has it really been that much of a bad day?"

'I harked back to the things that I've seen in my career and said, "Look, it will make another nice little circle on it!" I really can't get overly fussed about that ... and I hope that's the lesson all the soldiers take out of it.'

Chapter 7

FIRST BLOOD

It happened just after 5 p.m. on 6 October.

The first volley of high-powered shots smashed into the two SAS soldiers, grazing a third. The men were escorting a convoy of detainees to the West Timor border near Suai when suddenly the two lead vehicles pulled away. The passengers in the truck and bus looked to the left into the bush — then all hell broke loose.

Trooper Ron Juric was the gunner in the first vehicle and he took two rounds, one in the shoulder and one in the lower leg. Sitting next to him was Warrant Officer Greg, whose camouflage shirt was grazed by a militia bullet.

In the second vehicle, driver Corporal Mark Hogno was hit in the upper shoulder close to his neck.

Back at INTERFET headquarters in Dili, Major General Cosgrove had been wondering when the militia would try something against his men, and the time had clearly arrived.

'I couldn't have picked the moment,' says Cosgrove, 'but I knew sooner or later they were going to have a go, either through some policy or through the adventurism of a particular group. These were people who had shown a propensity to kill, without mercy, admittedly defenceless people, but they were well armed ... so it stood to reason that sooner or later one of our combat elements would cop something.'

And cop it they did. The ambush had been well executed and the diggers came under heavy and sustained enemy fire.

The SAS convoy included two Land Rovers and a Unimog truck and about eighteen soldiers. Patrol medic Trooper Brook Burgess was riding in the Unimog at the rear of the convoy. Burgess, a thoughtful and softly spoken amateur rock musician, had been in the SAS for just on two years — the average length of service is ten years. He hit the floor as the ungainly truck shuddered to a halt.

'There's no real cover, just concealment from view,' he recalls. 'I bobbed back up, put in a bit of covering fire so the guys in the Land Rovers could organise themselves and the guys in the front of our Mog could actually get out, because from the cabin of a vehicle you can't do a lot. We knew where the shots were coming from but I didn't see anyone. A few of the guys saw other people, saw people out there, but I was just shooting at likely positions.'

The men jumped off the truck and took up positions in a 20-centimetre-deep drain that ran along the roadside. At that stage no one from the Unimog knew that there were any casualties. As soon as word came back that men had been hit, Burgess jumped up under covering fire, retrieved his patrol medical kit and went straight to the nearest casualty, who was Ron Juric. Burgess was under constant fire and could hear the *crack* of bullets all around him. He recognised the sound of the rounds as 7.62 mm, which is the ammunition used in the standard issue assault weapon favoured by the Indonesian Army and the militia. When he reached Juric he found that another trooper, Dean, had already begun treatment with a compression dressing over the top of Juric's camouflage uniform. 'However, you don't really want to do that,' explains Burgess. 'You want to clear the site and remove anything out of the way. So I quickly took that off and got rid of his cams.'

The bullet had passed through Juric's calf and shattered the tibia and fibula. 'A good analogy for it is, you know when you get a stocking of sand and you squeeze it really tight, and all the sand disappears out of the middle and it's just left with a floppy skin, and it's hanging in the breeze — that's what his leg was like. It was a closed fracture, it was a nice small entry wound, nice small exit wound, just that everything inside was mush. I was surprised, because it didn't look that bad, but I was surprised once I felt it and looked at it how it had just vaporised everything inside the leg. It was so violent in its action but at the same time, in being so violent, it didn't look as traumatic.'

During the initial treatment, which was taking place under enemy fire in the roadside drain, Burgess noticed a small dirt bank, or berm, a few metres behind his position. He made a mental note to get his patient behind that as quickly as possible. In the meantime he stuck to his doctor 'ABC'.

'He was conscious, so I knew he was in pain, and his airway and breathing were good to go. Circulation's next, you're looking for major haemorrhage, stuff like that, so you're looking over his body, asking him, because he's conscious, "Were you shot anywhere else? Is there pain anywhere else?" "No, no, it's just my leg." His arm wound was fairly minor, so the leg was the major concern. The human body's amazing, there was no profuse bleeding or anything, contrary to what you see on the movies — when someone gets shot there's blood everywhere. It was nice and clean and all the vasoconstriction, all the blood vessels were just *whssst*,' Burgess says.

Although he was under fire and in real and immediate danger, Burgess's patrol medic training kicked in. Each SAS trooper is either a medic or a signaller — 'chook' — as a core skill; they specialise during their initial training. The medics undergo an intensive six-week training course and regularly spend time helping out in civilian hospital emergency departments.

'It should be longer to let things settle in, but time with this place runs at a million miles per hour — it's a jam-packed six-week course just of cramming. You've got to pass numerous tests and scenarios and are drilled constantly,' Burgess says. At the end of the course they are expected to be able to keep a wounded soldier alive until he can be evacuated from the battlefield.

So the drills came to him automatically as he delved into his patrol medical kit for more treatments for his wounded comrade. The kit includes equipment to take care of airways, breathing and circulation, and a range of antibiotics and medications in the form of oral tablets and a pouch of injectables. It also contains blood pressure cuffs, stethoscopes to monitor and evaluate the patient, and bags of fluids for drips.

The other wounded digger, Corporal Hogno, was in better shape and receiving treatment from another patrol medic, Trooper John Boyd. Because of the position of his wound — so close to his neck — they didn't want to tie on any dressings and instead used a dressing clasped over the wound. 'He was sweet, the bullet hadn't hit his collarbone or anything like that, it had just passed straight through the fleshy part,' says Burgess. Eventually Burgess and two other soldiers picked Juric up and dragged him behind the berm, where his treatment continued.

Soon afterwards, two light armoured vehicles from the Darwin-based Cavalry regiment arrived and sprayed the enemy with chain gunfire as the troops continued to clear along the road. Two troopers stayed with Burgess, Boyd and the wounded diggers as the rest of the force fanned out to attack the enemy.

The medics transferred the patients into the back of one of the armoured vehicles and waited until the all clear was given. By that time Juric was in heavy pain, so Burgess administered morphine. He then handed over primary care to a Kiwi corps medic who was attached to the Australian Light Armoured Vehicles (ASLAVs). She eventually called in a Black Hawk for a medical evacuation to Dili.

On the ground in Suai, James McMahon was wondering how to get the wounded diggers off the battlefield and to the hospital in Dili: 'I was thinking, "Get the people we've got there out", both from a casualty perspective and from saving more lives if required. Again it was back to that position of, strategically, a bunch of Australians getting killed is not really what the general would want or Australia would want. So that was pretty high in my mind.'

As he arrived at the ambush site soon after, McMahon looked across his right shoulder and saw the militia shooting at him from pretty close quarters. The first thought that went through his head was, 'Shit, I'd better watch myself here or I'm going to get my bloody head shot off!'

The second thought was, 'Gee, it's good to see the blokes working in pairs.' This was the way the SAS trained, but McMahon was thrilled to see it working in a real battle.

The Suai incident marked the first time an Australian SAS force had fired a shot in anger since Vietnam. 'And the fact [was] that I didn't give detailed orders about how we were doing that, people just did their thing from all the training we did and away we went. I remember the bushes were just flicking down and that's when I thought, "I'd better bloody watch properly and focus on my front, because I don't want to be a bloody casualty". I think that's a natural survival thing, I think you've got to understand that humans want to live.'

It was a tense time for James McMahon. The day before the raid, one of his patrols had been shot at by militia. 'They [militia] knew the patrol was there, they were shooting into the bushes indiscriminately to make them move,' he says. 'I can laugh about it now, but it wasn't laughable when you were sitting back in the headquarters hoping the patrol would be all right, because we knew we were going in the next day. But they were providing us with great intelligence.'

One tactic used by the militia — as it had been by the Vietcong in Vietnam — was to fire into the bushes where they suspected the Australians might be 'lying up'.

McMahon thought the technique was probably linked to the hunting strategies employed by East Timorese when stalking deer or wild pigs, to make the prey move.

'The tactic made sense, because I suppose some people would move,' McMahon says.

A number of SAS patrols were subjected to indiscriminate shooting in their general direction throughout their time in Timor. The militia knew something was out there but they couldn't see the well-hidden and camouflaged diggers. 'The blokes had to be very steadfast,' says McMahon. 'They could smell us, we never underestimated them,' says McMahon. Despite every attempt to smell like their surroundings (a drill learnt in Vietnam), the diggers had a distinct body odour that the militia could pick up.

'It's not a good feeling having people bloody firing all around the bushes where you're trying to lie up,' McMahon continues. 'We can be a silent as we want, but we're not that silent. And smell is another one. Whichever way you cut it, you've got to be in the bush for a long time not to smell unusual.'

The troops sweeping through Suai later recovered two enemy bodies, and intelligence reports indicated that two more militia killed in action had been removed.

Reflecting on his first ever enemy contact, Brook Burgess says he was reassured by the way everyone involved had reacted: 'No one panicked, no one was freaked out by the situation, everyone seemed to be very methodical in what they had to do, it was like, "Okay, we're being shot at, where are the guys? They're over there, okay you look after that", and it all sort of clicked. Not a lot had to be said. If something needed doing, if you weren't doing it then someone else would just go, "Yep, I've got it." Everyone whinges about training — not, you know, seriously, but you can see why we do it. It was very, very reassuring.'

As for his medical training: 'The scenarios they run for us at work are heaps harder than the real thing. It's always a massive bleeder and you can't control it, and people are screaming in pain, and it's very dramatic and Hollywood, and it is hard to deal with if it's like that. But the reality of it was that the guys, although in a lot of pain, were coherent, knew what was going on, could give you honest responses to how they felt; and the wounds in those particular cases — because they weren't arterial bleeds — were very, very easy to manage.'

The ambush was the climax of an SAS operation to confirm Falintil intelligence that militia were killing and terrorising many people is the Suai district on the island's south coast. An SAS patrol, inserted by helicopter on 2 October, had corroborated the intelligence. The militia looters were returning to West Timor every evening.

So on 4 October coalition patrols were deployed to the area, and the next day a troop, under the command of Captain Jon Hawkins, mounted a vehicle patrol that left Dili for the first overland operation into the troubled Ainaro Regency, the district around Suai. At the same time Tim McOwan convinced Cosgrove of the need for a so-called 'brush and block' raid on Suai. The idea was for response force patrols to sweep through the area pushing militia forces back into the SAS blocking forces.

Early on 6 October the force, which included McMahon's headquarters group and two troops plus the Kiwis and Brits, launched the operation. The Immediate Reaction Force remained on stand-by in Dili with four Black Hawks, and the Navy frigate HMAS *Adelaide* was positioned about 25 kilometres off Suai in the Timor Sea. The blocking elements needed to be in place well before the helicopters arrived and alerted the enemy.

'The blocking element was positioned in accordance with the intelligence gained from the previously inserted SAS patrol,' McOwan explains. 'As soon as the helo assault force arrived, I knew any element of surprise would be lost, [so] it was critical that the blocking element and the vehicle element should arrive at their forming-up places clandestinely. Fortunately all forces arrived securely. We approached on three different axes converging towards the centre of the township, and pushing any likely elements towards the blocking force now in position.'

Watching the operation unfold, the SAS commander was impressed with the discipline of his men. As five armed militiamen ran away from the centre of town, the SAS soldiers remained hidden, their weapons at the ready. They could easily have engaged and killed any of the militia, but their rules of engagement — which allowed them to fire only if they were in imminent danger — did not permit it.

'Under these tense circumstances, the discipline and control of SAS soldiers has to be seen to be believed,' says McOwan. 'I later reflected that the SAS blokes from the Vietnam era would have difficulty understanding this more controlled form of military operation, although they too would have been equally as disciplined had it been required of them.'

The sweep through Suai was effective, and as the force approached the blocking position, there was a burst of automatic gunfire. James MacMahon radioed ahead to determine what had happened: Captain Carl Marning had ordered his mini gunner to fire on and stop a vehicle which had attempted to 'run' his blockade.

By the time McOwan arrived at the scene, Marning and his men had secured 116 detainees. The women were all sat down in the shade and the men were plasticuffed. The medics were treating three people who had been lightly injured in the short burst of gunfire.

McOwan had a Falintil commander called Dekker with him who asked the local fighter to try to identify any militia members amongst the detainees: 'Dekker and his translator indicated ten detainees whom they believed to be militia. I then took these detainees back to Dili by Black Hawk helicopter for subsequent questioning and directed James to release the remainder back close to the West Timor border. The looted goods were to be left in the town.'

That was when the ambush happened and the SAS took its first hits.

Afterwards Major General Cosgrove was quite philosophical about the Suai ambush: 'I am a child of the Vietnam era. I had been an infantry platoon commander. In battle, people get hurt. I was relieved they had not been killed.

'The SAS reacted emphatically and swiftly. They had very shrewdly brought along with them ASLAVs, which were a very heavy weapons platform to assist to dominate that battle. They conducted a good old-fashioned up-the-guts infantry assault to put an end to the militia.'

Trooper Brook Burgess was subsequently awarded the Commendation for Gallantry for his work at Suai.

The sequence of raiding across East Timor was described by hardened senior SAS soldiers as incredible, as the squadron adopted Major General

Peter Cosgrove's strategy — formulated on day one — of never taking a backward step.

The 3 SAS Squadron raided towns including Maliana, Alto Lebos, Fatu Lulik and Bobonaro, which had been hard hit by rampaging militia mobs, as well as the Oecussi enclave when it was still an unknown quantity.

Not since Vietnam, thirty years earlier, had SAS patrols been deployed in anger, without support, over long distances, to put eyes on targets deep inside 'enemy' territory.

The early targets were selected using strategic intelligence. The combination of Cosgrove's 'no backward steps' strategy, Tim McOwan's aggressive leadership and SAS tactics honed over many years paid off in spades.

In East Timor a highly professional relationship developed between the SAS and the Black Hawk pilots from the Army's 5th Aviation Regiment. This, combined with night-vision gear and the latest radios, took raiding and deployment tactics to a very advanced level.

The tempo continued when 1 SAS Squadron replaced 3 SAS Squadron in December 1999. While less glamorous than some of the early raiding operations, many of its patrols, especially in the Oecussi enclave, were arduous and dangerous.

Deadly force is a core skill of an SAS soldier, but the range of talents that he brings to a military campaign are far more sophisticated than simply killing people; in Timor they were all put to good use. The soldiers experienced the challenges of long-range patrolling as well as close personal protection, hearts-and-minds and medical work, and sea and airborne raiding.

The SAS commanding officer, Tim McOwan, was determined to rotate the three SAS squadrons into East Timor to develop their operational maturity, and he did.

Lieutenant Colonel Gus Gilmore was operations officer at Special Forces Operations Headquarters in Sydney during the early part of Operation Stabilise, and became SAS commander for the endgame in November 2001. Tim McOwan was promoted to a job in Canberra and, as a brigadier, was appointed Deputy Commander, Special Operations Command in Sydney in 2004.

Gilmore said that, prior to the operation, the government had been looking for a range of options for East Timor and it was the SAS that was able to provide two or three rational and effective alternatives: 'That really came out of a lot of the training and preparation we'd done over the years,' he said. 'The CT [counterterrorism] arrangement had helped, but SAS isn't preoccupied with the counterterrorist storm trooper-type mentality; it's something we have had from the late seventies. The legacy was this discipline of being, at very short notice, able to move in, palletise and be out the front gates for any operations in a matter of hours, which is quite unusual in the ADF.'

At the same time the regiment wanted to convince all stakeholders, including senior military commanders, that it was more than just a special reconnaissance force; that was its Vietnam legacy, and apart from the counterterrorism capability — which had never been used — the new generation of officers was keen to prove the regiment's broader value.

'I think most current-generation special forces or SAS commanders viewed it as a special operations force which has far broader, longer, strategic-type missions and goals and roles,' says Gilmore. 'So we were keen to say that Timor proved that we were more than just a reconnaissance force — let's actually continue to develop our skills so that we can offer good utility to [the] government in a broad spectrum of operations or circumstances.'

It was the pace of operations, particularly the raids and the hearts-and-minds patrols, that put the regiment out in front and proved to Peter Cosgrove that he could call on them to do almost anything. Cosgrove also recognised that he had to tailor their tasks and support them 100 per cent to avoid what he described as the 'wing and a prayer' option: 'They can do some incredibly difficult things, but it is incumbent on senior commanders not to become fanciful in the use of them.'

James McMahon, the man on the ground with tactical responsibility for the 'chicken stranglers', compared the early days of the operation with the first quarter of an AFL footy game. His men conducted fifty-six full mission profiles in the first forty days, and applied deadly force on thirteen occasions. That is more than one major troop deployment a day, and even the smallest of them usually required considerable planning.

'So we were working very, very hard and we were working in a time frame that in some cases we hadn't trained for,' McMahon said. 'I'll go back to the AFL first-quarter football: the fact is, we were out there very quickly on the border, and some major key areas — I mean Suai, Maliana, a whole range of areas where we put recon in there — see what's going on in a clandestine way and then we'd back it up with a troop movement.

'I think the big thing is about setting the scene. I believe that if you don't set that scene, if we weren't moving quickly or we weren't making a display of confidence, things could have been different and people [the militia] might have been more ready to have a go.'

However, that could have resulted in a more drawn-out campaign and increased the risk of escalation with the Indonesians. Therefore the risks — and there were serious risks taken — were not only worthwhile but necessary. Something like dropping foot patrols from helicopters deep into militia-controlled areas without support is dangerous, but it is fundamental to the 'Who Dares Wins' philosophy of the regiment.

Not that there was much time to think about risks: 'Some people would say, "Boss, we need more time to prepare", and I'm saying, "You don't have it!" It's just the reality of the situation, and I think the greater good by being out there was worth the risk because it could have been a different campaign if what I call a certain "information operation" wasn't achieved.'

The military focus was on Dili, but SAS troops were scattered from one end of the province to the other, undertaking tasks as diverse as tracking militia, providing medical help to the locals and liaising with Falintil. McMahon's biggest worry in those early days was having a number of patrols in the border areas with no support at all. The Immediate Reaction Force was on 24-hour stand-by, but the bottom line was that the enemy knew the ground much better than his troops did. Even with the best luck and planning in the world, support was always at least a couple of hours away — provided the weather was clear enough to allow the Black Hawks to cross the mountains that run the length of the island of Timor.

Just how vulnerable his men really were hit McMahon when a patrol was attacked in the Lebos area close to the western border: 'The particular patrol commander was talking to me on the radio saying, "They're getting closer, the shots are getting closer, I'm going to have to fire soon, I won't fire until the last safe moment." I mean, this is over the radio!'

On 13 October, a six-man patrol led by Sergeant Steve Oddy was flown into an area to the northeast of the town of Aidaba Salala, close to the West Timor border. They spent three days moving in a clandestine manner towards the town, which was a hotbed of militia activity. Oddy, thirty-two, was a twelve-year veteran of the regiment. He is a very good commander, a 'lead-from-the-front' style of senior soldier and a well-respected and highly skilled special forces soldier.

The patrol spent an entire day undetected in one village of several hundred people, and on the morning of 16 October the men crossed the dry bed of the Moto Meuculi Creek close to Aidaba Salala. The bed was about 10 metres wide with 2- to 3-metre banks covered with scrub, lantana and long grass; the creek was used as an escape route to West Timor by militia raiding parties.

As the troops began clearing an observation post overlooking the dry bed, a group of half a dozen militiamen appeared in the creek. The lead man was moving cautiously, with his weapon at the ready. Patrol second scout Lance Corporal Keith Fennell was spotted by the militiaman, who moved to fire on the digger. Fennell opened fire with his M4 carbine, using half a magazine and hitting three of the enemy. Oddy moved beside him and fired several rounds from his 40 mm grenade launcher at the fleeing militiamen. He then ordered Fennell and the patrol medic/machine gunner back across the creek to watch for further militia activity. It wasn't long in coming: just a few minutes later the medic spotted two armed militiamen in the creek moving towards the SAS position in the same direction as the earlier group. The medic shot and killed one of them and fired several more shots in their direction.

Oddy realised the patrol was in trouble so he recalled the men from across the creek and ordered his men into an all-round defensive position, with each man assigned an arc of responsibility, an area within which they would engage any enemy venturing in. He had also radioed Reaction Force headquarters in Dili requesting immediate assistance.

Several minutes passed before patrol members reported militiamen moving towards their positions. The militia raiding party had left the creek bed and was attempting to surround the diggers. The patrol's second in command opened fire on five militiamen approaching in an extended line. He hit two enemy and the others fired randomly in the direction of the Australians.

Up to thirty or more enemy now joined the fight, with one leader providing specific fire and movement orders. Realising that he faced a larger force obviously prepared to take casualties, Oddy decided to break contact and quietly led the patrol back across the creek bed. His men left their heavy packs behind and walked for about 300 metres before spotting two Immediate Reaction Force Black Hawk helicopters. After they set off a smoke grenade, one of the machines landed in an open area and the six soldiers scrambled aboard. They flew back to where the contact had taken place and landed in a nearby clearing. Three diggers left the helicopter and collected their packs, plus several weapons found near a dead militiaman.

The battle had lasted for about ninety minutes and the diggers had fired about 200 rounds from the Minimi machine gun and just sixty-seven shots from their M4 carbines. One soldier had not fired a single round because no enemy ventured into his arc of responsibility.

Just six hours after the fight, an infantry company from 2RAR, which was based at Balibo, swept through the area but found nothing.

Reports from villagers suggested the militia had suffered five dead and three wounded, although the official figure was four enemy killed.

James McMahon says that the experience of the Oddy patrol showed that the SAS training, tactics, techniques and procedures dating from the Vietnam era were not only alive and well, but they worked. A small patrol, a long way from support, had looked after itself in conflict.

'It showed the true grit of the people in the patrol. It was dire at one point, but they didn't give up.'

He says it also typified what the Australian soldier was about: courage, determination and teamwork. 'Without teamwork they might not be here today,' he believes.

The ferocity of the militia's repeated attacks had surprised the Australian commanders; the militia seemed to be 'desperate to kill an Australian soldier'.

For his actions and leadership on the battlefield that day, Steve Oddy was awarded the Medal for Gallantry.

After witnessing and hearing the horror stories of evacuees escorted out under Operation Spitfire, many troopers had some inkling of what they would find when they returned to East Timor for Operation Stabilise. Even so, the wanton destruction of the towns and villages came as a huge shock to young soldiers such as Trooper Brook Burgess.

'The biggest cultural impact there was that it was totally obliterated. The whole thing was destroyed,' he says now. 'Even speaking to aid workers who'd done Bosnia and other warzones around the world, they couldn't believe it. I was speaking directly to one guy who'd been to all those places and he said, "You know, you walk down a street and there might be a building in this block burnt, go to the next block and there might be one or two and the next block after that might be something destroyed, but go to Dili and a few other major towns and absolutely every single thing was burnt and destroyed."'

Chapter 8

THE LANTANA LUCKY DIP

Sergeant George, born in New Zealand of Samoan parentage, was posted to East Timor in August 2000 as a reinforcement. The then lance corporal, who is married with two daughters, was second in command of a patrol and eventually became a patrol commander during his tour. On one stint with the Immediate Reaction Force, he and his patrol were sent on a 'screening' operation to try to intercept an escaping militia force.

George, a big man with a ready smile and cutting wit, was rudely reminded on this mission of why the SAS selection course is designed the way it is.

'They dumped us in lantana which was . . . 2.5 metres high, and it was a clearing but all around us for a good 200 or 300 metres was this very, very thick lantana and it's very prohibitive to move through,' he recalls. 'I'd say 100 metres would take us an hour. And from where we were dropped, which looked like an excellent position and it was a good landing site, for us to get to the objective took us a good four or five hours. I remember thinking to myself at the time that selection has got nothing on that sort of thing! You could see why we do selection because it was really demoralising stuff to get through, because we knew we had to get to that point in order to do our task.'

During the lantana torture, George's mind went back to the Bindoon army training area northeast of Perth and the ironically named Lucky Dip phase of the selection course. He had not only experienced it himself, but had subsequently supervised other candidates.

'You have a five- or six-man group and they give you a task that would take maybe two more men, eight men, to do and not quite enough time to do it. They're not really tasks that are designed to be achieved, more to embugger [sic] the people. By the time they get to that stage they're quite tired, it's like a veil has been lifted and people's true traits come out. You can see someone who's going to be jack and lazy and sit back and say, "Bugger this, I've had enough." You can see people who are going to be shifty and try to slide out of work, and you see people who really, really buckle down and do their job. And the lantana reminded me of that because it was heinous, it was at the time one of the hardest things I've done.'

Lantana was the bane of a number of patrols in East Timor and George remembers his 300 metres and five hours of lantana hell as if it were yesterday. Because it was a night-time rapid-response task, he selected an area 300 metres square and instructed the pilots to land his patrol there.

'He didn't even land, actually, we did a hover dismount, he came in and he got as high off the deck as he thought was appropriate. We told him to go a bit lower because we had our packs on and didn't really want to jump off and hurt our legs.' During a similar insertion earlier on, a soldier had broken his leg jumping to the ground.

Once they hit the ground, the five troops were confronted with walls of lantana in every direction. Out came the Army-issue secateurs — machetes would have been too noisy — and they began the biggest pruning exercise any of them had ever undertaken.

'That's probably why it was so torturous, because we were just cutting through it, pushing it aside and making our way through that,' George explains. But, adopting the SAS mantra of always looking on the bright side, he thought, 'Well, at least it's not wait-a-while palm', whose sharp tropical foliage is a nightmare.

'Lantana is just an insidious mess of vines and the vines just go on and on . . . there's tons of little hair-like things that burn and scratch and get in everything. Your cams [camouflage clothing] would be all pilled and torn all completely, through travelling through it. It's not so bad if you're up the back, but we'd have to rotate the guy up the front because it's very exhausting. And it is noisy and it's very tough for the scout, who can be cutting, he's really got to take his time and look ahead.'

Lantana wasn't the only challenge faced by the SAS patrols. Local hunters and their prey, inaccurate information, and the rough terrain all threw up unique challenges.

Corporal Shane had been in the regiment for just three years when he was deployed to East Timor. The 34-year-old father of two and Perth local was a patrol 2IC when he arrived in November 1999.

During one operation he was lying up in an observation post when a wild pig, closely followed by a couple of dogs, rampaged through, knocking everything flying, including a camera and tripod.

'I could hear some people running down, first some dogs came and then people, they were hunters obviously after the pigs, so we thought, "We're going to get compromised here,"' says Shane. 'So we just sort of lay flat and one guy came right up, he would have been not even four or five feet from us, and he looked around and kept on walking. I'm 100 per cent sure he didn't see us. So we were lucky there.'

Building a 'hide', 'lying up position' (LUP) or 'observation post' (OP) as good as that one is another core skill of the SAS soldier. In this case the OP had been in situ for several days, so it had been refined to a high level.

'First you choose a location where it's not going to be seen — see and not be seen — so you're looking for your camouflage there,' Shane said. 'Hopefully it's under a bush or somewhere nice and camouflaged. Then as you are lying there you can work out where you can or can't be seen, so the next person who comes down brings a bit of extra camouflage, so you're not ripping it out where you are building it from. You slowly build on it while you are there, so you get a feel for it — what you can see and what you can't see. Our biggest problem there was the odd camera as well and getting the sun, the gleam, and putting a bit of cardboard over the top to stop that.'

Keeping track of their own people and avoiding the dreaded 'blue on blue' — friendly fire casualty — was another constant worry.

In one incident, Shane almost shot one of his mates. They were lying up late one evening when he heard a noise that sounded like a pig. When he heard the movement again, Shane knew it was no pig, so he clipped down his night-vision gear and decided to take a look, thinking one of his comrades should have been onto it so there must be nothing wrong.

'As I looked around I could see a dark figure walking with a weapon and coming around straight at us,' he said. 'I thought, "Here we go, we're on here!" So I went "instant" ready to fire, finger on the trigger, and I was about to shoot and I reckon I was within a millimetre of firing, and I shouted, "*Berhenti!*" which is "Stop" in Indonesian, and nothing happened. I said, "*Berhenti!*" again and this guy stopped and said, "It's me, it's me", and what had happened was, one of our guys who was sitting in the same thing as us went out to go for a shit. He reckons to this day that he told me and I can't remember. So, my heart was going a fair bit because I reckon I was so close to shooting him; I reckon I even had the pressure on the trigger ready to go in an instant — so that would have been a disaster. It just goes to show — simple drills, you've just got to follow them.'

It was the first time such a thing had happened to Shane.

'We normally do really have good communication between one another, and it's such a small group, and there's so much movement, moving up and in, but it happened at an unfortunate time. So it shook us up for the rest of the patrol.'

Accurate information, or the lack of it, was one classic problem of working with other army units or coalition forces that reared its head in East Timor. A near disaster occurred when a firm called Lloyds Helicopters, contracted to provide casualty evacuation services, was conducting a night evacuation exercise at one point when Shane's patrol was on a humanitarian assistance patrol up near Maliana, west of Dili on the border with West Timor.

Says Shane: 'The helo was not too far from us and it was hovering, and you could see the white light on one side and red on the other.

I heard over the radio one of the 6RAR guys radioed up and said, "I can see a white flare in the air, there's a white flare!" And he gave a directional grid and I worked it out that the directional grid he's given is where the helo is.

'So I radioed up and said, "Look, just be aware there's a helo flying around there and it's Lloyds and it's friendly, blah blah blah." Their platoon commander jumped on and said, "No, no, that's a flare, I can see it, I'm backing you guys up, that's a flare", and so on, and I said, "Fair enough, I can't see a flare."'

As the chopper turned around its red navigation light came into view and the radio crackled to life again.

'"Now I can see a red flare, there's a red flare!" So I said, "Have a look, have a look."'

Just in time, the regular soldiers realised what they were looking at.

Another time, Shane's patrol received a call from 6RAR (which had arrived in April 2000), saying that they had found an enemy position that looked like a militia training camp 'bigger than Ben Hur'. The SAS patrols were called in and told there would be a major offensive against this position high up in the mountains. The safest way in was from above, so Shane's patrol would be dropped on top of a high feature and would rope down and attack the position from above.

'It took a few days to go down towards where we were going, and every time we had to go down to these places we'd rope down; we'd hook our ropes on, rope down, leave our ropes there and continue the task. Remember, this is the biggest militia thing that's happened and they're worried about their info.

'We finally got there after about three days of pretty hard work. There were even times when I remember looking behind us and seeing the mountains and thinking, "I can't believe we walked down that with all our packs, clinging on to the sides", and I remember saying to [fellow SAS member] Jonesy, "Look at that! Did we walk down that?"'

After three days of merciless slog, the patrols reached the grid reference point and prepared for the attack.

'We're all sort of lying down in an extended line and we thought, "This is it, we're on here, this is going to happen", and everyone's revved up and giving the thumbs up and we were all pretty excited.'

As his patrol approached the site, Shane saw cut-down trees.

'They'd [6RAR] explained there were trees cut down because there were fire lanes for the militia and stuff like that, but ... there were little bunker things built. We soon worked out what it was — it was a coffee plantation and the locals had cut the trees down so that the sunlight could get to it.'

As the patrols were moving out that night, another 6RAR soldier reported torchlight flashing on the hill they had just cleared.

'I'm looking around and thinking, "I can't really see the light they're talking about", and then I realise what they're seeing. They're seeing the stars and a tree sort of waving in front of the stars. So it's a star — and they're reporting all this torchlight stuff up there!'

Shane put the false alarms down to a simple lack of training, although he believes the troops did the right thing by reporting what they thought they saw.

On another occasion troops from 5/7RAR reported seeing people creeping across the border.

'We went down to have a look and it was a herd of cows coming through,' Shane says with a chuckle. 'So we called them the "cow passus" [Indonesian special forces are called Kopassus]. That was the nickname — the "cow passus" are coming!'

Chapter 9

EYES, HEARTS AND MINDS

One soldier was pulling antibiotic capsules from a child's rancid ear; another was killing a militia fighter somewhere else in a jungle firefight. One SAS patrol escorted 'specialists' deep into hostile territory, while others were lying up in jungle hides for days, taking photographs through a long lens.

The tempo and mix of operations in East Timor was a special forces soldier's dream, and would harden the regiment for the challenges that lay ahead. In late 1999, Trooper John got the news that his squadron, 1 SAS, would be rotating into East Timor. For John, this news was 'fantastic'.

The squadron had done a 'build-up' — an intense pre-deployment exercise — and the young patrol medic and his comrades were raring to go. As was the case for many of the SAS men, East Timor was John's first overseas operational deployment. And while he didn't have a lot of call to treat his own fit and healthy troops (other than for dehydration, leg injuries or diarrhoea), the medic became closely involved with the local community through the humanitarian assistance program, which each overseas military deployment establishes where possible.

That meant setting up first-aid posts in isolated towns and villages and dealing with all sorts of weird and wonderful medical conditions.

'Being the patrol medic, I was in charge of that,' says John, 'which was excellent for me because I got to see a lot of things and work on a lot of people that I wouldn't [otherwise] have any exposure to.'

Soon the gangly redhead with the mischievous sense of humour was being called 'Doctor' by the locals and treating conditions as diverse as leprosy, malaria and fractures.

'It was the first time I'd seen a leper and had to work on a person with leprosy which, being from a nice Western culture, I'd not run into before.

'They hadn't seen anyone to help them out medically in a very, very long time, since basically when the Indonesians were running it properly. And some of the places we went to, other people hadn't been to for years, like little villages up in highlands. It took us about four days to get there, lugging this medkit up, and I'd bolster up the medkit if that's what we were going to do.'

In some areas the target communities were not only isolated but also quite primitive. In one case John was confronted with a sick child covered in burn marks. The local witchdoctor had tried an age-old remedy of lighting match heads on the child's skin. Infection had broken out, so John issued a course of antibiotics. But he soon learnt that he had to be very specific when telling the locals how to use the treatments he was giving them. One village had received a visit from a doctor about six months beforehand and a local child had been treated for an ear infection.

'He'd diagnosed the infected ear and given the correct dose of antibiotics for the small child,' John explains. 'The language barrier must have stopped at one stage, because when I got there they said he had a sore ear and when I looked in — he was a child of about four — I just couldn't see. I started taking stuff out, and they'd been putting the tablets into the ear!'

The message that the tablets had to be swallowed had not translated, and the tablet-filled ear had become dreadfully infected by the time John arrived.

'Once I'd cleaned all of that stuff out and irrigated it, the ear was in a very bad way. So I had to redo antibiotics and inform them that they're going to have to go to a doctor at some stage, which is difficult for them, but there's not much else you can do.'

Another chronic medical problem was dehydration. Because East Timor grows very high-quality coffee, the locals would drink cups and cups of it all day long, but no water. They would then suffer serious headaches from dehydration. So John would give them antibiotics and say, 'You have to drink this with water.'

'Can I drink it with coffee?' would come the inevitable reply.

'No, water.'

It was hard for him to get the message through to people whose entire system was based around drinking coffee during the day.

John also treated Falintil fighters and men who had been abused by Indonesian forces. As the word spread that an Aussie 'doctor' was in the area, people would come from miles around.

One victim of a savage beating came to be treated for a sore back, but when John placed him on the table, the man could not straighten his leg. As well as the beating, he had fallen from a tree and his knee had fused almost at right angles.

'The reason his back was sore was because he had to keep landing on this leg that wouldn't straighten,' John says. 'So we had to make up a crutch for him, and once we did that, a couple of days later his back wasn't sore — but he had to walk with a crutch for a while.'

John found the hearts-and-minds work he did in East Timor very rewarding. 'We do a lot of the strategic sort of stuff, a bit like a scalpel rather than a sledgehammer. So when you get to go and help out civilians who haven't had medical aid in so long, it really makes you feel a lot better.'

Trooper Shane was physically very uncomfortable as the clock struck midnight on 31 December 1999. He welcomed in the new year while treading water in the mud of the Oecussi enclave in East Timor. The enclave is a patch of land west of the East Timor border, which is East Timorese territory surrounded by Indonesia and the ocean.

Having heard reports of widespread abuse by the militia, the SAS had been keen to push into the area from the early days of INTERFET, but General Cosgrove was reluctant to move too fast because of the enclave's strategic location and distance from support. However, the regiment deployed a reconnaissance patrol into the area in the last few days of 1999.

Due to the extreme wet weather and the nature of the terrain, Shane's patrol was falling further behind schedule as the last hours of the year ticked by. They also had the added burden of escorting two non-regiment 'specialists', who were expected to keep pace with the fittest men in the Army.

'They probably thought they were on a selection course,' Shane says drily.

After days of slogging up and down 45-degree mountain country, patrol members — and particularly the specialists — were becoming weary.

Late on New Year's Eve they approached a small village that lay directly across their path. Given the condition of their guests, they decided to wait until after dark to proceed through behind the village. At about 10 p.m. they fitted their night-vision gear and set off. Just then the heavens opened and a tropical downpour enveloped the patrol.

'You couldn't see a metre in front of you,' Shane recalls, 'and people were slipping, and the two specialists we had with us were having a bit of a hard time getting through, and they were buggered from the previous couple of days, they were suffering a bit. The rain was that bad, we decided we'd better stop and wait a bit for the moon to come up a bit more so we [could] see a bit better and go through the main village. I remember at midnight someone waking up and saying, "Happy New Year!" And here we were just lying in this mud, just sort of treading water trying to get some sleep.'

Things went from bad to worse as the rain intensified, until finally, at about 3 a.m., the moon came up. The patrol set off through the village — dogs barking, roosters crowing — when one of the specialists began to stagger. Shane thought, 'Jesus, he's not too healthy, we've pushed them a bit too hard!'

As he says now: 'He collapsed right in the middle of the village and we thought, "We have to get out of here because people are starting to wake up."'

The man was suffering from heat exhaustion, so the patrol dragged him out of the village and down to a river.

'We got to a river and threw him in the river to cool him down and dripped him up, put a bag [medical drip] into him, and things were okay.'

Eventually the patrol reached its objective close to the West Timor border, two days behind schedule, and then it was time to turn around and go home. They couldn't retrace their steps through the village and the tough terrain, so they decided to risk a river bed they had noticed on a map.

'We'd copped a lot of rain, so it probably wasn't a good choice at the time, what with speed of movement and what we were going through, but we jumped in anyway.'

At first they used the river stones as stepping stones, keeping themselves reasonably dry. Then another huge tropical downpour began and Shane heard a loud roar. He turned around in time to see a flash flood bearing down on the patrol. The torrent picked up him and his 45-kilogram pack, and he was swept down the river. Somehow his comrades managed to cling to the bank, but Shane could not catch hold as the water roared down on him.

'I was swept under for a bit. At the time it was bad, but afterwards you can have a laugh about it,' he says now. 'After a bit I popped my head up and I was about 40 or 50 metres down the thing and I could hear everyone laughing at me, so I think I copped it the worst, being the first one. But I've never seen anything like it, like a flash flood coming down like that. We took the risk and paid the consequences.'

In this case the SAS men had dared and Shane had almost lost. Eventually, however, he managed to clamber out and rejoin the patrol.

'I felt sorry for the two guys who had the job to come with us, because I think they deserved a [SAS] beret by the end of it. It was one of the hardest patrols I've ever done.'

The patrols in Timor were not lengthy — they tended to last from two to ten days — but each day in rain and mud is a long one. Each soldier has his own bugbear, and for Shane it was mosquitoes. 'It's like a pet hate for me. You're always around the water and there's nothing worse than getting bitten all night and not being able to sleep,' he says. 'It doesn't help getting up and doing picquets — guard duty while your comrades sleep — every couple of hours, not sleeping. You're not in a very good sleep pattern anyway, and you've got mozzies eating you as well. I think I prefer the rain to the mozzies.'

Adding to the problem was the fact that SAS soldiers tend to sleep with one eye open, with their sleeping gear and packs ready to move in an instant.

'You don't want to set [up] ... anything too elaborate — if you need to bug out really quick you want to be able to pick up. You're always thinking about that, specially at that stage, we were parking pretty close to the border and it was our first trip there and we were getting the feel of the place, so sometimes it's better just putting up with it.'

At times it was difficult for the men to tell the difference between militia raiding patrols and simple hunting parties. Indonesian troops and militia often went on hunting trips into the jungle, chasing deer or pigs.

During one patrol, Shane and another comrade had left the OP to find a suitable landing zone for a helicopter extraction a couple of days later. As they came back into the OP, they noticed the patrol lying on the floor and facing out in defensive mode.

At first Shane thought that the pair had surprised their mates. Then they noticed about ten armed men, some in the classic militia outfit of camouflage pants and T-shirt, facing off with the patrol.

'There was a bit of a standoff there for a while, and they were running around looking at us and we were running around looking at them,' says Shane. 'We walked in behind, and we could see them running around us and beside us, and we thought something might have happened then. We weren't sure whether they were hunters or they were militia, and we didn't want to open fire or do anything hostile, so we watched it, but we were concerned [that] we had been compromised, so we decided that we would leave the area.'

The patrol radioed for an extraction and, in the heat of the moment, it must have sounded as if the patrol was surrounded. The IRF soon arrived from Dili. Soldiers rappelled down and the patrol was taken out by suspended extraction, hanging from the ends of ropes under the Black Hawk.

'To this day we can't say who they were, and I think they might have been hunters,' Shane says.

Some SAS soldiers are specialists in the ancient art of tracking. Lance Corporal George's SAS patrol tracker came in very handy. There had been a contact — a firefight between opposing forces — and his tracker, 'old John', was peering at the ground, searching for clues.

'He just studies the ground,' explains George, 'and looks for all sorts of signs like disturbances of the earth, imprints, bruised vegetation, things like that, any signs of people dropping things, and I remember I had a quite laugh with John about that. Because we stood and looked together, he and I were just standing at the site and there's blood on the ground and some rounds, expended shells, and John was looking quite intently and I was looking at him and looking at the ground, and I really couldn't see anything. "No worries, John, what's this shit?" And he's going, "Look, look, can you see that sign there, a bit of transition" — that is where earth has been picked up and dragged across and scattered.

'I'm going, "Yeah, no worries, John, that's great", and he eventually took us along a little path and found more signs, and it was quite credible stuff, such as more expended cases and some very definite footprints further on, and I was quite amazed at that skill.'

Tracking is not without risk, though, and it is vital that someone is keeping watch for the enemy while the tracker's focus is 100 per cent on the ground. A Kiwi soldier was killed during a tracking operation because everyone else was, apparently, looking at the ground.

On their mission, George and old John tracked the militia patrol into a valley that led them towards the West Timor border. That allowed them to call in troops from the 1st Battalion, who blocked the militia patrol the next day. The result was one enemy killed.

When George's patrol was recalled from the valley, they had to negotiate a small deserted village of about five buildings. George remembers that, 'By the time we got to the third building there was this horrible noise from inside and we were thinking, "Okay, what's going on?" It turned out to be about three buffalo that were inside the building, had occupied it and were moving out and around. That reminded me, I was thinking about Denehy [SAS Corporal Paul Denehy, who was gored to death by an elephant in Borneo in 1965] and wondering how we would explain shooting up a buffalo in the middle of the hills!'

Surveillance and reconnaissance (SR) patrolling was the main game in East Timor and for men such as Sergeant Nick, who had been in the regiment for twelve years, it was a golden opportunity to apply skills that he had only ever used during exercises. As a patrol commander, he had to apply virtually the full special forces 'mission profile' — the range of SAS skills and activities — in one form or another, from battle preparations to how to handle prisoners.

'Going in at three o'clock in the morning in a Black Hawk or going in at three o'clock in the morning across a beach — that's the exciting thing for me, going into an area that you don't really know anything about,' Nick says. 'Even though nothing may happen on the activity, as in nothing significant in the eyes of the media, like a big contact or a big shoot-up. But at the end of the day you've gone in on something quite complex, quite dangerous, and you've come back safely with all your blokes with no incident. You haven't been busted when there was a chance you could have been busted on numerous occasions.'

The result of such SR missions was that good information was passed back up the chain of command, and on to all supporting agencies.

'Arguably, providing proven, high-value intelligence is the most effective contribution the SAS can make to an operation,' former SAS commanding officer Tim McOwan says. 'No other military unit can do it quite as well.'

During one operation, Nick's patrol was sent into the Oecussi enclave to check on alleged incursions by militia fighters. 'We saw up to eleven or twelve militia, but what do you do? You watch, report, stay undetected and get on with the job. That's what we did for several different patrols, and to me that's the exciting part about it. And it also makes you proud, being the patrol commander, to watch your blokes go through a period out in the field with little or no support, maintaining their vigilance, to ensure they get the job done, and that's extremely rewarding.'

The last SAS soldier left East Timor in November 2001. By then the many lessons learnt were already being put to use in the regiment's new challenge in Afghanistan.

AT HOME

Chapter 10

THE OLYMPIC EXPERIENCE

The 'killing house' at SAS headquarters in Campbell Barracks, Swanbourne, WA, used to be a ramshackle hut that had to be virtually rebuilt after every counterterrorism training session.

It was assaulted, blown up and shot up as SAS troops honed their skills for resolving a terrorist or hostage problem, and it was where they 'killed' simulated bad guys using live ammunition.

These days the recovery or counterterrorism (CT) squadron practises in state-of-the-art live-fire ranges, where troops from the Tactical Assault Group (TAG) — which is part of the squadron — fire thousands of rounds, sharpening their highly specialised skills. The black-clad and masked soldiers move through the modern-day killing house — a 360-degree live-fire range called the 'room floor target complex' — with drilled precision.

The series of interconnected rooms with thick, rubberised walls offer the men a variety of target scenarios. Some are 'hostile' and some are 'friendly'. The troops have a split second to decide who's who in the zoo and then — *bang!* — the baddies (they hope) fall in a hail of bullets, their hostages left untouched.

A former commanding officer of the SASR, Governor-General Major General Michael Jeffery, said the SAS was the main reason why the 1978 Hilton hotel bombing in Sydney remains the only fatal terrorist attack ever perpetrated on Australian soil. 'The terrorists would have a low risk of survivability,' explains the Governor-General.

The fact is, however, that the SAS Tactical Assault Group would only be called out to a terrorist hostage situation if it were unable to be resolved through negotiation. The SAS would be the last resort: once the situation is passed over to the TAG, negotiation is over.

Indeed, the SAS CT mission is spelt out in plain language on the wall of the preparation area where troops don their black gear and double-check their specialised close-combat weapons, such as Heckler and Koch submachine guns and pistols. The document says that they are the government's last-resort siege/hostage resolution force. The message is blunt: 'Our job is to save hostages and survive.'

Two more live-fire ranges and an enclosed mock-up of a wide-bodied aircraft make up the complex of counterterrorism training facilities at Swanbourne. The urban combat range tests the soldiers against moving targets. The adjacent interactive cinematic range presents a variety of on-screen 3D hostage scenarios for the troops to resolve. On the big screen a swarthy, gown-clad terrorist emerges from behind a chair, another enters the room behind a hostage and a third springs up from a group on the floor. One wrong move and the hostages are dead.

The SAS training facilities are regarded as cutting edge. In addition to the special recovery (CT) squadron, Campbell Barracks houses two 'contingency' or war-fighting squadrons for special reconnaissance or offensive operations. It is also home to an Operational Support Squadron, Base Squadron and the 152 Signal Squadron.

All SAS soldiers working in the reinforcement cycle are trained and deployable in any of the three sabre (operational) squadrons.

Base Squadron is responsible for transport, medical support, catering, logistic support and technical support. Operational Support Squadron is the training squadron and it runs many courses a year in conjunction with the Special Forces Training Centre at Singleton in NSW. The 152 Signal Squadron provides all SAS communications.

The facilities at Campbell Barracks, which stretches along 6 kilometres of prime coastal real estate in between some of Perth's most exclusive suburbs, are supplemented by a much larger facility at the Bindoon army training area, about ninety minutes' drive north of the city. That facility, which was purpose-built for the SAS, includes a small town shopping centre, a large embassy building mock-up, robotic targets and a high climbing wall, and two multi-storey sniper towers for practising the full mission profile. The Bindoon facility is next to the SAS training centre where the twice-yearly selection courses for new recruits are concluded.

Controlling a terrorist situation such as an aircraft hijack or mass hostage-taking is, under Australian law, a matter for state police forces. If they can't fix it, the state government can ask the Commonwealth to call on the SAS for help under special Commonwealth powers called Defence Force Aid to Civilian Authorities.

The SAS takes its counterterrorism capabilities very seriously, and during the dark days of the 1970s and '80s, when the regiment's very existence was being questioned during a period of post-Vietnam cost-cutting, it was the CT funding that kept the place alive and ticking over.

SAS veteran Terry O'Farrell, who joined the regiment in 1966 and retired in 2004, says the SAS survived for 'quite a long time' because of its CT role.

'A lot of us realised that we were never going to deploy the CT role here in Australia. But it was a lifeline and it sort of brought focus back on the place and, more importantly, it brought resources and cash and some facilities, and it gave the younger brigade here a purpose in life,' he said. 'And they became very good at it. They overtrained. It was ridiculous. We were training two nights a week, five days a week down there, shooting and bashing in doors and blowing things up, but that was the only thing to do.'

The counterterrorism focus continued through the 1980s and into the '90s, until the Somalia famine and civil war in 1993, when the regiment's broader skills came to the fore. Close links were forged with special forces around the region, including the Indonesian Kopassus regiment, which is responsible for counterterrorism in our huge neighbouring country. It was clear to the SAS that the most likely scenario involving Australian hostages would be played out in a foreign country, and probably not very far from home. If the local force couldn't handle it then the SAS might be invited in.

Once East Timor came around in 1999, the pendulum swung back to the historical patrolling, special reconnaissance and raiding roles, and the need to properly equip the regiment for that job. However, the 2000 Sydney Olympic Games — which had been on the SAS screen since 1998, when they were given a key role — was a major test for the Recovery Squadron and its CT capabilities. It was the biggest counterterrorism task ever given to the regiment.

The Games also marked the start of an intensely busy period for the Special Recovery Squadron, which included the capture of a rogue fish-poaching vessel, the MV *South Tomi*, by an SAS boarding party after a trans-oceanic pursuit; the infamous MV *Tampa* refugee incident; a Commonwealth Heads of Government Meeting in Queensland; the seizure of the North Korean drug-smuggling ship *Pong Su* off Sydney; and the official visit to Canberra by US President George W Bush. The SAS was deeply engaged in all of these activities.

But it was the Olympics and Operation Gold — the name given to the Olympics mission — that was front and centre for 2 SAS Squadron, which was given the job of providing high-end counterterrorism support to the biggest sporting event in history.

Major Dan was put in charge of Operation Gold, and he spent more than three years of his life planning for the biggest show on earth. Born in Western Australia, the lean and cheerful young SAS officer was one of the rare beasts who had joined the regiment as a digger and had then returned to complete selection as an officer in 1992. Married to a Perth woman, the father of two daughters led 2 SAS Squadron's preparations.

These began in earnest in September 1999, with the focus on ship-underway capability: where the SAS board a hostile vessel under way at sea with opposing forces on board. It is possibly the most difficult and dangerous of all SAS insertion skills, depending on the size of the ship and the state of the sea. On a smallish ship in huge seas it is incredibly difficult, as scaling the sheer side of a ship in such seas, or dropping onto the deck from a helicopter, is extremely hazardous. Given that Sydney is the 'harbour city' and that a large number of cruise ships were expected for the Games, the ship–underway skill was regarded as essential. It became the focus of their training.

'It [terrorism] was seen as a potential threat, given the number of cruise liners visiting Sydney, and one the ADF should prepare for,' Dan says now. 'If there'd been an incident on board, what was the ADF, what was the government, going to do? So it was something that we spent a lot of time and effort [on] and relatively high–tempo, challenging training developing the capabilities for.'

They also trained on the usual range of CT scenarios, and to make life even more interesting, they embedded some Allied special forces troops into the squadron. The foreign troops weren't authorised to deploy on operations, but were there to observe and assist, given the global nature of the event.

It was a period of intense training, long spells away from home and, so Dan says, without the glamour and kudos of a 'real' operation such as East Timor, which was ongoing during 2000.

There is a large degree of luck in any military deployment, and in the close–knit world of special forces, luck — or the lack of it — can grate on the men. In the case of 2 SAS Squadron, their luck ran out. Because of Operation Gold, they were the last into East Timor and Afghanistan, and they didn't make it to Iraq at all.

For commanders such as Dan, this created some special leadership challenges.

'The best squadron, in my view, is the one you're in. I've served in all three [SAS sabre squadrons], and the best one's the one you're in. And those that are lucky go away and get the opportunity — good luck to them. But that doesn't necessarily mean they're more capable than the squadrons that weren't given that opportunity.'

It was Dan's role to make sure that 2 SAS didn't feel less capable than the other squadrons. Happily, the 2000 Olympic Games gave the troops in 2 SAS Squadron a focus and something to aim for. It also provided a whole new skill set that would come in very handy in the years ahead.

'We had a high-profile event with a lot of resources,' says Dan. 'So it was fortuitous in that sense, but at the same time the reality was you were going out to the back of Luscombe [a suburb in outer Sydney] — we used to call it Camp John West, from the TV advert: "The one the rest rejected"!

'If you remember, there was the controversy at the time regarding the refugees from Kosovo. Amongst the refugee families there were some complaints about their accommodation at Puckapunyal, and on their arrival they refused to move in and sat in the buses. When we turned up to Sydney in May, late on a miserable night, and realised we were in fifty-year-old barracks that had been literally picked up from one place and put in another, I was waiting for the boys to sit in the buses and refuse to get out!'

Six months before the Games, the squadron moved to the Holsworthy army barracks in southwestern Sydney and began rehearsing in earnest. That included not only ship-underway, but also helicopter insertions, road and rail scenarios, and a huge variety of drills based on Olympic venues and events. A crucial new skill set was developed to counter the threat from chemical, biological or nuclear weapons (CBR). As Dan explains: 'It involved decontamination and containment of a potential CBR incident as part of a counterterrorism seize-hostage scenario. That was new ground for the command and the TAG.'

A Joint Incident Response Unit (JIRU) was formed to develop a response capability, should terrorists unleash some kind of dirty bomb during the Games.

'The JIRU was to do not only the high-risk stuff, but also the broader consequence management, support the rest of the government and provide some sort of cutting-edge capabilities in disposal, detection, diagnosis.'

That unit has since become part of the Special Operations Command, which oversees all arms of Australia's Special Forces, and since the standing start in 2000 it is now a key weapon in the government's counterterrorism arsenal.

Despite being on call for the duration of the Games as part of the counterterrorism Joint Task Force led by the NSW Police, Dan was determined that his men would enjoy their Olympic experience. The troops conducted exercises all around Sydney Harbour, spending time at North Head and Manly, and when the Games began they went on to a lower training cycle so they would be 'rested and ready for anything'.

They also developed a highly tuned sense of situational awareness based on 'tactical-site surveys', in which all venues had to be physically surveyed.

'We were all fully accredited, we had the go-anywhere accreditation [for Games venues], so I would send about a dozen per day, a four-man team per troop plus the support staff and the aviators,' says Dan. 'It was a formal process, because we had to make sure we had an audit trail on our accreditation and who was accessing the venues, but the team would be going out to gain situational awareness. So we'd go to the venues, go to the Games, have the experience.'

The men also conducted recall exercises to test how long it would take them to muster when they were dispersed at various locations.

During the two-week period the Games were on, the soldiers met Olympic legends such as Ian Thorpe and Grant Hackett, and even managed to give them a taste of the 'SAS experience' at the conclusion of the swimming events. A special visit to the SAS unit was arranged for the swimmers, who were given a demonstration, a Black Hawk flight and a ride on the harbour in the Rigid Hull Inflatable Boats (RHIB).

'We rubbed shoulders with the Olympic heroes, they rubbed shoulders with the SAS CT guys and did what you would expect young blokes to love doing — shoot guns and drive boats and enjoy the buzz,' Dan says.

★ ★ ★

The ship-underway capability developed for the Olympics would be used to good effect by the SAS during several high-profile special forces operations at sea after 2000.

The first was in April 2001, when the Togo-flagged fishing vessel *South Tomi* was caught poaching Patagonian toothfish in Australia's economic zone near Heard and McDonald Islands in the Southern Ocean. The rogue boat was chased for 6100 kilometres before being boarded by an SAS troop in international waters off the southern tip of Africa.

However, the most notorious operation was that conducted aboard the MV *Tampa* off Christmas Island on 29 August 2001, and potentially the most dangerous op was that targeting the North Korea-flagged *Pong Su* off Sydney on 23 March 2003.

Both the *South Tomi* and *Pong Su* were regarded as classic special forces operations in the maritime environment. Both vessels were noncompliant, under way and suspected of criminal activities.

SAS Sergeant Nick says the *Pong Su* op showed the versatility of the regiment in being able to conduct two very different operations, almost worlds apart, at the same time. As he and his men rappelled onto the heaving rust bucket in a rough sea, 1 SAS Squadron was beginning to relax at al Asad air base in Iraq.

The *Pong Su* operation was run by the Navy's Maritime Command, which is based at Potts Point in Sydney. It tasked the recovery squadron with boarding the ship, which was suspected of carrying heroin, and taking control of the vessel.

The operation would require the TAG to provide a boarding party, and a raiding party would rope onto the ship's deck from a Sea Hawk helicopter.

Nick led the airborne raiders. 'One minute we were sitting here [in Perth] getting ready for Easter leave, and a few hours later we were in Sydney. Several hours after that we were on a Navy ship and then we seized this vessel with potentially some criminals who've bloody done some pretty nasty stuff,' he recalls. 'I was just bloody pleased to see our government and defence force prepared to be serious about something and be serious about stopping knuckleheads bringing drugs into our country. And for our organisation to be able to react at short notice and resolve the situation with support from higher [up] and the Navy was bloody outstanding. It wasn't a picnic with the conditions — the conditions were against us, time was against us — and it came off and it was bloody well executed and achieved everyone's aims.'

The conditions for a ship-underway job were indeed far from ideal, with high winds and rough seas, but the North Korean captain had refused all demands to heave to. The ship's crew remained noncompliant throughout, until a bunch of black-clad diggers got on board and were in the captain's face.

'Then they became extremely compliant,' Nick recounts. 'During rehearsals it was up to Sea State 6 [winds of approximately 30 knots and waves of 4 to 6 metres] and when you're in a little rubber boat it's not bloody much fun — when you've got to climb up and down boats and bloody rope out of helicopters and the like. And once again it was just the guts and determination of a lot of blokes who just got on and did the job regardless of how seasick they were.'

The assault force secured the ship and stayed on board until the vessel was handed over to the Federal Police in Sydney Harbour.

A former Special Operations Commander, retired Major General Duncan Lewis, said the Olympics, *South Tomi*, *Tampa* and *Pong Su* were all excellent examples of the utility and value of the SAS. As the man who oversaw the greatest investment in new high-technology kit in the regiment's history, Lewis got a major wake-up call from the *Tampa* and *South Tomi* operations, which he describes as 'barrier protection operations'.

'That barrier around the island, the protection of the borders of Australia, I think will be a central issue for us. And so, again, we have in the special operations world capabilities which have direct application, as you saw with the *Pong Su*.'

Protecting that barrier has been a central theme of John Howard's prime ministership. His government has employed the SAS in more diverse roles than any previous government, and he has given them more money than his predecessors. Howard receives a hero's welcome whenever he enters the gates of Campbell Barracks.

While he has used the SAS for high-end military and political roles in places as diverse as East Timor, Afghanistan and Iraq, and lower-end political roles such as the *Tampa*, Mr Howard believes it is the regiment's anti-terrorism role that has brought the SAS into its own.

'One of their great roles is anti-terrorism,' says the PM. 'When I think of SAS collectively, [I] think, amongst other things, of the siege at the Iranian embassy in London where the British special forces [SAS] were used, that was a counterterrorism operation.

'The need for very effective, elite special forces in an age of terrorism is overwhelming. One doesn't know what hostage-taking crisis you will face, and in that way circumstances have given them a centre-stage role. They are extremely valuable in the anti-terrorist situation. We haven't faced civilian hostage-taking, but we might one day face that and they'd be absolutely crucial. They would be the one group that you'd have to ultimately rely on. They are the most highly trained force in the country.

'The point I am making is there could come a time when that capacity will be tested and needed.'

Chapter 11

THE *TAMPA* — THEIR STORY

August is always a busy month for the SAS Regiment.

It is selection time, when everyone from the commanding officer down is immersed in picking the next batch of recruits, and it is also the month when the annual SAS art show is conducted.

The show raises thousands of dollars for local community charities and is one of the highlights on Perth's art and social calendar.

So the regimental gym at Campbell Barracks was a hive of activity in August 2001, with many of the partners of SAS members busy with preparations, including Gus Gilmore's wife, Lisa.

Gilmore, the commanding officer of the SAS, wasn't there. He was in the bush at Lancelin, north of Perth, examining a group of would-be SAS troops, when he got a call from Special Operations headquarters in Sydney warning him that a ship called the *Tampa* had picked up more than 400 'Unauthorised Boat Arrivals' (UBAs) and was heading for Christmas Island. Thirty minutes later a call came through from special forces commander Brigadier Duncan Lewis.

'I think you'd better get back to Perth and get a squadron back in so you've got them in case you need them,' Lewis ordered.

With barely a few hours' sleep in the previous two days under their belts, Gilmore and his weary senior staff drove straight back to Swanbourne. They arrived about mid-morning, and by then the picture had become clearer.

'We had a bit more information through our systems back in Perth, had a quick planning group, and by that time the first C-130 was on its way across to pick us up,' Gilmore recalls now.

On his way back from grabbing his gear, the CO went to the gymnasium, about 200 metres from his office in the headquarters building, to tell Lisa the news.

'Look, we're heading off,' he remembers telling her. 'I don't know when we'll be back. See ya and good luck with the art show.

'She was really happy,' he says, tongue in cheek.

Before he even had time to contemplate just what the mission would be, Colonel Gilmore, his senior staff and their vital equipment were on an RAAF Hercules bound for Christmas Island, a dot in the Indian Ocean just south of Java.

They arrived on the island, set up shop at the local basketball stadium, and still their mission was unclear. But by the next morning it had become stark, with a huge ship parked just offshore.

The Norwegian container ship MV *Tampa* had been steaming from Fremantle to Singapore via the Sunda Strait when she responded to a distress call from Australian rescue authorities. They asked the ship, which had a crew of just twenty-seven and was carrying $20 million worth of cargo, to go to the assistance of a sinking Indonesian people-smuggling vessel, KM *Palapa 1*. The floundering 20-metre wooden boat was carrying an estimated eighty people.

This turned out to be a huge underestimation. In a textbook rescue operation, the *Tampa*'s captain, Arne Rinnan, and his crew transferred an incredible 438 souls onto their massive 44 000-tonne cargo ship.

After the ship had set course for the Indonesian port of Merak, a delegation of asylum seekers visited Captain Rinnan on the bridge to demand passage to Australian territory, specifically Christmas Island. The delegation was quite aggressive and agitated, and Rinnan realised his crew was well and truly outnumbered. So he altered course for Christmas Island, an Australian external territory that is closer to Jakarta than to any Australian city.

Rinnan ignored the Australian government's decision to deny his ship entry into territorial waters, and the *Tampa* heaved to off the island early on the morning of 27 August 2001.

The SAS men could see the ship clearly on the horizon off the island's port, Flying Fish Cove. Meanwhile, the task group was getting mixed signals from Canberra and the media, but it was clear to Gus Gilmore that he had better start planning for an operation to provide some form of assistance to the captain of the ship and his crew.

The troops had taken just one Rigid Hull Inflatable Boat (RHIB) with them on the first aircraft. It was already assembled, and squadron commander Major Vance Khan began planning the tactical side of the mission: what gear he would need, how many men he should take, and who should be on the first trip out to the *Tampa*.

Gus Gilmore was talking to Duncan Lewis in Canberra, and during the conversation it became apparent that medical and language skills would be crucial for the initial boarding party. Gilmore had a Pashtu speaker, an Arabic speaker and a number of troops fluent in Bahasa Indonesia. The regiment had also brought along the Acting Regimental Medical Officer, reservist Dr Graeme Hammond, two highly qualified medics from the Army Medical Corps and several patrol medics.

The men had seen the widely published photo of the UBAs lined up on the deck of the ship, and they knew conditions must be fairly grim. Gus Gilmore had been angered by some media reports that the SAS had lined them up like that, when in truth the troops had not even reached the ship at that stage.

Gilmore had listened to a phone conversation between Captain Rinnan and authorities on the island about the medical condition of the rescuees, and this supported the CO's view that medical care would be the number one consideration.

'None of [the refugees' conditions] struck the medical authorities that were present on that telephone discussion to be life threatening,' says Gilmore now. 'From a purely military sense, it would be a bit like me saying, "Look, we're going to do a UN mission into this displaced persons camp — what's that going to be like when you get there? Okay, you're probably going to find that sanitation's pretty bad, because you've got lots of people living in cramped and uncontrolled-type circumstances. They're probably going to be hungry, they're probably going to be angry, some will have dysentery, possibly there'll be other viruses and illnesses that have just generated through the close contact with people. So therefore, what sort of capabilities would you like?"'

Gilmore knew that the boarding party would need a doctor to look after the more serious cases, a security element to ensure that the mission was peaceful, and extra sanitation supplies, especially disinfectant. 'It was really no different from the way we plan any operation.'

As with any military plan, it was reviewed and revised hourly in the knowledge that, once the operation commenced, the plan would probably change quite significantly.

Because the basketball stadium where the SAS was based was close to the port, Gilmore was surprised that the large media contingent that had gathered on the island had not discovered them.

'When we deploy we would normally try to keep a fairly low profile, to enable us to focus on the job in hand, and I think as it turned out we used those normal procedures, for no particular reason apart from that's the way SAS normally deploy. We managed to find ourselves sitting in our holding area with not too much exposure.'

Gilmore looked out to sea early the next morning and saw that the *Tampa* was much closer to shore. Then the order came from Canberra to board it — 'Now!' It was 20 August 2001, and by this time the task group included the TAG, communications and other logistics and support staff, who had travelled from Swanbourne.

Major Vance Khan led a boarding party from the TAG aboard the fast RHIB, while a local barge followed carrying other soldiers, the medical team and more supplies.

'I used the TAG because they were available, had the right kit and were current in ship-boarding, not because of their CT skills,' Gilmore explains. 'We deliberately downscaled the usual CT garb — the type of helmets, no body armour, etcetera — as we did not anticipate any form of strong opposition. But we could not afford to be entirely unarmed, due to the limited intelligence [we had] and consequent uncertainty. Additionally, we were very conscious of striking the right balance between "walking softly but carrying a big stick" as General Cosgrove once said, versus appearing overwhelming and losing the trust of those on board.'

Everyone from the CO down was aware of the sensitive nature of the mission: 'There was a national interest, therefore potential for strategic implications if we didn't do our job professionally, and so it was incumbent upon us to make sure we did it as professionally as we possibly could. We are always aware that anything we do could have some form of strategic impact.'

Given that Gilmore and his men had been on the go for four days with very little sleep, he thought it was crucial that they understood the strategic intent rather than try to interpret the political implications. He focused on the job and, particularly, on the reception his men would receive on board the *Tampa*.

'At that stage we [recognised] that one of the potential scenarios was that the rescuees posed a potential hazard — I wouldn't call it a potential threat, but they were an element that needed to be assessed.'

His questions for himself and his men were: *Are they manageable? And what are the conditions on board, including the conditions of the rescuees?*

Squadron Executive Officer Captain Chris was on the barge about ten minutes behind the RHIB. As they approached the ship his main thought was, 'Nothing is going to stop me getting on that boat.'

'We had some concerns,' says Chris, 'because I think the ship had given the impression that the [UBA] group could have been hostile and they were under threat. They more or less said they were under threat, and I don't think they really were, at any stage. [But] the crew had secured themselves within the accommodation area of the ship.'

The 26-year on-and-off SAS veteran, who had served in both the soldier and officer streams of the regiment, says the troops did not know what the situation was. 'In the back of our minds [was the fact that] we could have met hostility on coming on board, and we were prepared to deal with that, mostly by nonlethal means, but we had lethal means there if required. It never got close to that.'

Dr Graeme Hammond was also sitting on the barge as it lumbered through the choppy sea. He had left behind a surgery full of patients in his suburban Perth clinic when he received the call from SAS headquarters the previous afternoon, summoned because the Regimental Medical Officer was away on a course. Dr Hammond, an experienced reservist who had served with the Army before on overseas deployments, was pleased to be there.

Sergeants Alex and Dan, from the Army Medical Corps, were underwater specialists and among the military's most highly trained medics. They had been posted to the SAS for five years, and as part of the TAG they listened intently to the progress of the boarding party through their headset radios. Their first responsibility was the medical welfare of the SAS boarding party, so they were tense and focused.

As Dan explains: 'Your ears are trying to hear over the top of the engines of the boat, trying to hear what's going on, trying to get an understanding of what we might face, whether any of the guys were going to be hurt, like there's a lot of people on the ship, and then you've just got that sort of stuff running through your head.'

The barge arrived alongside the massive wall of steel that was the *Tampa*. They were all relieved to see that the captain had lowered the Jacob's ladder, which meant that the men on the RHIB had not had to board the ship using their ship–underway skills.

It was a steep climb. Once the medical team reached the top of the ladder at 9.25 a.m. there were still another eight flights of stairs to climb to the tank deck. The medics were weighed down with their full military rig, which included weapons and their heavy medical kits. Once they knew the initial boarding party was fine, they kept an eye out for the doctor.

'Our main concern probably turned into making sure Graeme was okay, because . . . he was the main asset medically on the boat.'

The pair gave the doctor a hand up with his gear and waited to receive their next instructions over the radio. Dr Hammond had briefed the two medics after he had spoken with the ship's medical officer from Christmas Island, and they all expected to find some very sick people.

Once on board, Captain Chris joined his boss, Major Khan, on the bridge, arriving just as Major Khan and Captain Rinnan reached a classic Mexican standoff.

The Australian government wanted the ship to leave Australian territorial waters, and the Norwegian captain wanted the 438 rescuees off his ship.

'He [Khan] had directed the captain of the ship to return to international waters, and the captain of the ship said no, he wasn't going to do that. They'd drawn their line in the sand, we'd drawn our line in the sand, and then negotiations started at the higher level in the next three or four days,' says Chris.

Meanwhile, the SAS troopers from the TAG were busy securing the vessel. Once they were reassured that there was no threat, Alex and Dan decided they needed to find out what medical supplies were available on board.

'So off we went to the bridge — that's where the medical kit normally is, and the stretcher and all sorts of stuff,' says Alex. 'Generally, international ships have a considerable amount of medical stores on them, and we wanted to utilise those stores ... It's a first principle of any mass casualty to accumulate all your stores in one spot, and all your medical people, and then you can use that as a base to treat people. So that's what we did, and we rocked up to the bridge.'

They also wanted to find the ship's sickbay, which was likely to have oxygen supplies and other equipment.

'Apart from the stuff that we'd med-packed on, we needed to find these items so that we could become more of an asset.'

The medics arrived on the bridge in the middle of the heated discussion between Vance Khan and Captain Rinnan.

As Dan recalls: 'Graeme stayed down below, and Alex and I probably felt a little bit privileged to be in that situation, to be witnessing what I consider to be a piece of history.'

Through their headsets the medics could hear all the conversations between the ship and the shore. They stayed for a while, fascinated by the exchanges they were watching and hearing, but the mission beckoned, so they found the sickbay and relieved it of some supplies, including stretchers, before rejoining Hammond on the deck.

The medics found the rescuees in squalid living conditions. The ship's crew had provided what they could in the way of food, shelter and medical aid, but nothing had been done about sanitation by either the crew or the rescuees. Human excrement slopped about inside two containers that had been used as toilets, and it was spilling out onto the open deck.

The SAS troops established a barrier between the rescuees and the side of the ship so that no one could jump or be thrown overboard; then they opened a couple more empty shipping containers among the hundreds on the deck to provide extra shade and shelter.

The medics then turned their attention to the 438 boat people inside the barrier, who might have any manner of medical condition. The *Tampa*'s medical officer, First Officer Christian Maltau, had told Hammond by phone the previous day that fifteen of them were unconscious, another had a broken leg, and that there were four pregnant women requiring urgent attention.

The medical team split up and began an initial triage assessment of the rescuees.

'We were very surprised to find that [their] medical condition was very good, given their circumstances,' Dr Hammond remembers. 'There were many people with dehydration, exhaustion and minor ailments [but] this was to be expected as they had been at sea for a number of days. I could not identify any unconscious casualties.'

Dr Hammond believed that the medical condition of the people on board had been overestimated or exaggerated by the ship's crew. 'I would put this down to inexperience, but I noted it would be in the Norwegian best interest to off-load these people as quickly as possible.'

Dr Hammond and the two medics embarked on an arduous regime of treatment. At night — despite the offer of a cabin and a bunk — the doctor opted to stay with his medics and all the SAS troops, sleeping on the deck without blankets and practically working around the clock.

The two specialist medics, Alex and Dan, learnt a great deal from the doctor. They felt protective of him and admired him greatly.

'We were sleeping on the tank deck, so it was hot, and at night it was cold,' Dan recalls. 'We didn't have any sleeping material ... so there were times there when it was hard. And there were times when we woke up and the doctor was down there doing his own medical parade, by himself, with a few escorts as guards. And that was at five o'clock in the morning — we're trying to find out where our doctor is, and he's already down there doing work himself!

'He had the option to go and sleep up where the captain of the ship was sleeping and the OC, [but] no, he stayed there with us. Lay down on the tank deck and slept on this bloody grate and did everything that we did. For an Army Reserve doctor to say that they didn't want to go and sleep up on a bed in the air conditioning or in the heating overnight, he wanted to stay with us, is just mind-blowing, it's fantastic.'

Gus Gilmore says that sleeping on the deck and living rough was a deliberate tactic to build bonds between the troops and the people they were helping. 'Through those measures they were able to not even have to worry about the security situation, because they developed a rapport and a firm but friendly approach to managing the situation. And the focus was very quickly on all those different types of humanitarian things. In some ways, I suppose, the UN experience of the '90s [working in places such as Somalia and Cambodia] helped there, but they are the types of guys you have.'

Dr Hammond and the two medics administered intravenous fluids to twelve patients, including four pregnant women. A list of the conditions they treated over the five days reveals sixty-one cases of scabies, forty-six of head lice, twenty-four of gastroenteritis, fifteen of dermatitis, fifteen of boils/skin infection, nine of headaches, six of sore throats, six of conjunctivitis, four pregnancies, two of backache, two of weakness, two of heartburn, one ankle and one knee soft-tissue injury, one fever, one congenital defect, one cracked skin, one chronic kidney problem, one case of warts and one of painful urination. This was out of a total of 369 men, 26 females and 43 children.

'They were dehydrated, malnourished, unhappy — but, really, the medical emergency stuff that they'd talked about wasn't there,' says Hammond now.

'We checked everybody, we did medical rounds four times a day and formulated a preventative health plan and also set up treatment areas, treated their minor illnesses, who needed blankets, food, water, got all that organised. At no time was I ever alarmed about anyone in terms of serious medical conditions. There were lots of people who needed attention, but none who were that desperately ill that they needed specialist treatment or hospital treatment.

'If someone was really desperately ill, we could have moved them off the ship onto Christmas Island, but it just wasn't necessary. No one told me I couldn't evacuate anyone, and it was my understanding that if they were ill enough they would be transferred off the vessel. We're not cold, ruthless bastards — if someone [had been] that ill, we would have moved them off the ship.'

The medical team decided that the best time and place to conduct checks was in the queues at meal times. But they soon learnt that the rescuees had their own hierarchy, and that some women and children were not allowed to line up. There was also something of a schoolyard atmosphere, with bullies taking food from children and the less robust.

Dan explains how they got around this situation: 'We started implementing that everyone walked the line so that we could have a physical examination — minus the pregnant ladies, whose husbands were getting food for them. They were our main concern, so we spent a lot of time with them, and I think three out of four of them at some stage were on intravenous fluids. And we had monitored them for a long time, obviously with the chaperone of their husbands, because of their cultures. Pregnancy was an area we weren't overly used to.'

After all, there are no women in the SAS. In comparison, however, Graeme Hammond was an expert — he had safely delivered hundreds of babies.

While the medical staff set about treating the sick, the rest of the SAS boarding party got on with cleaning up the place. They arranged high-pressure hoses, supervised the cleaning of the toilet containers and set up more hygienic toilet facilities using garbage bins and plastic liners.

'Over the next twenty-four hours we tried to build sea toilets,' says Gus Gilmore, 'so that they'd have a means of going to the toilet over the side of the boat, rather than on the deck. [The diggers] started looking at ways of increasing the hygiene, so they set up wash points.'

The soldiers also set up food points and started cooking the first hot meals provided by the SAS. About that time the Special Forces commander, Duncan Lewis, put in a call to Gilmore on the secure phone to find out what was happening on board.

'They're cooking,' Gilmore told him.

Lewis was amazed. 'I guess I'd been expecting some detailed military explanation of how the ship had been secured and so on. But they were cooking! And, of course, in the wider sweep of history that was absolutely the most important thing that had to be done at that moment in time, to look after this cargo of human misery that was on board. And it showed me the sort of flexibility of the soldiers, the fact they could turn their hand to anything, and that's what's special about them.'

Soon a food shuttle was set up, with hot boxes flown out by helicopter from Christmas Island. Bread, fresh fruit and stews were the staples. The soldiers also ensured that the food was distributed so that everyone was getting a fair go, including the women and children whom the dominant male rescuees had relegated down the chain.

Before the SAS arrived, the crew of the *Tampa* had flatly refused to allow the boat people to use their toilets or to go anywhere near their accommodation. Dr Hammond thought the crew members were frightened of the UBAs: 'They wanted them off there as well, and a few of them physically threatened them and that sort of stuff, and they would not allow them to use the toileting facilities on the boat.'

Dr Hammond had initially been puzzled by the condition of two patients.

'There was one fellow in particular who said he was paralysed, and really, when we looked at it, it was a hysterical paralysis. He didn't really have a neurological injury. However, there was one guy who was fairly drowsy, reasonably drowsy when we got on board, and it turns out that the Norwegian guy, [Christian] Maltau, had been injecting this guy with sedatives. What happened was . . . when I first got on board [Maltau] was quite cooperative and we went over what he'd done and all that. There were a few things that I took issue with . . . but I didn't speak to him about it at the time — I didn't want to inflame the situation.'

Pressed further about the drowsy patient, Maltau gave Dr Hammond an empty drug vial with packaging similar to drugs of the diazepam family but labelled in Norwegian, a language Dr Hammond did not speak. Maltau would not give a straight answer about whether he had injected the man, and if so what with, other than to say the patient had had a fit or a seizure.

Says Dr Hammond, 'He was drowsy because of the sedatives he'd been given, so we stopped that, and the guy got better just with normal care.'

Maltau, an engineer by training with limited medical experience, told Dr Hammond that he had discussed treatments by phone with his father, Jan Martin Maltau, the professor of anaesthesia at Tromso University in Norway.

Dr Hammond did not believe Maltau administered the treatment in order to have the man evacuated from the ship. 'To be honest, I don't think that would be the case. I think Christian was trying to do the best job that he could, but he was just overwhelmed. He had 438 patients and with not a lot of experience in medical terms, certainly not the training that we get, and he had just, I think, overestimated the casualties.'

The medics quizzed Maltau about how he was treating the drowsy man. They explained that he didn't need to keep injecting the patient.

'Once you stop injecting a person with a drug and the body starts to get rid of it, then it's a slow come-around, depending on how much drug's been given initially,' Dan says. 'I think we saw that there was either three or four vials missing, so I think it took three days to get the person back on his feet.'

Maltau later publicly accused Dr Hammond of lying and labelled him a 'complete arsehole'. Dr Hammond had undertaken to provide the Norwegians with a written report on the medical situation on the ship, but in the end the Australian Defence hierarchy refused permission for its release, so there was no official way Dr Hammond could refute Maltau's accusation.

As Dr Hammond was leaving the ship, Maltau threatened him in front of the two medics. 'I'll make sure I get you,' he said. This hostility was in contrast to relations between the rest of the task group and the ship's company.

Dan and Alex believe that Maltau took a set against Dr Hammond because he was awake to what the Norwegian had done. And once relations had broken down, it seemed as though Maltau was trying to make their lives as miserable as possible. He refused to provide any more medical gear — even rubber gloves — and turned off the ship's water while the rescuees were being washed after a particularly bad outbreak of diarrhoea.

This time the diggers had made the refugees clean up their own mess, directing them to use fire hoses to wash out the containers.

'We organised for everyone to have a bath on deck with hoses and soap and stuff, so they'd showered with their clothes on and cleaned themselves up. And then [Maltau] came along and turned off the water supply because he said we'd used too much water,' says Dr Hammond.

Some of the soldiers contracted diarrhoea afterwards. This added to the misery of scabies, which some of them also caught from the rescuees.

The medical team was well aware that there was a chronic shortage of water on the ship, which had to be under way to make fresh water from sea water. But, says Alex, in the end Maltau was even getting upset when the Australians washed their hands. This made their work difficult, particularly when they ran out of latex medical gloves.

'The ship's company refused to allow any of the Australians to use water,' he says. '[Maltau] took back the stretchers and all these types of things that we'd borrowed to use for initial triage and he didn't allow us to use any of the ship's equipment thereafter, once these conversations were had.'

The two medics felt very protective of Graeme Hammond, who went above and beyond the call of duty for about twenty hours a day under very trying conditions — the filth on the deck, the howling gales that upset everything whenever the ship turned into the wind (the ship was not anchored due to the depth of the water).

The mild-mannered Dr Hammond remains philosophical about Maltau, whom he believes was under a great deal of stress, but he is very proud of what he and the two medics achieved during five days on the *Tampa*.

'When we got on there, lots of people were sick. After that five-day period, they all got off that boat, they were all fine. When they were transferred, they all got up and they all took off, even including — and this makes me laugh — the guy who had the reported broken leg, who I thought at the most had a small flake fracture. He spent that five days sitting down and not moving, saying his leg was broken, [but] as soon as the life jackets came on and we said the transfer's on, he was — *shwoosh!* — almost running to get off.'

There was a false start to the transfer to HMAS *Manoora* — the Australian vessel that was to transport the refugees to Nauru, where they were to be detained under the Government's so-called 'Pacific solution'. This, combined with the troops cancelling a meal, caused tension and some of the detained men briefly became aggressive. Just before the transfer to the *Manoora*, another group of men decided they weren't leaving. They soon changed their minds, however, when Captain Rinnan said he would off-load them at the first Indonesian port he came to.

The harbour master at Christmas Island expressed amazement when Gus Gilmore told him they were allowing just six hours to transfer the 438 people between the two ships. He was even more amazed when it took only about two hours.

As Gilmore recounts, 'He was full of praise for the military precision that was demonstrated. And that was largely due to the crew of the *Manoora* ... and the RHIB drivers that moved back and forth between. The other thing is the fact that the SAS troops on board [the *Tampa*] had developed a sufficient enough relationship with the people who needed to be moved that it was done compliantly.'

The *Tampa* operation presented a number of significant challenges to the SAS. The fact that they were the only government asset available to do the job at such short notice, and that they conducted it with distinction, is a matter of historical record.

What is less clear-cut is how the politically charged operation impacted upon the regiment. Some SAS men felt privately that the regiment had been used for partisan purposes.

Prime Minister John Howard says that he took the advice of experts. 'It wasn't the case that at the beginning of it I thought, "Oh, this is something the SAS could do." When we started it, we didn't necessarily think that the ship's master [Rinnan] would behave in the way he did. At the point we realised that we had to take some action, then it was suggested. [Admiral] Chris Barrie [the chief of the ADF] was there and Max Moore-Wilton [the head of the Department of Prime Minister and Cabinet]. I said, "What have we got to do to stop this?" They said, "Oh well, we'll send an SAS detachment." To the best of my recollection, that's how it arose. Once he [Rinnan] saw that we were going to use military force, he didn't argue with that. I just would have taken Barrie's advice on that.'

The main positive element for the SAS troops involved in Operation Gaberdine — as the Department of Defence's support to the Department of Immigration's effort to counter UBAs was called — was the satisfaction of knowing they had contained a potentially volatile situation, cared for 438 people and done a first-rate job in the best traditions of the regiment.

Squadron Executive Officer Captain Chris and the men didn't get much thanks from those they had helped, but they understood that for many of the rescuees it would be difficult to respect anyone in a military uniform, given what they had been through.

'We did improve conditions for those people,' he says, 'we treated them fairly and looked after them while the situation was being sorted at the higher levels. For all the high-level stuff and for all the things that SAS soldiers are supposed to do, it ended up a pretty dirty job without any kudos or glory.'

Chris felt a certain satisfaction when he later saw some of the people being allowed to settle in Australia after their lengthy stay on Nauru. 'I feel pretty good about it. To be honest, the way I rationalised what was happening to a degree at the time was, I looked at this group and I thought, "This is a very divisive group. They are conditioned very differently [to] Australians. I don't know how they're going to fit into Australian society." Then, seeing later interviews of how they're getting on in New Zealand, in Australia, and seeing how they've changed — given a normal lifestyle, most of them will.'

Gus Gilmore's most satisfying moment came when he escorted the Norwegian Ambassador to Australia, Ove Thorsheim, and a representative from the International Organisation of Migration, onto the *Tampa*.

'Both of those parties, I believe, were genuinely impressed with the efforts of our troopers and commanders on board,' he says now. 'Of course, it was a political hot potato, as the media might describe it. But we had a job to provide a fairly level playing field until our next direction was given, and the guys did that immaculately, and that's what I'd like to bring out.'

When the ordeal was over, the SAS presented Captain Rinnan with an SAS plaque and a framed map of Christmas Island, and Rinnan gave them a company flag signed by himself and his crew.

The exchange indicated that there was a mutual professional respect despite the difficulties. Gilmore was reminded of ceasefires in previous wars, during which soldiers in opposite trenches sometimes came together to exchange gifts.

Gus Gilmore stayed on board the *Tampa* into the evening of the last night. The people traffickers had been taken off the ship by the Australian Federal Police, the ship itself had been cleaned and sanitised by the SAS troopers, and there was one last boatload of five Australians ready to go.

Gilmore and Vance Khan were up on the bridge with Arne Rinnan when he received a message from the people of Christmas Island over the radio, thanking him and inviting him and his wife to take an all-expenses paid holiday on the island.

Rinnan thanked them in return, but said he did not think he would be rushing back.

'I think it was a reasonable end to the situation,' Gilmore says reflectively. 'We shook hands, got on our boat and wished him the best for the rest of his career, and off we went. And as they cruised out to sea, we went on the RHIB back into Christmas Island and were gone very early the next morning.'

AFGHANISTAN

Chapter 12

AFGHANISTAN OR BUST

Gus Gilmore was at home in Perth, watching television, when he saw a news flash saying that a plane had flown into the World Trade Center in New York.

Like many people, the commanding officer of the SAS Regiment — who had just returned from Christmas Island and the *Tampa* operation — assumed that it must have been an off-course Cessna. However, as he surfed the channels, he was confronted with the horrifying images that shook the world.

'I remember saying to Lisa, "This is big",' he recalls.

Gilmore, who had been running the regiment since January 2001, had come into the job focused on how he could improve the unit's unconventional warfare capacity to counter so-called 'asymmetric' or non-conventional threats (threats that came from an unknown enemy rather than an opposing army). He was continuing a trend established by his two immediate predecessors, Tim McOwan and Mike Hindmarsh, and espoused by the commander of Special Operations Command, Major General Duncan Lewis.

'We felt there were more opportunities to use the unique skills of the troopers that we had in the regiment and we were exploring ways that we could present them to government,' Gilmore says. 'If you're going to face asymmetric threats you need a whole lot of tricks in your bag nationally. So although perhaps the political agenda hadn't swung that way, I suppose part of our responsibility as military officers is to ensure that we are able to offer a range of appropriate response options to government, and, really, this was all part of that.'

Duncan Lewis had been pondering how to best structure those 'response options' for years. He saw the changing nature of conflict as the major reason why special forces in general, and the SAS in particular, were moving to the centre of Australia's conflict options. To use large conventional forces to attack a terrorist force would simply give the terrorists what they expected — and wanted.

History had conspired to make special-operations forces highly useful in that sort of situation, but the deployment of such forces is always a high-risk venture.

'If it's going to be done, it's got to be done right,' says Gilmore. 'And we have earnt the confidence of the Australian government, if you like; that if they want something done, we'll do it right.'

Prime Minister John Howard puts it slightly differently. 'There are a group of people, thank heavens, who are prepared to take enormous risks and when circumstances require it, in the national interest, to behave in a ruthless fashion and protect that interest ruthlessly — within the laws of war, obviously.'

At the time Gus Gilmore witnessed the most audacious asymmetric attack in history, the regiment was already in good operational shape in the wake of East Timor, the Olympics and the *Tampa*.

'We certainly didn't foresee September 11, but I think we did foresee that there would be a need for us to be assisting Australia's national security in different ways to the old,' Gilmore says now.

On the night of the attack he went to sleep with just one thing on his mind: *What does this mean for us?* The next day he spoke to his men about the new threat and the need for the counterterrorism squadron to be as well prepared as possible.

'I also thought [the attack] might globalise our reach,' he says.

With the politically charged *Tampa* operation already consigned to his personal history basket, Gilmore was able to focus on the wellbeing of the 500 or so men under his command. This was just as well:

September 11 triggered an intense period of preparation and planning at the SAS barracks at Swanbourne.

By early October, Gilmore and his operations officer, Major Pete Tinley, had left Australia to begin selling the wares of the Australian SAS to overseas defence forces. Before deploying to Afghanistan — which a coalition of forces would attack in retaliation for September 11 — the pair would spend weeks positioning the regiment for a central role.

The politics of the Coalition operation (codenamed Slipper for the Australian forces) meant that niche units such as the SAS had to convince the Americans that they could offer not only a unique but a useful capability. Fortunately, the Australians had already built up solid relationships with their US counterparts through various special forces exchanges and appointments to key offices in various US commands.

The SAS also had close links with the British SAS and Special Boat Service (SBS) and the New Zealand SAS. Afghanistan would become a special forces jamboree, and after missing out during Desert Storm in 1991, when they were used only in a search and rescue role, the Aussies were determined to be at the forefront of the new war against terrorism.

Other special forces participating in the Afghanistan mission included American SF units such as the Navy SEALS, Army Green Berets and US Rangers, Canada's Joint Task Force Two, the German Kommando Spezial Kräfte (KSK), and operators from Poland, Denmark, France, Italy, Lithuania and Norway. Throw in the CIA's Special Operations Group and the field was pretty cluttered.

Unlike some of the Coalition units, the Aussies were vehicle self-sufficient. Their Australian-designed LRPVs would prove ideal in the harsh Afghan environment, as they could stay on patrol for weeks on end without needing to return to base. And it wasn't just the vehicles that managed very nicely on their own: in the US, special-operations skills tend to be sectionalised within each unit; in Australia, most of the skills — such as for water, air or land operations (SF soldiers specialise in one or the other) — tend to be available in a single five-man SAS patrol.

The international special forces task group present in Afghanistan would eventually combine for the biggest operation of the Afghan campaign: Anaconda. They were part of the task force known as K–Bar, under the command of veteran US Navy SEAL Captain Robert Harward. The task force contained 1300 special forces troops, many of whom had fought in the two earlier large-scale battles of the war — Tora Bora in the mountains, and the capture of the northern city of Mazar-e-Sharif.

When he arrived in the Middle East to begin the lobbying process, Major Pete Tinley — a tall, laconic officer who had joined the Army from his home in Fremantle as a private soldier and risen through the ranks — discovered that it was not going to be an easy task.

Tinley, Gilmore and Australia's Ambassador to Saudi Arabia, Bob Tyson, were keen to find a location and a role alongside the US and British special forces teams. At the same time, a diplomatic flurry was in motion, trying to convince Kuwaiti authorities to allow the SAS to bring some 150 soldiers, plus vehicles and gear, into their country.

Establishing a base was a headache for the Australians throughout the campaign as the Gulf States walked a diplomatic tightrope between their obligations as US allies and their support for Arab unity.

As Osama bin Laden had pointed out on more than one occasion, the conflicts in Afghanistan — and, later, Iraq — were to be seen as a struggle between Islam and the West. Therefore, much secrecy would surround Australia's basing arrangements in the Middle East during both of those campaigns.

While America's power and might meant it could virtually insist on any location, Australian officials had to dance on eggshells with one eye focused on the lucrative trade deals that could be at risk. Diplomatic assent for the Australian SAS presence was finally granted by Kuwait, but only on the basis that Australian troops were there to help defend the country.

'So a third of the force stayed in,' says Pete Tinley, 'which was a bitter pill for some of the guys to take, and I was the deputy commander, so I took command of that group and stayed in Kuwait for a while.'

At the same time, planners were examining possible options for operations against al Qaeda strongholds elsewhere in the region.

While all this was happening, the senior Australian liaison officer, Brigadier Ken Gillespie, was working hard at Central Command headquarters in Florida, in the US, to try to convince the US commander, General Tommy Franks, to incorporate the SAS in his war plans. Central Command was an unknown quantity to the Australians at that point, because most of the Australian Defence Force's focus had naturally been on the Hawaii-based Pacific Command.

Major James McMahon — who had distinguished himself in East Timor — took his place in a team working directly for the blunt but inspirational US general on an overall strategy to fight the war against terrorism.

As McMahon recalls, 'He [Franks] was good to work for, and if you didn't produce what he wanted, he told you, and if you did, he would give the appropriate accolade, so he was good like that ... You accepted that if your plan was not good, in front of a forum of fifty people he'd tell you, but if it was good he'd also tell you that and say, "Well done, thank you" ... [I]t was great to work with a boss like that, because you knew where you stood all the time and, also, you didn't waste your time if you weren't on the right track.'

Meanwhile, Gilmore and Tinley shifted to Kuwait, intent on getting into the 'sandbox'. They arrived at Camp Doha, the vast US desert base, and worked the halls, telling anyone who would listen about the SAS's capability.

'We were an unknown quantity,' says Tinley. 'We were known for exercises, and a few Aussies were a bit of a novelty factor, but in terms of actual runs on the board, you had to go back to Vietnam to say, "Well, these guys are good guys", and there are not many Vietnam guys around who have had those personal experiences at the command level.'

Tinley armed himself with his laptop and spent days knocking on doors at the 2000-man Middle East land headquarters.

'I would open up my laptop and give them a presentation. "This is the SAS, this is what we come with; this is our capability!" Close it up and walk on. I had to be quite entrepreneurial.'

It was already late October 2001 and the Afghan Northern Alliance — entrenched in a battle against the ruling Taliban — and their US special forces buddies were pushing south towards the capital, Kabul. According to Tinley, there was a real fear in the SAS ranks that the Afghanistan operation would be over before the regiment could make a meaningful contribution.

As soon as he heard from his commanders about a possible start for the SAS supporting the US Marines, Gilmore flew down to US Maritime Central Command headquarters in Bahrain to talk to the Marine Commander, Brigadier James Mattis. The 34-year Marine veteran and CO of the First Marine Expeditionary Brigade instantly recognised the value that the SAS could bring to his push into the deserts and mountains of Afghanistan.

Mattis, an unmarried, tough-talking Marines officer, later came to be highly regarded by the SAS troops. After a session with him, one SAS trooper emerged and announced, 'I have just met my father.' A thoughtful and well-read officer, Mattis regaled the Aussies with tales of Breaker Morant and the legendary World War I Australian general, John Monash.

In Bahrain, despite being preoccupied with the massive task of getting his brigade into southern Afghanistan, Mattis gave Gilmore a half-hour hearing, which enabled the Australian to explain the six specific capabilities that the SAS could bring to the Americans' operation.

'That was difficult because I had no idea of what their task was,' Gilmore says. 'So it was more of an explanation of the unit's capabilities.'

Mattis told him that he could definitely see a few things he would like the SAS to do for him as he fanned out from Rhino, the Coalition's forward operating base (FOB) in southern Afghanistan.

'He took us on and then we got the resources we needed to project ourselves into the country,' says Tinley. From there the SAS was able to commence operations. Finally, the regiment had found its niche in the first phase of the so-called War on Terror, and a very busy few months were about to begin.

During any US-led military campaign, the movement of troops, equipment and materiel is a huge task; non-US forces usually fall a long way down the roster. But, thanks to a lot of effort by Australian liaison officers in various American commands, the SAS made its way quickly onto the precious US movements tables, which determine who or what move and when they move. Just two weeks later the number came up and Gilmore was able to order 1 SAS Squadron into Kuwait to prepare for the move into Afghanistan.

In the meantime, Mattis had briefed Gilmore on his intent for the SAS: they were to become his eyes and ears.

'Look,' he told the SAS CO, 'what I'd like you to do, Gus, is to dislocate the Taliban that are in Kandahar at the moment. I want you to psychologically and physically dislocate them. I am also concerned about this area up here to the northwest — we don't know what's up there, we feel that there might be a chance that a significant push could come down because they're conscious that down from the north, the northeast, that's where the main Coalition push had been.'

Finally, after more than a month away from home, Gus Gilmore and his team had a real job. And what a job it was.

Between FOB Rhino, about 100 kilometres southwest of Kandahar, Kandahar itself and the capital, Kabul, about 400 kilometres to the northeast, there had been virtually no ground operations at all by Coalition forces. It was tiger country, and apart from satellite imagery and manned and unmanned spy plane flights, it was unknown territory. Despite all the technology available to modern commanders, the 'Mark One eyeball' (the human eye, any soldier's most vital asset) and the man using it remained a crucial factor. As they prepared for the job, the SAS men realised they would have about half a country to use as a blank canvas.

Says Gilmore: 'I was very conscious at the time about, "How are we going to paint the canvas to achieve the task of psychologically and physically dislocating the Taliban and al Qaeda while ensuring that we meet our national strategic intent?" A key part of that was to demonstrate how potent the force was that we had in place.'

That would mean classic long-range, unsupported SAS patrols, exploiting — by occupying or destroying — al Qaeda training camps, exploring and destroying key sites identified by intelligence planners, and ensuring that all movement in particular areas was monitored and reported. 'A lot of that invisible work that goes to toppling a regime or whoever,' Gilmore explains.

As the build-up continued, back in Australia there was a quiet debate about the value of using SAS troops for what some military planners saw as a conventional operation. The head of the Special Operations Command, Major General Duncan Lewis, rejected that notion.

'We had to work within a very complex, very divided and fractured society, work out exactly who were the good guys and the bad guys in order to get information on where Taliban or al Qaeda fighters were located, and then range over extraordinarily long distances, in the order of hundreds of kilometres on some occasions, in order to take action against them. Now, that's quite beyond the capability of conventional infantry forces in the current context.'

The SAS and Australia's senior military commanders would learn many lessons from the Afghanistan campaign, and Gus Gilmore was later awarded the Bronze Star by the US Armed Forces. According to General Cosgrove, by the time the SAS left Afghanistan in December 2002 several keen judges — men he respected in the US military — had named the Australian SAS troops as among the best in the world.

'Fraternal rivalry being what it is,' says Cosgrove, 'this is a big call.'

Chapter 13

OPENING THE DOOR

The first time he saw FOB Rhino in southern Afghanistan, Gus Gilmore was reminded of the Apollo 11 moon landing.

It was about 2 a.m. on a still, moonlit November morning as the American C-130 Hercules transport came to an abrupt halt after a vigorous 'tactical' (steep and sharp) approach to Rhino's dusty airfield. With 3000 Taliban and al Qaeda fighters allegedly on the loose in that part of the country, no one was taking any chances.

The aircraft was blacked out and the flight crew fully kitted out in body armour just in case of hostile fire from the feared 'man pad' shoulder-fired surface-to-air missiles. As the rear ramp dropped, the battle-ready soldiers were greeted by a blinding cloud of bull dust — a talcum powder-like dust that infiltrates everything — hurled up by the plane's four massive propellers. The bleak outpost was also blacked out, but its features were visible under a near-full moon.

'You could just see through the haze, and off to the side was this pimple feature — it really looked like one of those small pimples that you see on photos of the moonscape,' recalls Gilmore. 'It was very still and quiet and quite cold — it was an isolated place, there was no noise, there was no wildlife, there were no trees, there was just desert.'

Rhino was a walled compound set in a barren landscape. According to Duncan Lewis, its remote airstrip had previously been used as a node for the export of opium, the profits helping to fund terrorist activity.

With the SAS boss was the commander of 1 SAS Squadron, Major Dan McDaniel, a logistics expert and a signaller. The C-130 also carried a single SAS LPRV to provide inherent mobility should the advance element need to relocate and just in case Rhino was overrun by opposing forces and the Australians had to bolt for the border.

Prudent planning dictates that every SAS operation has a patrol rendezvous point (RV), an area of operations RV and a theatre RV in case of emergencies. If a patrol were broken up, the troops would first aim to get to the patrol RV; if that didn't work, to the AO RV; and, finally, to the theatre RV, for a predetermined extraction rendezvous.

'Escape and evasion is something we're all trained in, and it's something that you always plan on,' Gilmore explains.

'Welcome to Rhino,' said the US Marine who greeted the men as they piled off the Hercules. The SAS advance party went to the operations room to announce their arrival, before unfurling their sleeping bags to grab a couple of hours' precious sleep.

The next morning Gilmore's first contact was with a US Navy SEAL sergeant who had done some advance reconnaissance around the base. He then met with Brigadier General Mattis, who provided a broad overview of what he expected from the SAS. Satellite communications were established with Australia and Gilmore set about the task of getting his squadron group plus more than twenty LRPVs and their logistic support into Afghanistan, while supplying Mattis with numerous tasking options.

While Gilmore was otherwise occupied, his logistics officer, Dan McDaniel, was liaising with his American counterparts, trying to acquire the necessary supplies to sustain the Australian force.

Rhino was still in the very early stages of development and the Americans were frantically trying to move the rest of the Marine Task Group into the base. There was no power, no water and no fuel, and flying could only be done at night. Ammunition and vehicles were the priority. The Australians had wisely kept their shopping list to the absolute minimum, with a key focus on their vehicle fuel supplies.

Gilmore explains further: 'In many ways [McDaniel] was able to develop a relationship in the first place because we'd said, "We're coming in with enough rations to cover us for a couple of weeks, we're coming in with first line of ammunition, some fuel, but we do need this, this and this." So he could start the logistics planning — because, of course, without logistics you can't do anything.'

The squadron had been building in Kuwait, with giant leased Antonov transport aircraft ferrying vehicles, equipment and men in from Pearce RAAF base just north of Perth. The vehicles were fully serviced so they could hit the ground in Afghanistan ready to roll. The troops also spent valuable time acclimatising in the desert environment while they waited for orders to proceed to Rhino and the front line in the war against terrorism.

'Although the third country's [the 'base' country — in this case Kuwait] climate is quite different, it is a different part of the world, so they can switch their heads over from Swanbourne — if you have that luxury, you use it,' says Gilmore.

At that time Kandahar was still in the hands of the Taliban, and great chunks of the south and west of Afghanistan had not been explored by troops from the US–led Coalition. Added to this was the possible threat from chemical and biological weapons, the fast-approaching winter, and the fact that within days Australian troops would be sent hundreds of kilometres out into the unknown.

'Early on it's the patrols, in particular, who bear the brunt of it,' says Gilmore. 'They've got to go out and interface with the population, they've got to be isolated by a couple of hundred kilometres. I'm sure that they have all those thoughts initially running through their minds when they roll out on their first patrol.'

In their first few days in the country, SAS patrols pushed hundreds of kilometres in three directions from Rhino. This surprised many Americans who were not familiar with the regiment's capability. Gus Gilmore sensed that some American officers were dubious about what his men could do — so he pushed the envelope, and the sceptics came around.

'It certainly surprised the Americans, and that was great in terms of winning the confidence of our Coalition commanders. That gives you access to all the resources that you might require to conduct future operations — greater access to fast air and to insertion and extraction assets and so forth. Because they feel it's a worthwhile investment, and that's a decision any commander would make — do you waste your good investments or good assets on troops that may not use them effectively? So ... those first few weeks for the patrols really set up the operation in its entirety in Afghanistan for the Australian SAS.'

And the patrols were not easy. The diggers had to drive through villages flying recently hoisted Afghan flags from buildings and had men armed with everything from armoured vehicles to heavy machine guns and rocket launchers. Troop and patrol commanders — whether young captains or experienced sergeants — would have to decide how to deal with the situation in terms of their rules of engagement and the commander's intent.

'That's where you get the true benefit of the SAS soldier, which is that the commander forward on the ground can make that very important operational decision about opening up an area or exposing their presence or remaining concealed,' Gilmore says. 'On that can swing a whole area of operations, really — if their judgment is wrong, you would need in that instance to divert a whole range of other assets to support the ensuing action. So that can be a real problem at times. If you didn't have a good squadron commander, if you didn't have good patrol commanders, if you didn't have troopers that can make those judgments when it's a one-on-one confrontation with someone, then there are so many opportunities for mission failure, as opposed to mission success, that you just can't count them. They do such a good job because of the selection process, because of the training, because of our ethos, the ethos we try to live on a daily basis in the regiment — all those things make the difference, so that when you do get to a battle or ... a situation it's automatic, it's not something you have to think about.'

★　★　★

As the build-up gathered momentum, Gilmore and his senior staff were getting to know their new boss, General Mattis. They were all impressed by his no-nonsense and very loyal approach to warfare and by the affinity he had with his troops. As Gilmore explains: 'You'd go across to see him and he'd just be coming back in, in the middle of the night, with his webbing on, having just walked around the perimeter — the perimeter's a kilometre out — to see his Marines, and he really had an empathy for them, he connected with them very well.'

Mattis's 'office' — a rudimentary space with no windows, full of dust from sandstorms and with hardly any furniture — doubled as a bedroom. 'He'd just sleep on the floor, because his soldiers in the pits didn't have any better,' says Gilmore.

Mattis's colourful language also had an impact on the diggers, who were used to more subdued tones from senior Australian officers. One of the general's favourites was, 'I don't want any eaters and shitters here' — meaning that if you were just there to eat and shit, you'd be on the next plane out. That same rule applied to weapons: 'If I see anyone not carrying a gun, they're on the next plane out.'

The SAS men were left in no doubt that Rhino was a fighting base, and everyone had to have rounds in the barrel so if shit came to trumps they would fight. The diggers took an immediate liking to their hard-talking commander and, in return, Mattis was to become deeply impressed by the SAS men.

Gilmore's aim was to convince Mattis that he had at his disposal a potent force that could do virtually any job that he wished to throw at them. And in the weeks ahead, the tough Marines commander would not be disappointed.

In a letter to Duncan Lewis in February 2002, Mattis wrote:

> Dear Duncan,
> As the Commander Task Force 58 it was my pleasure to
> serve alongside the Australian Special Air Service
> contingent during active operations in southern Afghanistan

from November 2001 through February 2002. At this time I desire to acknowledge the high qualities of leadership, devotion to duty and aggressiveness displayed by the men of the SAS. Uncritical in their acceptance of missions, the sun has seldom shone on soldiers as competent and confident. I am familiar with the standards set by the fighting men of Australia. No Marine can fail to be impressed by your force's combat achievements from Gallipoli to North Africa and beyond. The performance of Lieutenant Colonel Gus Gilmore and these super fighters continues that tradition. The conduct of your officers and men has earnt them the full admiration of the Sailors and Marines of Task Force 58. Please pass to them my personal respect and appreciation for a job well done. We Marines would happily storm Hell itself with your troops on our right flank.

Semper Fi,
James N Mattis, Brigadier General, US Marine Corps

Once they'd received their commission from Mattis, the SAS patrols began fanning out from Rhino in search of Taliban and al Qaeda strongholds and training camps, weapons caches, supply routes and a myriad of other tasks, which included getting to know the local tribal people. They patrolled extensively around Kandahar, which was still in Taliban hands, and across into the Helmand Valley close to the Iranian border. The patrols were mostly covert, and troops would establish a 'hide' (another name for an OP) and spend several days observing and reporting.

As they explored territory formerly occupied by al Qaeda, the SAS troops were exposed to the constant threat of land mines and booby traps. Many enemy camps consisted of concrete bunkers with 1-metre-thick, 8-metre-high walls dug into a mountain side with full-size shipping containers set into the walls or buried underground. This was a well-armed, well-equipped and highly motivated enemy.

One of the first SAS patrols in the area was tasked with getting to a point on a main supply route just south of Kandahar. Gus Gilmore recalls this as a crucial test, not only of SAS capability, but of their credibility in the eyes of the American high command.

There were only really three ways to get to Kandahar from Rhino: one was via the Pakistani border and past a couple of towns that were regarded as 'hostile' at that time; another was to the north from Lashkar Gah, a stronghold of Taliban leader Mullah Omar; the shortest and most direct route was across the desert through the Margon dunes. These giant, rolling sand dunes were clearly visible on satellite images and presented a formidable barrier.

The vehicle-mounted experts, who knew the capabilities and limitations of the SAS vehicles, and Troop Commander Greg assessed the Margon and decided they would go that way.

Says Gus Gilmore: 'I think there was real scepticism ... probably from the US high command, although Mattis never expressed this directly to me — that it would be a very difficult task and they would be surprised if we could complete it. And of course the patrol was across there well in advance of any projected time frames.'

Thanks to that patrol, the Coalition soon had eyes and ears on one of the main routes out of Kandahar. Suddenly maps on the walls of US command posts featured Australian flags popping up all over southern Afghanistan. For a very small force, the SAS was covering a lot of turf.

'Within the first week, I reckon, we had gained Mattis's trust,' says Gilmore, 'and I think that really set the tempo for the rest of our time in Afghanistan. And from there the guys, through their successes, went from strength to strength.'

Crucial to the regiment's success in the campaign were its unique LRPVs. First developed in the 1970s when Series 2 Land Rovers were modified to suit SAS requirements, the modern-day six-wheel versions came into their own in Afghanistan. They had been deployed to Kuwait in 1998, but Afghanistan proved their value beyond any doubt.

Experienced SAS vehicle operators say the next overhaul of the fleet should include a 40 per cent boost to engine power. Depending on the task, each of the vehicles in a troop carries enough food and water to last anywhere from several days to several weeks. A typical load would include fuel, spare parts, and ammunition for vehicle-mounted weapons such as the 50 calibre machine gun, MAG 58 machine gun, Javelin anti-armour missile system, 66 rockets, Carl Gustav 84 mm rocket launcher, plus ammunition for personal weapons including the Colt M4 and 40 mm grenade launcher.

Then there would be an array of batteries for all the electronic kit: radios, laptops, global positioning system (GPS) and beacons. These days a laptop in the vehicle is permanently connected to a GPS so that each vehicle in a troop knows exactly where it is to within a few metres. Most vehicles also have a jury-rigged battery charger in the cigarette lighter.

The Australians made regular contact with Coalition air crew on the ground-to-air radio network; American air crews were extensively briefed by SAS soldiers on what the Australian vehicles looked like and what their call signs were. Understandably, avoiding friendly fire was a major preoccupation of SAS planners.

It is rare for troops to train with operational loads, and the same applies to vehicles. Extra ammunition, rations or some other form of 'mission creep' — items such as cigars, chocolate bars and even soft drinks — meant they were almost always overloaded. And, certainly, the SAS LRPVs set off on patrol in Afghanistan at their maximum weight, which was an extra challenge for the mechanics who had to keep them running under arduous conditions.

As the winter deepened and the patrols pushed further into the snowcapped mountains of the Hindu Kush — the country's major mountain range — fuel quality became a major issue.

Captain Neil was 1 SAS Squadron Executive Officer in Afghanistan. The former Regimental Sergeant Major joined the Army at the age of seventeen as a private soldier in 1973, and was selected for the SAS in 1976. A fair-complexioned, solidly built, typical Aussie, his dry sense of humour and sharp wit were handy traits when it came to running a vital piece of kit: a go-anywhere truck known affectionately as 'the mother ship'.

Neil says fuel quality was a major concern in Afghanistan. As temperatures dropped below minus 17°C the diesel supplied to one troop was so poor that when it froze it turned to sludge and blocked up all the filters and engines. 'We had to pull all the fuel filters out of the motors, drain all the tanks and then boil the filters in unleaded petrol over a fire to clean them.'

The next fuel resupply was supposed to include higher-quality fuel with an anti-freeze additive, however, says Neil, 'This fuel was worse than the original fuel, and the filters in the cars looked like they were coated in raw animal fat, like a fat trap in a drain.' So the troops were stranded at an airfield while the filters and engines were drained and cleaned again. The problem was finally solved when they were supplied with JP1 jet fuel, which they used on the proviso that top-end power (maximum power levels) would suffer as a result.

'There's a lesson learnt there about the quality of fuel and having a multi-fuel engine, which the Americans have,' says Neil.

The troop was lucky to have several former RAEME (Royal Australian Electrical and Mechanical Engineers) mechanics in their number and one of them, a soldier who was with Captain Neil, spent much of his time up to his elbows in fuel — so much so that his clothes disintegrated and he suffered industrial dermatitis.

Fortunately the LRPVs are mechanically straightforward, so even soldiers with an elementary knowledge of cars could keep them going. 'You didn't have to be a rocket scientist to work on them,' says Neil. 'If they were complex — fuel-injected electronic timing and the rest of it — well, trying to repair something like that, trying to do a diagnosis of what was wrong, would be very difficult. When they're quite simple, and there are parts available in the Third World for some of these vehicles, you can jury-rig a few things.'

The Unimog mother ship was central to maintaining the SAS concept of self-sufficiency. It carried anything and everything, from extra rations to batteries. But the vehicle proved to be a bitterly cold ride because, as Neil explains, 'The brain-dead mechanics had removed the heater!'

The soldiers tried every trick in the book to help themselves to the mother ship's supplies. 'Every time I'd pull up or pull over, they'd just come over and decimate the truck looking for extra food, and they'd get batteries . . . you name it, they'd be pilfered,' says Neil.

Two of the items always on the target list were smokes and cigars. Back in Perth just three or four of the squadron's troopers smoked, but on active duty that figure was reversed and just three or four stayed off the tobacco.

As Neil recounts: 'Some blokes in the cold were almost chain-smokers. [But] they would come back from operations and give up smoking, no problem. I've always envied smokers, because when I first joined the Army you were few and far between if you didn't smoke, and I've always envied the smokers to see the satisfaction they get from smoking and that feeling of ecstasy they get when they inhale a cigarette.'

Both of Captain Neil's parents had died from cancer, so he refused to join in.

Chapter 14

DEVIL CARS WITH ONE LONG EYE

There were just a few hundred US Marines at FOB Rhino when the bulk of the Australian SAS force arrived at the barren outpost in early December 2001.

With reports of several thousand Taliban and al Qaeda fighters on the loose in the neighbourhood, being at Rhino was, as SAS Troop Sergeant Nick put it, 'pretty full-on'. Right from the first night there were reports of enemy 'probes' close to the base. In response, the Marines fired mortars and launched helicopters.

'The next morning we were standing to and thinking, "We're pretty vulnerable here",' recalls Nick. 'At the same time, as a soldier it was pretty exciting to potentially go through that kind of scenario.'

The SAS men would have felt more secure in their traditional small patrols, relying on their own capabilities, than in a big FOB. After learning base-security procedures so that they could enhance the overall defensive position if attacked, the men settled into a patrolling regime to secure the immediate area. General Mattis wanted clearing patrols done so that he could get some accurate information about what was going on 'outside the wire'.

'He had no other force element to do it and we could just get out there and do it,' Nick says. 'Essentially, it was a 25-kilometre clearing patrol around the whole FOB.'

The SAS troops discovered that the area was clear, and that some of the Americans had been firing at shadows or even at shooting stars. It was the diggers who realised that shooting stars in the northern hemisphere traversed the night sky almost horizontally.

The incident gave Gus Gilmore's men the opportunity to impress upon the Americans that they were skilful at gaining situational awareness rapidly, which in turn enhanced the quality of reports they sent up the chain of command. And the SAS men knew they had to grab every chance to build American confidence in them.

During those early days at Rhino, the diggers went to 'stand-to' — being at full alert and ready to fight — on numerous occasions. Not one alarm turned out to be accurate, but it was all part of being there.

Fortunately, a sharp-eyed Marine saved the Australians' bacon several weeks later when Nick's troop was returning to Rhino from a patrol. They were making a dash back so as not to miss the 21 December move to the new FOB at Kandahar airfield, and were speeding across the desert when two of the vehicles became airborne with a huge Australian flag flying above them.

'I just looked across and thought, "Fuck, that's funny", and it has just stuck in my mind,' says Nick.

But it soon stopped being funny. A communications breakdown resulted in the Australian vehicles trying to pass through perimeter security at the wrong point. Suddenly the troopers in the first car noticed a Marine Humvee with a Tube-launched Optically tracked Wire-guided (TOW) surface-to-surface missile aimed directly at their vehicle. The American operator had 'locked on' and was just about to pull the trigger when he noticed the Australian flags and realised just in time that the convoy was friendly. It was fortunate for the Aussies that the Marine was a professional who followed his procedures, or there could have been a classic 'blue-on-blue' friendly fire disaster. (The term 'blue-on-blue' comes from the British armed forces; blue forces were friendly during war games.)

They compared notes afterwards. 'The lads had a chat with him and he said something like, "Oh, you goddamn Aussies! Yeah, I was about to let one go in your ass!"' says Nick. 'They laughed about it, we laughed about it, and everyone was dandy and got on with it.'

Originally from Nowra in New South Wales, Nick is a self-contained, no-nonsense character who doesn't suffer fools or bullshit gladly. A man of few words, his intense demeanour and cutting humour were forged during the Black Hawk disaster near Townsville in Queensland in June 1996. He was on one of the downed machines and earned a Commendation for Brave Conduct for his work on that terrible night when fifteen SAS soldiers and three Army aviators were lost. The father of three is a medic and water operator, but like most SAS troops he has done the free-fall insertion (advanced parachute jumping) course as well. He was reminded of that awful night in Townsville during a patrol in Afghanistan, when he was acting patrol commander of the reconnaissance element for a squadron action against a possible former al Qaeda camp.

'Once again, you're going into the unknown and stepping off a helicopter at bloody 7000-odd feet with a bunch of people you've never even worked with — and things got a little bit hairy,' he recounts. 'The CO of the bloody aircraft nearly crashed the rest of the patrol into us on the ground, and it was like, "Shit, here we go, Black Hawk all over again."'

Fortunately the pilot landed the rest of the patrol safely and they got on with it and did the job.

Humour — a key ingredient for any SAS patrol, even in the most dire situations — came into play on one occasion when Nick's patrol was in a vehicle which was surrounded by hundreds of Afghanis bristling with weapons, including rocket-propelled grenades.

'The reality was, things could go bad real quick,' he says. 'And just the comments blokes made, like, "Well, fuck it, it's going to be interesting anyway!" Or "If they get rowdy we'll throw 'em a chocolate bar!" Or just taking the piss out of your Australian rations, just little one-liners that blokes throw in that make you go, "Well, actually, I'm not really worried."'

Another time Nick was lying up in a hide when a local tribesman came in on his camel. 'He was really no harm, no real threat at all, but the first thing that happened was his fuckin' camel started spluttering and I said to my mate, "Fuck! He's got breath like such-and-such!" [referring to an SAS soldier with very bad breath] and from there, do you think we could pay attention to the job at hand? We were just laughing our heads off.'

It didn't take long for the Australians to get a reputation among the locals. The diggers' ability to overcome language and cultural barriers and engage the locals — a key part of every SAS trooper's training and a tradition upheld by Australian diggers serving anywhere in the world — came into play constantly in Afghanistan.

To the locals, the SAS became known as 'devil cars with one long eye' after one particularly devastating night-time firefight. The phrase was their way of describing the long night-sight on the SAS night-vision gear. But the Australians' preference was always to talk rather than shoot. They were, after all, Mattis's eyes and ears, not his blunt implement.

Trooper John, a gunner and patrol medic who was a veteran of East Timor, arrived at the base at Kandahar airport on Boxing Day 2001, from Kuwait. His first task was to find the vehicle he would be using and set it up. That meant making sure everything was okay with its primary weapon, the 50 calibre ring-mounted machine gun.

'I also had to make sure that I could get my medkit at any stage if anything went wrong,' says John. 'And make sure everything's set up — I had enough ammo, the spare barrel was working, I could get to it easily — all those ... simple procedures that you've got to do. Once all of that's squared away, I feel happy that I'm ready to go on patrol.'

Then there was the vehicle itself: checking who had it last; if the spare tyres were okay; any mechanical issues; checking over the whole vehicle to see what was there and what was not there — 'What you'd prefer to have on it, what you can do without, things like that.'

John says that the preparation for the vehicle was really just an extension of the drills that every good infantry soldier goes through before a patrol, making sure that everything is packed, and packed in orderly fashion so it's simple to get to.

'It's not just a case of, "Oh yeah, I just grab everything, pour it into this big sack, put it on my back and walk, and then when something happens I run and shoot things." It's the act of hunting humans and doing that sort of stuff — you've got to prepare yourself. So [when] infantry guys prepare their packs, they don't want it too heavy, they don't want to leave stuff behind — you've got to find that happy medium. And that's what we do with all of our stuff, and then we've got to do it with the extras we use and with [the] car as well.'

Weapons and equipment took first priority, followed by water and then food.

'Working with vehicles it's a bit different [from foot patrols],' explains John, 'because you've got the space, you can really stock up on the food because you can go out on long patrols. It's not unheard of to have a month's worth of food in the vehicle. You'll be out there for a month, and then once you start running short of food, the patrol's coming to an end, and if you need to go longer you can get a resupply dropped in by air.'

For the SAS soldiers, trained to go without food or to make do with very little for long periods, a biscuit and sip of water could become a gourmet meal and glass of fine wine in the hands of an imaginative trooper with the right sense of humour. Food tales did wonders for morale in one group of starving, half-frozen diggers when one trooper — a part-time amateur comedian — conjured up images of his mates' favourite seafood restaurant or steak house back in Perth.

Luckily for their palates, in Afghanistan the SAS troops were able to supplement their Australian ration packs (or 'rat packs') with some American Meals Ready to Eat (MREs) — or 'meals rejected in Ethiopia' as they are affectionately known — and some local tucker, especially freshly baked flat bread. Most patrols had stories about going into a village, pulling up outside the 'bakery', running in and throwing down a US$10 bill, then scooping up an armful of the still-warm bread, leaving the local shopkeeper stunned and wealthy beyond his wildest dreams.

When Trooper Brook arrived in Afghanistan with his squadron, in March 2002, he was impressed by the local cuisine. He says there was nothing better than a nice goat curry with flat bread after days and, sometimes, weeks on MREs. 'I loved it — I love the spicy stuff. [There are] a lot of Indian influences there because of Pakistan [being so close]. It was great. We'd get invited in, and with their culture they have to look after you, so you're always offered a feed.'

Warrant Officer Steve had a different take on the local tucker. He was working as a liaison officer with US Special Forces, living in an old fort close to the Pakistan border. He had been living on ration packs for almost two months, so the fresh food on offer every third night was a real treat.

'I was a bit suss with this to begin with,' he admits. 'I thought, "The war's still going on", but I remember there were thousands of crows all over the fort and over the period of time, because they were feeding 400 local forces and sixty or seventy of us, it didn't occur to us until six or seven days later that the population of crows died down and this meat that we thought was chicken, in fact, was fucking crow. They'd been feeding us crow for about two weeks and we didn't even know!'

The locals cooked the crows with chicken, lamb and rice, mixed it all together and served it on fresh pitta bread. Says Steve: 'It was shit, but it was fresh.'

Patrol Commander Macca saw food as a way to get acquainted with the locals. Whenever his patrol was offered local fare, they would try to eat with the tribal people. Then they would break open a ration pack and show the bewildered villagers what the soldiers were forced to live on. 'By doing that, I think they found it easier to talk to us as well,' Macca says.

It came in handy that the Australians were used to eating highly spiced food. 'From the few that did come across Americans or British, it was always mentioned, "Are you sure the food's all right, because the British and Americans won't touch it."'

One simple custom that also helped strike a cultural chord was that the Aussies were used to drinking hot black tea. In America, tea is usually consumed ice cold with lemon.

'Americans probably drink it and go, "Uurgh, cripes, what's this?"' says Macca. 'Whereas we go, "Oh, yes, it's a cup of tea", and drink it down. The Afghans respect that — it's being quite friendly to them, I suppose.'

Food was just one of the cultural aspects of the job in Afghanistan. Another was language, and with most locals speaking Farsi and no Farsi speakers in the patrols, it was usually a mix of hand signals, gestures and rough Arabic that got the troops through. Sometimes a US Special Forces linguist would be attached to SAS patrols, and occasionally a good English speaker would emerge from the throng.

When approaching a village for the first time, the Aussies would usually check it out cautiously.

'After we'd seen the initial reaction was quite friendly,' says John, 'we'd just do a quick look through, and a couple of guys would dismount and go through ... trying not to put the locals off. Once we got our vehicle up close to a wall ... I could stand up on the turret and look down with my personal weapon, as opposed to the machine gun. And that way you can see into their ... back yard, which is where they keep animals and stuff as well. You could see they're just like everywhere else — there's a couple of kids playing with chickens and such. Give them a wave and they'll wave back and go on and look for something a bit more substantial.'

One thing that stuck in John's mind was the women and the fact that they remained covered from head to toe despite the removal of the Islamic fundamentalist Taliban regime. 'It was so ingrained by that stage that they stayed covered up. And when you'd catch them out — little girls weren't covered up, obviously they weren't into the stage where they had to be covered, but you'd see all these little girls and they'd be all shy and wave and stuff, and then the mother would pull them away so that they couldn't be seen.'

Trooper Brook remembers seeing very few women, and being shocked at the attitude of the males. 'You can just see how ingrained it is in their society — when you see a brother and sister and the brother, the little boy, will come straight up and talk to you, shake your hand, very manly for an eight year old, and he'll turn around and his sister's crept up too and he'll give her a clip behind the ears, pick up a rock and throw it at her and tell her, "Get back out of sight!" When you see kids doing it, it's even worse than seeing adults doing it.'

The soldiers had been trained not to react to local customs, but to simply observe and report what they saw, and 'in no way make out that it's alien to you,' says Brook. They knew that they could not afford to show any disapproval or get the locals offside. Cultural-awareness courses were an essential part of pre-deployment training for the men, who would face very diverse experiences each time they went on a new job.

'You can't be judgmental,' says Brook, 'you've got to adapt as quickly as you can to new things. If you see something you don't like, just totally ignore it, just block it out.'

Patrol Commander Macca found the locals' attitude difficult to ignore during a bomb clearance in a village in the north of Afghanistan. A 650-pound unexploded bomb was discovered next to the village, and after lengthy negotiations between the troopers and the village headman, it was agreed that the Coalition forces could destroy it.

Macca requested that the village be evacuated and the locals consented. As detonation time drew near the troops did a final sweep, looking for stragglers, but, as Macca recounts, 'Every single house had women and kids looking out of the window. I've gone, "What the hell's going on here?" and they said, "Oh no, they're not important. They're just women and kids. The men are out of the village."'

The Squadron Executive Officer, Captain Neil, says that most of the locals he met were friendly, but he didn't understand the hierarchical nature of Afghan society until he gave some food to a group of kids.

'Some of the adults were quite hostile to the children receiving food, mainly because, if you're going to give anyone anything, you must give it through the chain of command to the village head and he distributes it. If you give food directly to people, you're undermining his position. There's a whole heap of skills [required] there and understanding about how their local tribal structure works.

'Kids were the common factor throughout — whether it's Timor or Afghanistan or Iraq — the kids were all the same, you know, they're happy, the innocence of their youth keeps them going.'

The diggers were also trained to stay away from local politics. But that was easier said than done, as Patrol Commander Shane discovered when, during one twenty-day patrol, locals offered up some very tempting information: they told the men that they knew where some Taliban were. So the patrol travelled with the headman and his convoy for two days — until Shane realised they had done a figure of eight. After another two days they decided there were no Taliban and parted company, only to discover later that the local warlord had been using them as an accessory to resolve a dispute with another village.

Says Shane: 'He wanted to look nice and strong — "Look what I've got with me now!" sort of thing. "Don't take me on, that's it."'

Trooper Brook encountered a similar power struggle between two warring villages in southern Afghanistan. Each side was accusing the other of being al Qaeda sympathisers. Matters came to a head when an SAS foot patrol had to be extracted from an area between the two villages. As the convoy approached the extraction point at night, it came under fire from a heavy machine gun and rocket-propelled grenades. The convoy fanned out and called in air support, which took care of the hostile fire. Fortunately none of it came close enough to do any damage.

'The guys came wandering down a creek line, jumped on the cars and we all skedaddled out of there with air cover on overwatch,' says Brook.

The next morning, the unhappy diggers went into the village looking for answers. 'We asked who owned those features [ridges and hills] up there where we had been shot from, and they said, "We do". This was the village we were closest to.'

When the Aussies explained about being shot at, the locals first denied it was their fault, and then admitted to engaging what they thought was an invading force from the enemy village.

'It was quite childish in a way, but that's how they work over there. So the excuses came flying, and the very next morning they took us up to the top of that feature themselves — we weren't going to walk up there because of the mine threat — and we occupied it from that day on for about a week, until we sorted out what was going on.'

One thing that struck many of the diggers working in Afghanistan was the incredible beauty of the place. Even in its most desolate regions, a splash of colour would bring it to life. In the Hindu Kush, huge snowcapped peaks framed against a blue sky provided a spectacular backdrop. Trooper John recalls travelling through one village in the middle of nowhere, about sixteen days into a patrol.

'The village was all really, really bright red ... the dust or the mud was red in that area, it was so bright. At the time we went through, the sun was just coming up over a mountain, because it was fairly high up, and I remember looking at that and going, "Oh, that'd make a good photo." It was just really very bright and with the sun hitting it, it just added to the whole effect, and all the snow on the mountains in the background.'

Captain Neil thought that the night skies were like those out in the Australian bush, except the stars were even brighter. On clear nights, the hour or so before dawn was the best.

'A lot of times at night you'd look up with the naked eye and the stars would be beautiful. Then you'd look up with the night-vision goggles and you'd see the amount of aircraft action [by] the Americans. Occasionally you'd see a B1 bomber come past, doing some fantastic speed, and you'd see a flash on the horizon and then the thing would come back.'

However, the beauty of Afghanistan's mountains was both a blessing and a burden. As the winter dragged on, the intense cold would test the men and their equipment as never before.

Chapter 15

THE BIG CHILL

The Hindu Kush in winter is no place for the faint-hearted.

For special forces troops conducting clandestine patrols in Afghanistan, the cold was almost a bigger enemy than al Qaeda or the Taliban.

Speeding down a mountain track in an open vehicle with a wind-chill factor of minus 35°C was an extreme challenge for the soldiers, who had trained mostly in the Australian bush and the steamy jungles of Papua New Guinea, and whose last job had been in the equatorial heat of East Timor.

Snow, ice and extreme wind-chill while riding in their LRPVs were experiences that few in the regiment had ever known. Some had been on the Arctic warfare training courses in Scandinavia and New Zealand, but that had been in snow — and snow is considerably warmer than the icy mountains of Afghanistan.

In some cases, as for Sergeant Matthew Boulliaut's patrol during Operation Anaconda, the men would have to 'lie up' for days in the one spot under freezing conditions, living on ration packs. The occasional brew of hot tea provided the only relief, but frozen water made brewing up in the morning a challenge. There was ice all over everything, including their weapons.

Patrol Commander Shane's worst cold-weather experiences happened during one of his squadron's most successful intelligence-gathering missions, when they uncovered a major al Qaeda stronghold just before Anaconda was launched. It was minus 18°C; they had been told to get off the mountain by a certain time because a massive air strike would be launched. Driving their vehicle without a windscreen, doors or a heater, at 50 to 70 kilometres per hour down the frozen mountain track, they had to stop every twenty minutes or so to get feeling back in their hands and toes, and to check for frostbite.

Shane was shocked by the cold. 'I remember coming back from one patrol, I couldn't feel any of my fingers at all, none, so I went to the doc and he said, "Look away", and he put pins in and says, "The pins are down somewhere in there."' But Shane couldn't feel them. 'At one stage we estimated as we were driving somewhere that it got down to about minus 30, with the wind-chill factor — and it felt like that too, everything was ice.'

Unfortunately there were no gloves on the market that allowed a soldier to stay warm and operate weapons and other equipment at the same time. The men always had their gloves ready to flick off at a moment's notice; when they approached a 'suspect' village, the gloves came off and within minutes their fingers were frozen.

'We had some weather experts around here who had dealt with the cold weather before,' says Shane, 'and they advised what gear to get, so the regiment acquired gloves and what you call puffy suits and things like that. I don't think we got the best, unfortunately, because I remember freezing heaps. I don't know how you can battle against those sorts of temperatures.'

The cold also carried an operational cost, and on one occasion SAS CO Gus Gilmore travelled up to join a patrol to experience the conditions first-hand, following a conversation on the secure satellite phone talking with his squadron commander, who was due to move into a certain area to coordinate close air support involving Apache helicopters.

As Gilmore recalls, 'I said, "Why haven't you moved?" I couldn't understand ... the delay. And he said, "It's just too cold."' It was minus 15°C, and with the wind-chill in the vehicles it would have dropped to minus 35°C.

Gilmore concedes that the stripped-down vehicles had limitations in the Afghani winter. 'We've since gone a fair way towards rectifying that. We had cold-weather gear — but it was clear that we perhaps needed a few extra things. But we've worked on that and that is now fixed up.'

Another limitation on the extreme cold-weather patrols was their diesel engines and the quality of fuel they received. During his stay, the boss saw for himself how the fuel glugged up in the cold, blocking filters and fuel lines.

'The mechanic had been working around the clock trying to fix the problem,' says Gilmore, 'trying different fuel types, cleaning the fuel filters and so forth, which were just gelled up. He had been up to his elbows in diesel constantly, and his arms were about twice the size they would normally be, just swollen and covered in sores from just constant freezing cold work ... He managed to find a solution to the problem eventually.

'It was only through his persistence and endurance, with all the pain that he would have been feeling, that he managed to get that solution. So that's something that I think is a testament to the quality of the Australian soldier, regardless of where they are.'

Convincing the higher-ups back at headquarters in Afghanistan and Kuwait of the depth and effect of the cold was often a challenge. During one mountain patrol of nearly a month's duration, Patrol Commander Shane reported back to headquarters that it was snowing — one of the 'abort criteria' for the patrols was extreme weather. Higher-up came back and told him, 'It doesn't snow there.'

'We actually built a snowman and sent a photo back saying, "Look, that's snow!" That was quite funny.'

Because it was 'sleety' snow rather than a full-blown blizzard, the patrol kept going. Says Shane, 'Sometimes it was better where it was snowing because the lower you got, the sleet and the rain was worse, so you were better off in the snow.'

Captain Neil had completed the Arctic warfare course during a two-year stint with the British SAS, but he had never felt as cold then as he did in Afghanistan. 'If you're in Europe, you're in snow ... so you become [accustomed] into it. I would have preferred snow to the conditions we had [in Afghanistan] because we were in sleet — it was just that middle ground between the two, a bit like Scotland in the winter.'

Captain Neil thought the worst part was having to get up every few hours to do gun picquet duty, guarding the camp and battling the cold. That disruption, combined with the snoring of some of the men, meant that lack of sleep was a constant, particularly during the cold-weather patrols.

'Some of the blokes sounded like bloody warthogs,' he says. 'They were so bad that some of the other guys in the tents with them had to wear ear protection at night. Normally you dig a hip hole and roll them onto their side.'

Picquet duty for the modern SAS soldier involves a lot more than just staying awake and scanning the horizon. 'There is always something happening, and nobody wants to be the person who lets anyone through. There is pressure on you,' says Neil.

The men were equipped with good-quality civilian Polartec and Goretex clothing, but most agree that wasn't quite enough.

Often the soldiers back along the logistics chain were unable to comprehend the urgency of the cold-weather gear issue. On one occasion the troops on patrol ordered so-called 'guerrilla masks', the trade name for neoprene masks that protect the face from windburn and frostbite.

'The logistics people thought we were having some sort of costume party at the other end,' says Neil. 'It wasn't till later — after some heated explanations — that the masks eventually arrived, but it was too late for that particular operation.'

Most of the camping gear used by the SAS in Afghanistan was off-the-shelf kit. Sleeping bags called Wiggies, rated at minus 5°C, were sourced from an American firm, and the tents were bought from a camping supplier. The US Marines had better-quality tents, but the

Aussie tents had two entrances, which meant that those going out on gun picquet did not have to crawl over the bloke by the door every time they went outside. The combination of the Wiggies and Goretex clothing allowed the men to at least snatch some sleep.

'[The weather] was by no means a perfect thing but it wasn't a war-stopper,' Neil says. 'I think each man learnt a bit about cold weather, but it was much worse for the guys who went up into the mountains.'

The SAS troops were trained to sleep in the open, sometimes under a hoochie (a single plastic sheet used for shelter), so they could keep an eye on things and be ready to react. Shane says it took a while for the men to adapt to sleeping in the domed camping tents. 'At that time it was something most of us had never done before, and because we were in a domed tent and it was closed, people were coming up with all sorts of methods to keep it open, but you just couldn't because it was that cold. You just had to have more people on picquet dressed up like big bears, because they had so much stuff on. You had to just endure the cold and keep on swapping over so you had people watching.

'It was daunting being in a tent and not knowing what's out there, and there were times when you were asleep, and the sleeping bag would be on your head, and because of the condensation everything would turn to ice, so you would wake up with a big slab of ice on your face. I didn't enjoy that part.'

Patrol medics were constantly treating men for frost-nip and chilblains, which were unknown conditions to many of them.

Because Afghanistan is a country of great extremes, heat was also a big problem for the second squadron who rotated in. Patrolling in temperatures up to 50°C meant carrying much more water and, at a kilogram per litre, much more weight. And with packs weighing around 36 kilograms, as well as 15 kilograms of webbing on their bodies, every extra kilogram was a burden. In some cases the men carried 18 to 20 litres of water as well as their packs. It's no wonder that their minds were drawn back to selection and the Lucky Dip exercise. The suffering they had endured during the selection course took on even greater significance.

ABOVE: SAS soldiers, led by Regimental Sergeant Major Warrant Officer Greg, confront Indonesian TNI soldiers in Dili, the capital of East Timor, in late September 1999.

LEFT: The chief of staff of Falintil's guerrilla forces in East Timor, Taur Matan Ruak, with Falintil leader Xanana Gusmao, soon after Gusmao's triumphant return to Dili in October 1999.

BELOW: Former SAS Major Jim Truscott and friends in East Timor during September 1999.

Unless otherwise indicated, all images are courtesy of SAS soldiers.

RIGHT: A map of
Afghanistan showing
the Australian SAS areas
of operations around
FOB Rhino and
Bagram air base.

Photo by John Feder, courtesy News Limited

ABOVE: An SAS vehicle
patrol at Bagram air base
in northern Afghanistan
in 2002.

RIGHT: A common sight
for members of SAS
vehicle patrols during
the Afghanistan winter
— everything in their
open Long Range Patrol
Vehicle (LRPV) frozen
solid.

ABOVE: Soldiers from the SASR pause to 'brew up' during a vehicle patrol in Afghanistan. The humble cup of tea can become a rare luxury, especially during extended cold-weather patrols.

LEFT: An SAS soldier leads pack donkeys 'Simpson', 'Murphy' and 'Roy and HG' on patrol into the mountains of Afghanistan.

BELOW: An SAS patrol moves through a village in Afghanistan.

ABOVE: (left) An SAS medic tends to a pregnant woman on board the Norwegian container ship MV *Tampa* off Christmas Island in August 2001; (right) a rare photo showing the desperate faces of boat people on board the *Tampa* as they receive medical care from an SAS medic.

BELOW: A military map showing the Australian, American and British special forces areas of operations (AOs) in western Iraq.

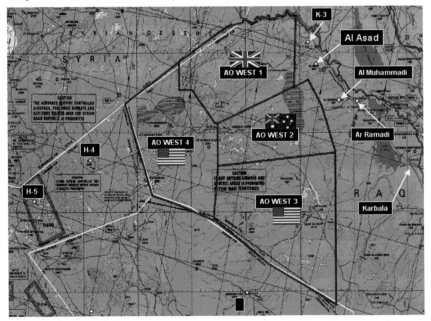

LEFT: A US Chinook special operations helicopter prepares to lift off carrying a troop from 1 SAS Squadron on the opening night of the Iraq war. They would be the closest Coalition forces to Baghdad for the first 96 hours of the conflict.

BELOW: Two LRPVs from an SAS patrol intercept an Iraqi taxi heading for Jordan on Highway One during March 2003.

LEFT: An SAS gunner fires off a Javelin missile during the Iraq campaign.

ABOVE: SAS soldiers repair the runway at al Asad air base in northern Iraq to allow Australian C-130 Hercules to land at the vast facility.

LEFT: The Kubaysah cement works near al Asad loom up out of the desert like the Temple of Doom.

BELOW: An Australian SAS LRPV tows an Iraqi Air Force Mig 25 at al Asad air base. The Aussies wanted to liberate a Mig and donate it to the Australian War Memorial, but bureaucracy and diplomacy thwarted their efforts.

LEFT: A patrol from 1 SAS Squadron takes a break in Iraq. One soldier takes the opportunity to indulge in some physical training.

BELOW: An SAS soldier armed with an M4 carbine conducts a clearing patrol of a building in western Iraq during March 2003.

ABOVE: 1 SAS Squadron proudly flies Australian and US flags as well as the squadron colours in the desert of western Iraq.

LEFT: Captain Quentin takes a moment to reflect at the SAS memorial known as 'The Rock' outside the headquarters building at Campbell Barracks. The names of the 42 SAS soldiers who have made the ultimate sacrifice are engraved on a large piece of granite. The last name is that of Sergeant Andrew Russell, one of the few to have died in action. Most have been killed during training accidents.

ABOVE: The only Australian fatality from the war against terrorism in Afghanistan, SAS Sergeant Andrew Russell, shown here with his wife, Kylie.

Photo by John Feder, courtesy News Limited

To conserve water, the patrols operated mainly at night and would lie up during the day. This upside-down schedule enabled them to see Afghanistan in, literally, a different light. Trooper Brook, for one, never ceased to be amazed by the country. During one foot patrol in 50° heat, he was lying up, observing the rocky moonscape, when he saw a man pushing a wheelbarrow to God knows where.

And, like most isolated places, Afghanistan had been infiltrated by that icon of American consumerism, Coca-Cola. 'You could get a Coke pretty much anywhere in the country — and it would be ice cold,' remembers Brook. 'In the peak of summer they've got ice and you can buy Coke. That's pretty weird.'

While a cold Coke was one luxury item that was available to the troops, the SAS men were largely denied the one thing that really gladdens a soldier's heart — mail from home. Since World War I, when war correspondent Keith Murdoch travelled to the front to expose the scandal of the legendary 'snail mail', generation after generation of diggers has had to put up with a hopelessly inadequate mail service. Afghanistan was no different.

The mail had become a big issue during the East Timor operation and the government and top brass had pledged to fix it. In Afghanistan the diggers went weeks on end with no mail deliveries, because, for months in the early part of the Afghanistan campaign, the RAAF did not fly into Afghanistan. Exacerbating the situation was the fact that personal email was, for the most part, out of the question for security reasons.

Mail has more significance than just 'news from home'.

'There is something therapeutic about actually putting pen to paper and opening a parcel,' says Captain Neil. 'And the other side about mail, from a command perspective — as I've always taught the guys when I was a warrant officer — is that the troop sergeant dishes out the mail and it serves two purposes. You can see who's getting a lot of mail and you can try to find out why someone's getting a letter every second day — is there trouble at home, or are they just happy to write? Or is someone not getting any mail at all who's married, so is there a problem there? So you can start to identify . . . a few combat indicators with mail . . . mail is a two-way street.'

At times Neil virtually dragooned men into writing. 'Regardless of whether you write to your mum, write to someone, keep a diary, just write things down,' he told them.

Many of the experiences of the SAS soldiers in Afghanistan were recorded in diaries and sketches by the men.

'Quite a few guys were diarists; one guy in particular, Eddie, was a good sketch artist and he kept a diary and made pen sketches which are quite good.'

Neil hopes that some of them will eventually find their way into the Australian War Memorial in Canberra, as such simple records have become a vital part of the nation's war history.

Chapter 16

THE VALLEY OF THE SHADOW

Leisa Russell never met her father, Sergeant Andrew Russell. She was not even two weeks old when he died in the service of his country, killed by one of the 20 million or so land mines that litter war-torn Afghanistan.

The death of Andrew Russell on 16 February 2002 hit the SAS hard. Because he was the regiment's first operational fatality since the Vietnam War, his passing also had a huge impact on the nation. Since Vietnam, hundreds of SAS soldiers and other Australian military personnel have been posted to conflict zones, but Russell was the only one who died in action.

Since the regiment was founded, forty-two SAS soldiers have made the ultimate sacrifice; all but nine have died while training or of natural causes. The biggest single tragedy to hit the regiment claimed fifteen SAS men, along with three Army aviators, when two Black Hawk helicopters collided during a night training exercise near Townsville, Queensland, in June 1996.

It was almost six years after that disaster when 33-year-old Patrol Commander Sergeant Andrew Russell was riding in the front passenger seat of an LRPV driving down a dusty track in the Helmand Valley in western Afghanistan.

His squadron had been conducting a routine operation and, according to Trooper John, the mission had been long and 'fairly boring'. Russell's patrol was providing security for the squadron headquarters when the front left wheel of his LRPV detonated an old Russian-made anti-tank mine. The blast, which was directional —

concentrated in a narrow column —and very powerful, virtually sheared off his section of the car, inflicting severe injuries to Sergeant Russell and minor wounds to other soldiers. His dazed comrades, including the patrol medic, began administering first aid and radioed for help.

As the patrol medic worked frantically to provide battlefield first aid, a US helicopter lifted off from Kandahar on a medical evacuation mission. By chance a USAF fixed-wing aircraft was flying in the vicinity with some medics on board, and the pilot offered to jump them in with some extra medical supplies. So three specialist medics conducted a highly dangerous night jump from the fixed-wing aircraft into the site, just under two hours after the blast. They compared notes with the SAS patrol medic, who had already done everything that could be done for Russell, and they prepared their patient to be moved. The chopper arrived soon after, but Andrew Russell died during the medevac flight to the US military hospital in Kandahar.

Russell's comrades were lucky to escape a similar fate. According to eyewitnesses, the vehicle's gunner was thrown from his spot on the gun turret and flew through the air before hitting the ground. He then stood up, but was told not to move before being prodded by his mates. Incredibly, he suffered only cuts and bruises.

After that, everyone travelling on the cars wanted to sit on the turrets as they traversed the mine-littered countryside.

The land mine had hit the front left tyre and the whole front left of the car, including the engine block, had been pushed up. The vehicle was virtually destroyed. The driver had been saved by his position in the vehicle — the parts of the car that were pushed up had stopped short of where he was.

That night the men slept in wheel ruts, and the next morning the damaged vehicle was stripped almost bare and then destroyed.

Andrew Russell was the second Australian mine casualty in Afghanistan.

Just a month earlier, on 17 January 2002, SAS Trooper 'Sal' lost part of his foot when he stepped on an anti–personnel mine during a mission to destroy a huge arms cache north of Kandahar.

His patrol had discovered three large bunkers filled with an estimated 15 tonnes of munitions including mines, mortars and artillery shells. They were clearing the area and preparing to detonate the cache when Sal stepped on the few square centimetres of ground that no one else had set foot on.

Trooper John was the patrol medic at the scene, but by the time he got his medkit out and reached his mate, six other soldiers were already working on Sal.

'Everyone's training just kicked in and there was some awesome hive of activity going on,' says John now.

The blast had taken several of Sal's toes with it and inflicted minor wounds to his hands and eyes. As the patrol medics moved him to a safer spot, treated his injuries and administered painkillers, the commanders radioed for air support to evacuate their wounded mate.

'At one stage I was going to go with him because I was the senior medic,' says John, 'but the Americans had two of their medics on the chopper, so it was better that I stay with the patrol. We put him on top of one of our vehicles, moved him down to where we could call the chopper in, and extracted him like that. It was all over fairly quickly. Then we finished the job, blew up the hill and all of the tanks and all of the equipment on there, and went from there.'

Andrew Russell's body was given a solemn farewell several days after his death, with a sole piper from Princess Patricia's Canadian Light Infantry playing a lament as his coffin was carried aboard a Hercules transport plane.

'Everyone, as you'd imagine, was really disappointed but unfortunately it's part of the realities of our job, we're well aware of it. It comes as a shock all the time when someone you know is injured or killed,' Trooper John says with quiet understatement.

The incident generated a debate in the Australian parliament about the quality of medical care available to the Australian troops. Some politicians — including Labor MP and war veteran Graham Edwards, who lost his legs to a land mine in Vietnam — suggested that the medical response time was too slow. Others said that a supply of whole blood might have saved Russell. But the soldiers who were on the ground say nothing could have saved their mortally wounded mate.

Squadron Executive Officer Captain Neil, who spent many cold hours at night on picquet duty with Andrew Russell, talking about his family and his aspirations for his children, says the entire system worked very well. 'They could have put blood into him, they could have done all that and I don't think he would have made it. The whole system wound into gear and worked well. The Americans, the PJs [parachute medics] that jumped out of the back of the aircraft out in the desert there, did a fantastic job jumping in there at night, being unsure where they were going to land.' One of those American medics was later killed in the war.

The SAS soldiers understood the risks of their work. They knew they did not have the facilities of a metropolitan hospital within easy reach. 'That's the risk you take,' says Neil, 'and it's always been, with SAS long-range operations, it's always been the risk. You'll never have a surgical facility or X-ray facility out in the field, and it goes part and parcel with our job.'

One thing that did change after the incident was that survivability enhancement kits (SEK) were fitted to the cars. The extra armour plate fixed underneath added considerable weight to a vehicle, thus boosting the stresses and strains it was already under, but as it protected the vehicle from mine damage, it did provide some peace of mind to soldiers riding up front.

Mine awareness had been a major preoccupation for SAS soldiers before and during their tours in Afghanistan, and never more so than after Andrew Russell's death. Gus Gilmore and his planning team had spent many hours poring over mine maps of the country, trying to make sense of the insidious threat.

The Russians had left the mines as a terrible legacy from their war against the Afghani mujahideen, and parts of the country were littered with their deadly devices.

'One of the early things that strikes you, apart from the climate and the terrain, is the mine-mapping,' says Gilmore. 'The initial mine map I got was next to useless, so I said, "Go back and get me some more information." Even the more refined mapping we received didn't tie it down, and so you end[ed] up with red dots on the map — quite [a] significant [amount] — and of course when you go to Afghanistan you see it. Every road has little stones on the side of the road painted white for the safe side and red for the dangerous side. Mines are everywhere and you therefore know, "Look, this is a reality of the environment we're operating in."'

Land mines are an important tool for infantry soldiers, especially for self-protection, but normal practice is to carefully map the mined area and then remove the mines once an operation is over. But the Russians — particularly small units that had used mines for protection at night — just spread them about without mapping. Thus the most sophisticated protection for the locals was rocks painted red on the side where the mines were supposed to be. Of course, this is not foolproof: rocks can easily be turned over.

According to Trooper John, most SAS patrols in Afghanistan had some kind of mine incident during their tours.

'They [the locals] always try to mark them with a row of rocks, some of them painted red on one side and white on the other . . . and the problem is, you never know which side is the danger side, because you don't know who put out the marker. So when you see them you go, "Okay, there's mines in the area and you're on one of the sides."'

'We'd been briefed that the red side was supposed to be the bad side and [we] go out there, and the locals, you'd see them all walking on the white side and . . . in another area they're all walking on the red side! . . . And there are all these vehicle tracks going through and they're all on the red side . . .

'You get a little bit of tension, but when you see yourself crossing over one of those lines, you're going, "This is probably not the best idea!"'

On one occasion, John's patrol picked up an SAS foot patrol that had been out for several days.

'I looked over the back tyre of our vehicle and there was an anti-personnel mine sitting on the road. It had been run over but it still looked as if it would work, and here I am picking up a foot patrol in a car and right next to my rear tyre is a mine! Yep, there are a lot of mines in this country! When you're on the ground, you try not to think about the possibility that there are mines out in front of you; you try and do the best you can.'

A lot of work went into mine risk-mitigation strategies. With just two casualties — Andrew Russell and Sal — given the thousands of hours of patrolling, they were clearly very successful. However, Gus Gilmore describes the lack of mine casualties as a 'blessing' rather than a surprise: 'Anyone who deals with risk management knows that you can mitigate, but it's very difficult to eliminate risks. So we were very fortunate and it was a blessing that we didn't have more casualties from mines.'

At the time of the Andrew Russell incident, John's troop had been doing a lot of patrolling for not much result. 'We were a bit disappointed with what we were doing at that stage, and then that incident had happened — it really wasn't good for morale,' he says. 'So after the Andrew incident everyone was more aware, but it didn't change any of the things we did or the way we patrolled, because basically that's what we do. As it happened I was thinking, "I don't get paid enough for this!" And there's always the thought in the back of my head that the compensation won't be anywhere near as much as if I was a politician on a pushbike.'

That lack of compensation would later generate a public dispute between Andrew Russell's widow, Kylie, and the Howard government, but while they were on the job, the issue was not one the men wanted to contemplate. As John explains: 'When you're on operations you're going, "Well, if I get injured or die, my wife will be getting bugger all and my kid will be living on bugger all." That's a big thing, once you start having a family, a wife and stuff, your focus on the job is still as keen as it was before, however you've now got extra responsibility that you have to think about. So you put your life on the line a couple of times and you start to think, "Well, maybe it's not worth it." But then you get back and you look at all your mates and you get straight back into work.

'The good thing about special forces soldiers, I think, is that the job comes first, basically. You're in a combat zone, you're doing the job on the ground — especially when you're on the ground. I'm sure people in Diego Garcia were disappointed [RAAF crews were based on the Indian Ocean island during the war] and saddened by the fact that someone had got injured, but when you're on the ground in the area where the mines are, you've got to just get up and keep going. You're going to be there for you don't know how much longer, you've got a job to do, [and] that's why you're special forces, because you can do the job.'

For Squadron Operations Officer Major Pete Tinley, who served with Andrew Russell, the reaction to his death was actually a fine example of the professionalism of the SAS.

'If somebody goes down, you deal with that right there with what you can, and just get on with it, go for it. Black Hawk's [the helicopter crash in 1996] another example of that. The day the rest of the squadron got back to Perth after the accident, they were reinforced: the mission was to have a fully capable counterterrorist squadron at very short notice to do what had to be done ... So the same thing happened here: they re-formed and just went on with the job. It's a mission-focused organisation and everything subordinates itself to the mission, the achievement of it. They just picked up, dusted off their shoes and walked on.'

It was about ten o'clock at night in Perth when news of Russell's death came through to Gus Gilmore. The SAS commander had returned from Afghanistan two weeks earlier, after handing over command of the task group to Lieutenant Colonel Rowan Tink.

Gilmore and his executive officer, Major Grant, went straight to SAS headquarters at Campbell Barracks to implement the very well-oiled plans for what to do in the event of a death in the regiment. Their immediate concern was for Sergeant Russell's widow, Kylie, and her baby daughter, Leisa.

'I don't want the name in the media until we've had a chance to speak to Mrs Russell,' was Gilmore's first message back to the brass in Canberra.

'That is protocol and procedure,' he says now, 'but sometimes in this media-hungry, public-information-hungry environment those things are often forgotten and, indeed, the last person who's often thought about is the wife.'

Gilmore was satisfied that everything that could be done in-country to safeguard the welfare of the squadron group was being done under the watchful eye of Rowan Tink. (Like Gilmore, Tink would later be awarded the US Bronze Star for his leadership in Afghanistan.)

'In some ways I wished I could have been there for that,' Gilmore states, 'but I think [that because of] the tasks that I had at home, in many ways it was best that I was there from a regimental perspective.

'I visited [Kylie Russell] soon afterwards and tried to explain to her what Afghanistan was like, what might have transpired, the information that we had available from the incident. Duncan Lewis said to me, "Look, my experience from these things is to tell Kylie as much as you possibly can and explain it in as much detail as you possibly can."'

The fact that Gilmore had literally only just returned from Afghanistan allowed him to tell her quite a bit about the nature of the place where her husband had died and what he and his mates would have been doing at the time. He was also able to explain, with great accuracy, the nature of Andrew's wounds and the care he had received.

'That's a very emotional thing — not only are you feeling your own sense of loss as a commander and as a member of the same "family", so to speak, but [I was] acutely aware of the much more personal loss of Kylie and of her daughter, Leisa, who her father hadn't even seen.'

One issue that took Gus Gilmore by surprise was the angry response of some of the other squadron wives regarding the lack of information they had received. He spoke to them about a week after the event and some were openly hostile because they hadn't been told that their husbands were unharmed.

'Many were appreciative of the information and just trying to talk, [but] there were a number who were understandably very angry about the fact that someone had been killed — it could have been their husbands — and why they hadn't been told that their husbands were safe. And that was quite a confronting issue.'

The official SAS procedure was to not tell the wives that there had been an incident and that their husbands had not been hurt. As Gilmore explains: 'One of the reasons for that — we push this very much — is that, initially, no news is good news and we will devote all our resources and effort to ensure that, as quickly as possible and as accurately as possible, you are advised if there is something wrong.

'If we try to spread those resources, or if we try to reach every wife and we can't contact people and so forth, then the pain of waiting is greater for many more. So, there's no good solution when something like that happens.'

The priority, inevitably, had to be the family who had suffered the loss.

'It's very difficult for Kylie and I wouldn't even hope to understand the trauma for her,' says Gilmore. 'That, then, went on for some time for a range of reasons and I suppose we just tried to remain as much like a family as we could, which is very difficult, particularly as the higher up you go in the organisation, the more distant you're perceived as being from the reality of the situation, and the closer you're perceived as being to the bureaucracy that sometimes provides varied support. That was difficult.'

Kylie Russell has since become a torchbearer for military wives seeking fairer compensation for the loss of their husbands. Like all women in her situation, she has received inadequate compensation and will be forced to rely on financial assistance from organisations such as the SAS Resources Trust (established after the Black Hawk tragedy) to provide for her daughter's future.

The impact of Andrew Russell's death would eventually reverberate all the way to the White House. His sacrifice was acknowledged on several occasions by US President George W Bush, including during a speech at the Australian War Memorial when he visited Canberra in October 2003. Sadly, Kylie Russell was not on the guest list that day, due to what the government said was an oversight. This omission caused considerable public outrage.

However, when Prime Minister John Howard and his wife, Janette, visited Campbell Barracks for the Unit Citation parade in June 2004, Mrs Russell was introduced to them.

Major General Duncan Lewis was in Hawaii for a conference when a late-night call came through on his secure communications system to inform him of the loss of Andrew Russell.

The inaugural head of the recently formed Special Operations Command had been bracing himself for just such a call, given that Afghanistan was a 'serious shooting war', as he called it. But 'that doesn't ease the shock,' General Lewis says.

The first thing he thought about, in what he described as a 'chaotic sequence', was Russell's family: 'How do we provide them with both the information about what's happened and the support that will clearly be required? What about the soldiers that are with him, what is happening with regard to them — are they now out of harm's way, are they being looked after, are they okay? What has been the effect on the wider force that's deployed, what about the others — have they been affected in any way [by] that? Then you look to the media back here. What is going to happen? There will be a frenzy about to start.'

There were the superior commanders to think of — they had to be well informed so they could provide the politicians with accurate information.

General Lewis goes on: 'It was a very sobering experience for all of us. And it renews and redoubles all your efforts: "Have we done everything that we could have done? And now, knowing what we know, is there any progress we can make on that?"

'So you go into a period of, I suppose, self-examination. Have we taken every possible step to make sure that we're looking after our people, that they are as secure as they can be, recognising that at the end of the day they're in harm's way?'

General Lewis was proud of the way the regiment went about its business at that time. He was also grateful for the support the SAS received, as it always does, from the people of Perth and the wider Western Australian community. This support will need to continue — because of its role as the government's force of choice, the SAS will be in the firing line and will suffer casualties.

General Lewis says he often thinks about the modern Australian community's tolerance for loss. Due to the nature of modern conflict and the effort that goes into ensuring protection of our forces, the skill of commanders and modern medical capacities, losses have been kept to a minimum.

General Lewis ponders the alternative scenarios. 'Bomber command in the United Kingdom lost 55 000 killed during the period of the bombing of Germany. I just happened to reflect as I was looking at the figure and compared that to the sort of losses that we've sustained over the last few years. If you were number 55 000, would anyone other than your immediate family and people who were associated with you … have known — would it have been a public issue? I dare say the answer is "No". Tragic and awful as that death is, it's exactly the same as the first one, but the first one was more public.'

He says the Americans often referred to 'wars of necessity' as opposed to 'wars of choice'.

'Obviously if it's a war of necessity [such as World War II] then the bar height is much lower and the threshold for casualties is higher. In wars of choice, where your nation is not directly challenged [for example, Vietnam], then the threshold is lower.'

Just outside the SAS headquarters building at Campbell Barracks is a large piece of granite bearing a plaque carrying the names of the forty-two SAS men who have made the ultimate sacrifice for their country.

'The Rock', as it is known, is a simple and solemn memorial and a reminder of the nature of the business the Australian SAS is in. The fact that all but a few have died during training says a lot about the commitment of the men who dare.

Major Terry O'Farrell, who retired in late 2004 after thirty-eight years' service with the SAS, knew almost every man whose name appears on the Rock.

Standing by the memorial on a clear spring morning, the veteran SAS soldier — who was himself wounded in action in Vietnam during one of his two tours — reflected on the names engraved for eternity.

'Anthony Smith was drowned in the Avon Valley during a river crossing during some training up there.

'Paul Denehey, he was gored by a rogue elephant in Borneo, across the border. The elephant had a broken tusk and it was the broken tusk that he took through the back, and two of the guys — it was only a four-man patrol — two guys went off to get help and one stayed with him. And eventually the guy that stayed with him, fearing that the other two weren't going to return, also went off to try and get help. So Denehey died alone out there. Pretty awful death.

'Hudson and Moncrieff, they were obviously again killed in Borneo but both of them died during a night river crossing. They'd heard some Indonesians across the river and they were trying to get across to have a look at what was there, and they were swept away in the swollen river. They never recovered their bodies.

'Copeman, he was shot in Vietnam and basically died in Australia, he was almost out of danger and got pneumonia or something like that.

'O'Shea died of sickness in Vietnam.

'Baines was throwing or getting rid of old grenades, right at the end of the tour to Vietnam with 1 Squadron. He'd been twelve months unscathed and one of these bastard things went off and he was killed instantaneously.

'Irwin drowned in the Collie. He was on the patrol course, so he'd got through selection, and he was swimming the Collie River at night in the middle of winter, so a strong swimmer, but he just went down at night and wasn't recovered until the next morning.

'Ronnie Harris, he was in my patrol in Vietnam and he was accidentally shot and killed by one of our own. He'd gone out with another patrol. Ronnie was an Aboriginal [sic] ...and always wore a tiger suit [camouflage uniform featuring tiger stripes], which was different to what most of us wore. Anyway, they didn't know him and there was a mix-up and "Harry" got shot. There were lessons to be learnt — first of all, do what you're told when you're out in the field, and it was a bit of a misunderstanding there ... We could see a bloke, if we knew him, just the way he stood, you know what it's like. You know people — and they obviously didn't know him.

'The next two, Eiler and Grafton, they were killed in a parachuting accident. They got entangled, exited the C-130 together and were entangled thereafter, and Lieutenant Eiler was killed when they hit the ground. Grafton was tough as nails and he lived for a few days, but he was so badly damaged, he died.

'Fisher — horrendous, never been found. He was in a patrol in Vietnam, they were in heavy contact with the enemy. They were extracted by what we used to call hot extraction which was a helo with some ropes dropped down. They hooked on — no one quite knows what happened, no one's even sure when he fell off the rope, but he's never been found.

'Brian Jones, great bloke, he was shot and killed again by one of our own. They'd found a camp, gone on a reconnaissance, were coming back to the LUP where the rest of the guys were, and they'd taken a guy out with them who was a new guy, green and inexperienced. He saw some movement and shot [Jones].

'Harry Green died in a vehicle accident. Dougie Abbott, a parachuting accident.

'Bernard Mealin died down at the Fremantle Powerhouse, fell down a coal chute at night. We were on a course down there and he went up on an area he wasn't supposed to go into and then disappeared down one of those big coal chutes.

'Pewee Williamson, he was shot here by one of our own. They were engaged in some counterterrorist drills and they were prepared to go into the room to shoot some targets. They got stopped and then started to do some dry drills on each other and, inexplicably, one guy shot him between the eyes.

'Tonkin, Miller and Fry were lost in the Philippines when a US C-130 Talon combat [plane] put a wing into the sea and went down.

'O'Callaghan was killed in Bass Strait in a diving accident. Rawlings in a parachuting accident here.

'Steve Daley was killed in an air crash in Nowra when a Pilatus Porter went in.

'Kench was killed in a diving accident.

'Holland, he died just over there, on a run of all things. It was just an early-morning run and, bingo, he died.

'Martin — tragically, we were put on a demonstration for the Defence Remuneration Tribunal and they did a skydive up [at] Bindoon — something happened to him, no one knows quite what, but his parachute was opened and on full drive, and he flew into a tree and was killed on impact right in front of the Remuneration Tribunal. They said, "Yeah, this is pretty dangerous, we'll up your dough!" What a way to do it.

'Then you've got Stevens, Ellis, Avedissian, Bird, Constantinidis, Oldham, Smith, Tombs, Callow, Hagan, Johnstone, Frost, Church, McDonald and Peters, all fifteen killed in the Black Hawk, and Andrew Russell, of course, in Afghanistan.'

It is clear that being an SAS soldier is a high-risk occupation. The roles and tasks these men undertake push them very close to the edge during both training and operations.

'You are very conscious that injury and death [are] often close at hand,' says Gus Gilmore. 'Therefore you are very focused on trying to avoid that through risk mitigation. But it remains, and if you look at the Rock at SAS, you realise it's a constant.'

The SAS ethos encompasses the possibility of death in a way that is difficult for outsiders to understand. Gus Gilmore recalls a memorial service held at the Rock for the families of the regiment's three soldiers who went missing in action.

'You have the families of these once-young men who never came home, and perhaps finality was never provided to them. You research a little bit about their lives and you understand that they're no different from the guys serving today. And you just realise what a history the regiment has in its short life. It really has been forged through blood, sweat and tears, and the guys serving there today are carrying on that heritage. But it didn't start yesterday, no, it started a long time ago and there's a real ethos that pervades the regiment that I think is one of its main contributors to its stability and its professionalism and the solid performance that you get from the regiment. You know, it's an interesting place.'

Chapter 17

THE BOWL OF DEATH

'This is fucked up,' said the veteran American sergeant. 'This is worse than Mogadishu.'

His assessment did not reassure the two veteran Australian SAS soldiers enduring withering enemy fire high in the Shahi Khot valley in eastern Afghanistan.

Most of the eighty-two troops pinned down by al Qaeda fire were raw eighteen or nineteen year olds from the US Army's 10th Mountain Division. The sergeant, however, was a seasoned campaigner, who had fought in the 'Black Hawk Down' debacle in Mogadishu in 1993. He was not happy and the two Aussie SAS men — 45-year-old father of two, warrant officer, Clint P, and Signaller Jock Wallace — thought the American's assessment was spot on.

Operation Anaconda, the biggest offensive of the Afghanistan campaign, involving hundreds of local and US forces and almost 100 Australian SAS troops, had run off the rails almost before it had begun. The operation was supposed to strangle enemy forces in the valley, hence the name 'Anaconda', after the giant South American water snake that crushes and drowns its prey, swallowing its victims whole, beginning with their heads. But the operation in the Shahi Khot was going wrong.

It was about 6.45 a.m. on Saturday, 2 March 2002 when the two Aussies were dropped in the valley with a company of 10th Mountain Division troops. As soon as they jumped off the giant twin-rotored MH-47 Chinook transport helicopters they came under a blistering barrage of enemy machine-gun and rocket fire. Alarm bells started ringing inside the Australians' heads.

When a rocket-propelled grenade whizzed past Clint P's arm and landed a metre behind him without exploding, those bells turned to sirens.

'There was no cover and eighty-two people were looking for some,' he recalls now.

Unfortunately Clint had left his entrenching tool, a small spade, back at camp to reduce his load, so he found himself digging a trench with his bare hands in an effort to protect himself from the attack. As the fire intensified, both he and Wallace, racing against time, managed to dig surprisingly large holes with their hands and their knives.

Intelligence estimates given at pre-mission briefings had suggested that there would be 100 to 250 enemy fighters in the valley, mainly Uzbeks, located in the villages of Marzak and Zurmat. There was no mention of larger forces dug into sheer mountain sides high above the Coalition forces' landing zone. Enemy armoured vehicles had been spotted in the area weeks earlier, so it was a known enemy stronghold, but the strength and permanence of the enemy positions came as a complete and shocking surprise.

Clint had been worried when an American general announced just before the operation began that their so-called 'blocking force' — the Mountain Division force, which was meant to prevent any enemy withdrawals once the major offensive began at the other end of the valley — might have to deal with up to 500 bad guys. Later estimates put the number of enemy at closer to 1000 heavily armed and battle-hardened al Qaeda and Taliban fighters, dug into caves and bunkers on the ridges above the two diggers and their struggling American comrades.

Planning for Anaconda had been going on for weeks, and yet the most fundamental information — the estimated strength of the enemy — proved to be deeply flawed as soon as the opening shots were fired. The enemy was well prepared and had even evacuated women and children from the maze of caves and tunnels overlooking the valley.

Unbeknownst to the Australians, history was repeating itself. The Russians had landed a force nearby during their Afghan war in the

1980s, and it had been wiped out by mujahideen fighters firing from the ridge lines above. That disaster is detailed in a book called *The Bear Trap* — either US intelligence officers had not read it, or they did not believe that al Qaeda would use the same tactics against them less than twenty years later.

Those tactics included steel mortar base-plates permanently cemented into the ground and already zeroed in on likely landing zones.

Now the two Aussies and their eighty American colleagues were facing the same fate as the Russians, as accurate mortar and heavy machine-gun fire continued unabated.

'I was lying in my hole watching a B-52 flying over at 20 000 feet with its bomb doors open and hearing the pilot [through his radio headset] say, "Bombs gone". I hoped he had it right and I had more than seventeen seconds to live,' Clint P recalls.

No sooner had the dust settled from the aerial bombardments than enemy fighters emerged from their holes and resumed firing. Some even waved at the men pinned down below. After the first hour it was apparent to the Aussies that what was supposed to be a victorious offensive operation had instead become a survival exercise.

Things were even worse on the other side of a mountain — known as the 'whale feature' because it was shaped like a whale — that divided the valleys. There, a sweeping force led by Northern Alliance Commander General Zia was being given an even bigger hiding.

Warrant Officer Steve was the liaison officer (LO) attached to US Green Beret Stanley Harriman's Cobra-72 team working with local forces from a US Special Forces base in Gardez, in eastern Afghanistan. Four other SAS troopers were with him in the valley.

The nuggety senior soldier, who joined the SAS in 1985, is a classic special forces operator. His sharp wit, keen mind and ability to take the piss in most situations are valuable traits when things go pear-shaped. They would come in very handy throughout this day in Shahi Khot.

The Coalition's western thrust began at first light when, in Steve's own words, 'We got our arses mortared off'.

The plan had called for the local Afghani force to spearhead the attack and US Rangers to move in behind and secure the area. The 10th Mountain Division troops and the two Aussie SAS men — now fighting for their lives on the eastern side of the whale feature — were supposed to prevent any enemy from fleeing the scene.

'We were behind the indigenous forces, we were following their vehicle columns,' explains Steve. 'Essentially I was back there with the other guys just making sure these guys didn't push down south and conflict with our guys.'

Before they could even get into the valley, however, the local force was hit with a mortar barrage and pushed back to Steve's position. They could hear heavy fire from the valley where the two diggers were under siege. 'We could hear them getting fairly well shwacked on that side.'

Just before lunchtime the enemy launched a massive mortar attack. This forced Steve and his comrades into a fighting withdrawal from what became known (once the battle was over) as the 'bowl of death'.

Steve now describes the whole action as 'bizarre'. 'I remember looking up at the whale feature and thinking, "Oooh, okay, 82 millimetre mortar, 5700 metres, I don't think we're back far enough."'

As the morning wore on, a few mortars were landing within 200 or 300 metres, but they were only coming at twenty- to thirty-minute intervals.

'So we did this duelling mortar thing with them,' says Steve. 'We could see them on top of the hill, walking along on top of the hill, [and] the aircraft were flying around and smashing them.'

Things changed dramatically just after 10 a.m., when an American jet came in, bombed the whale feature and turned back in for a strafing run with its cannons. The men on the ground were astounded to then see a white snake curling skywards, chasing the American jet.

'The whole lot of us and the Americans went, "Shit! If they're firing a Stinger missile in there, they're either hiding something or they're going to be there for quite some time."'

By this time two Afghani fighters from the Coalition force had been killed and there were about fifteen wounded soldiers.

'Then, just after eleven o'clock, we hear this *whhoooo* and I thought, "Fuck, that doesn't sound right", and someone yelled out, "Incoming!" and everyone's running around looking for somewhere to hide. The only cover was under one of the fifteen sports utility vehicles or four trucks parked in the huddle. I've dived under this jingle truck [garishly decorated local truck], realising that it's full of fucking mortar rounds and thinking, "I'm an idiot!" But nothing happened — it was a dud. And probably about five minutes later was when we got smashed.'

Steve was operating alongside the US colonel who was in charge and an SAS captain. Of the leadership in the operation he says, 'It wasn't my train set — I probably would have done it in a different way, as I'm sure the other four Australians were thinking, but it wasn't our place to say, "Maybe we should do *this*". They obviously do things differently.'

When that mortar barrage began, it became a case of every man for himself because there were simply not enough vehicles to transport everyone away. Steve had three Aussies in his vehicle and several locals sitting on the roof.

'I remember looking back and seeing the locals running, you know, and just these bloody mortar rounds landing behind them,' he says. 'So we got back to what we thought was a relatively safe area, regrouped — that took about twenty minutes — and then we got hit again and I think they'd come around behind us and were using RPGs [rocket-propelled grenades].'

The force pulled out of the huge wadi, withdrawing 3 or 4 kilometres.

'Then we stopped, did a head count and realised — or the Americans realised — that a lot of the local forces weren't there. They pushed back, with trucks, got them all on the trucks and brought them back. They then did [another] head count, which bloody surprised me. I mean, the Americans, even though they've got a policy that they won't leave their own behind, if they've got other forces working with them, that's [also] their policy. And they did a head count for all the local forces, made sure they had them all, then we licked our wounds and went back to Gardez.'

They were back at the camp in time for lunch, with a casualty count of five dead and thirty-three wounded.

During the mortar barrage, Steve's main concern — apart from his own welfare, of course — was for his SAS comrades.

'We had our own little contingency plans throughout the morning — "Okay, [if] this happens we're going to do this and [if] this happens we're going to do that",' he says. 'Although the captain who was with us, the Australian captain, he was with the colonel all the time, 100 metres away, making sure [the American] wasn't doing something that would conflict with the 1 Squadron guys. I essentially had the other three [SAS] guys with me around the Land Rover, because you could see it was going to get fuckin' ugly.'

Meanwhile, on the other side of the whale feature, Clint P and Jock Wallace continued to fight for their lives. Despite massive air support from B-52 bombers, AC130 Spectre gunships and Apache attack helicopters, the enemy assault showed no sign of waning.

The technology that was supposed to give Coalition forces the edge was breaking down. Runners (soldiers carrying messages) had replaced radios, the number of wounded was growing and ammunition was running out.

Late in the afternoon the enemy launched a massive barrage of fire. As Clint P recounts: 'I was lying on my back in my hole looking up and the tracer fire was crisscrossing like the laser beam alarms you see in the bank vault of a movie. It went on for twenty or twenty-five minutes.'

Just on dusk there was a breakthrough when two Spectres — known by the locals as 'spitting witches' due to their pyrotechnic gun flame display at night — hammered enemy positions with their 105 mm Howitzers, 40 mm cannons and mini-guns. The massive firepower subdued the enemy for long enough to allow the rescue mission to begin.

By 8 p.m. the Coalition's thirty-four wounded had been evacuated by Black Hawk helicopters and by midnight the entire force was out of the valley. Clint is convinced that if the company had not been rescued that day, it would have been overrun and wiped out by the next morning.

Miraculously, the two Aussies had not sustained even a scratch, and not a single soldier was killed. Jock Wallace was later awarded Australia's third highest gallantry award, the Medal for Gallantry, for his courage under fire.

While the battle raged in the Shahi Khot valley, another SAS patrol was operating in the mountains more than 10000 feet above sea level, overlooking an al Qaeda stronghold on Takur Ghar mountain.

Led by Sergeant Matthew Boulliaut, the patrol called in deadly accurate air support throughout 3 and 4 March. Using direct and indirect fire power, Boulliaut was able to outmanoeuvre the enemy and significantly influence the outcome of the battle. His actions saved the lives of more than thirty US Army Rangers who had been stranded during an attempt to rescue a downed US Navy SEAL, Petty Officer First Class Neil Roberts, who had fallen from a chopper and been killed in action. Wave after wave of advancing enemy was wiped out as Boulliaut and his men called in pinpoint air strikes on attacking al Qaeda reinforcements who were trying to overrun the isolated and trapped Rangers. Up to 300 enemy were estimated to have perished as a result of the strikes.

The small Australian patrol spent eleven freezing days working in snow and ice. For his outstanding leadership during the operation, Matt Boulliaut was awarded the Distinguished Service Cross. His citation reads: 'He made tactically sound assessments and decisions and displayed excellent leadership qualities under arduous conditions.'

During the next ten days, Takur Ghar, the whale feature and the Shahi Khot valley were pounded by US air power: B-52 bombers, A10 Thunderbolts, AC130 Spectre gunships and attack helicopters.

Eventually, Warrant Officer Steve and his SAS mates returned to the valley with their comrades from the US Green Berets.

'That whale feature looked half the size. I reckon they just hammered it,' he says now.

The men spent a day pushing through the area, and apart from the occasional rifle shot, the opposition had disappeared. Strangely, despite the intensity of the air strikes and intelligence estimates of dozens of enemy killed, they found just three bodies.

Steve's explanation is that 'with the amount of bombs that went off down there, I would say that half of them were probably killed and their mates took them back to the caves. The other half probably got away. It's a long time, twelve days all up, from the time we first went in — and these guys know the bloody ground.'

One thing was certain: none of the enemy had been buried on the valley floor.

'They dragged them up in the caves, they didn't bury them [on the valley floor], I know that much, because we spent a whole day going over it.'

As a liaison officer working with the American special forces, Steve's most important job was to keep a close watch on where the Australian patrols were at all times and protect them from possible blue-on-blue incidents. That meant staying close to key headquarters staff at all times, and watching and listening intently to what the SAS troops were up to.

Steve had originally arrived at the US base at Bagram with his 1 SAS Squadron comrades, only to be told ten minutes later that he and four other senior SAS soldiers would be 'farmed out' as liaison officers. 'So essentially we had about thirty minutes to grab our shit, throw it in an American bloody armour-plated friggin' Land Rover — which wouldn't start — and race down to Kabul to link up with these guys.

'We grabbed one of our own [Land Rover] Defenders from the squadron and headed straight down to bloody Kabul, with an escort.'

The men knew Anaconda was going to be revved up, but their job was to get to Kabul, link up with the US special forces guys and tap into what they were doing to make sure their activities wouldn't adversely affect the SAS troops. And just as well they did.

On one occasion Steve overheard a radio call between the American officer he was accompanying and a Ranger patrol out in the field. The patrol had about 147 surplus 120 mm mortar rounds and they wanted to fire them off into what looked like an uninhabited mountain, so they didn't have to lug the heavy shells back to base. According to Steve, the captain had seen five men killed and thirty-three wounded ten days earlier, so he was probably thinking, 'I hope there is a shitload of Taliban up there.'

Approval to fire was being given when the Aussie intervened: Steve thought the location of the target hill sounded familiar.

'I pulled out my map and had a look at it and found we had a patrol sitting on that very hill, so I went straight over to the captain and said, "Will you ... give me a grid reference for where you want those Rangers to expend those rounds?" So he gave it. I said, "No, fuck it, stop, drop, no rounds are to be fired, I've got a patrol on that hill."'

The SAS foot patrol had every right to be there, too, because the hill was in the Australian area of operations and the men had been there for some days.

'That's why, as an LO, you're like fucking Blutac with these guys, making sure that any decision that they make doesn't conflict with our own guys or with what we're doing within a joint Coalition operation,' says Steve. 'I went up to that patrol commander in Bagram and told him he had to buy me a beer.'

Steve spent weeks with the Green Berets and Rangers, and that single incident proved beyond doubt the value of having experienced liaison officers attached to American and Coalition units. That sort of arrangement is manpower-intensive and requires confident and experienced soldiers, but its worth is proved by the fact that Australia was the only major player to avoid friendly fire casualties during both the Afghanistan and Iraq campaigns.

Friendly forces were not the only 'deconflicting' (preventing friendly casualties) issue during military operations in Afghanistan. The media also played a part, and one Australian patrol probably saved the lives of a carload of reporters and photographers during Operation Anaconda.

Patrol commander Shane was working in an area where the bombing from the Coalition air strikes had become so intense that the special forces troops had to use earplugs to try to get some sleep. According to some of the men, it was so bad that enemy fighters became shell-shocked, which caused them to become careless, and allowed the SAS troops to pinpoint their targets with even greater accuracy.

'They [the US] dropped a lot of bombs,' Shane says. 'They went a bit crazy towards the end there — but it worked for them, I suppose.'

At one point Shane saw two vehicles heading north, away from the area. Because Osama bin Laden hadn't been captured, Shane thought he might have hit the jackpot. 'I remember thinking, "This is a bit suss. You never know your luck — it might be the world's most wanted man."'

Two LRPVs gave chase to the unidentified cars and one of the gunners locked his Javelin anti-armour missile onto one of them.

'If something happens I'll just fire the Javelin off,' the soldier told Shane.

The vehicles split up and Shane, who was manning the Mag 58 machine gun at the front left of his car, was about to shoot out the tyres on one of the cars when it suddenly stopped. The occupants emerged with their hands up and told the diggers that they were journalists from *Time* magazine.

Ordered onto the ground, the American and Canadian newsmen appeared oblivious to the extreme danger in the area and how close they had come to being killed. They said they had simply wanted to get to the front line and 'have a look'.

Shane explained the dangers to them, especially the threat from the AC130 Spectre gunships and other aircraft, which had intensified their activity after the early Anaconda setbacks.

'The journalists were under the impression that if they put a big panel marker on their roof that they would be safe,' he says, but he has no doubt that if the reporters had met an American patrol, they would have been shot at.

Obviously seasoned campaigners, the journalists' predicament did not dull their enthusiasm for their story, and despite being asked not to take photos of the Australians, they proceeded to shoot some images. The troops were then obliged to remove their digital cameras and wipe their storage disks clean.

'We asked them for operational security reasons [not to] take photos,' says Shane, 'and they did.'

The commanding officer of Operation Anaconda, US Army Major General Frank Hagenbeck, later praised the work of the Australian SAS troops. 'They were there, did what they needed to do — a supporting role in the first days, but by the third day they were the main effort for the fight and they came through superbly.'

Other than a few small ambushes close to Gardez, the remainder of Anaconda was a mopping-up operation for the Australian patrols, cutting off the so-called rat lines used by the enemy to travel in and out of the mountains.

They uncovered more weapons stockpiles, including one that yielded, amongst other things, a mobile anti-aircraft gun. The patrols also found more evidence of the level of cooperation between the Taliban government in Afghanistan and Osama bin Laden's al Qaeda terrorist network.

The extent of the training camps, and the massive amount of excavation and other engineering works involved in hiding them, shocked seasoned SAS campaigners such as Captain Neil. In one case the troops discovered a valley shaped like a punchbowl, about 1000 metres in diameter. It was surrounded by sheer 200-metre-high cliffs and had just one entrance at the end of a zigzag road that climbed about 700 metres.

'Around every corner was this underground bunker looking straight down the road,' Neil recalls. 'Had they been armed or manned, they would have shot us up, and the [bunkers] weren't poorly made either — they were made out of reinforced concrete with high beams, and there were hundreds of them. We found shipping containers buried underground.'

They also found detailed training manuals and other valuable intelligence. The magnitude of the punchbowl complex was all the evidence the troops needed to prove that the Taliban regime had been working hand in glove with al Qaeda — and for a very long time.

'This was not an apparition or something that just started overnight,' says Neil. 'It must have been done with the acquiescence of the local government.'

Such was the quality of the work and the secrecy surrounding it that Coalition intelligence operatives had had no idea about the scale of the camps. And it was their sheer size that really surprised the Aussies, who were reminded of the film *Dune* when they saw the labyrinth of underground compounds, all built on opium money. Opium poppies are a staple crop in Afghanistan, and funds from the opium trade are used to fund local warlords and terrorist cells.

Neil continues: 'I walked up to one of the compounds at night and knocked on the wall to see how solid it was, because we were going to put a rocket into it, and there was reinforced concrete a metre thick and 8 metres high. Inside, again, they'd built shipping containers into the wall of the compound.'

The compounds allowed the well-trained and well-armed Taliban and al Qaeda fighters to cause mayhem against their high-tech enemy.

'You've got to give it to them on Anaconda,' Neil concludes, 'they gave the First World a run for its money.'

It was only US air power and the quality of the soldiers involved in the battle that ultimately saved the day. The diggers, whose lives were on the line, describe it bluntly as a 'stuff-up'. The campaign was supposed to last two days but went on for twelve, and when it ended no one could say how many enemy had been destroyed or had fled deeper into the mountains on the Pakistan border.

At a media briefing in Canberra at the end of the Afghanistan operation, the then head of Special Forces, Brigadier Duncan Lewis, who was the operational commander in Afghanistan, chose his words carefully when asked about intelligence shortcomings.

'You would always be trying not to have a situation like that develop, but intelligence is not a pure science. As you know, there is a large amount of art involved in that particular pursuit [intelligence], and you can't get perfect situational awareness. No matter what wizardry you have available to you, no matter what technology is available, it is not possible — and you would be foolish to think — that you can get perfect situational awareness.'

Lewis admitted to being surprised by the ferocity of the enemy response at the start of Anaconda. 'I don't know whether it was dependent on the amount of intelligence that the Americans had, but the ferocity of that engagement was surprising.'

Warrant officer Steve believes, even in hindsight, that the Anaconda operation had to be done.

'I think tactically the whole concept of the operation they had planned for was sound. I think the problem was that (a) there were more of them than what they thought, and (b) they stood their ground. They weren't prepared to be fuckin' pushed out. Overall it had to be done, regardless. Unfortunately a lot of guys got killed — Americans. Fortunately none of us got killed, but you can't say it should never have been done. When you've got that many enemy there, you can't just let them carry on the way they were carrying on. It's not right.'

On May 16, an SAS patrol from 3 SAS Squadron was involved in a fierce firefight in another valley close to Khost, not far from the scene of Anaconda.

Designated Redback Kilo Three, the patrol, under the command of a sergeant with twelve years' experience in the SAS, was observing a suspected Taliban armed position near a village called Zambar. The diggers had set up hides about 40 metres away from a heavy machine gun position. When an armed local fighter blew their cover and threatened to fire at them, the SAS opened fire.

Suddenly they found themselves under attack from heavy machine guns, small-arms fire and rocket-propelled grenades from three flanks.

An official Defence briefing on the incident given on 30 May 2002 reported, 'Now the Australians exchanged fire over a period of several hours while attempting to disengage. The hostile fire, from prepared defensive positions, was directed onto them from all directions, while a number of hostile groups attempted to close with and kill the Australians. There were no Australian casualties, but at least four of the hostile forces were killed.'

The patrol commander radioed for close air support. Unfortunately a nearby coalition F/A-18 Hornet fighter could not help because the patrol was too close to the enemy. But an AC130 Spectre gunship arrived and fired a few bursts from its 105 mm gun into the enemy positions.

Several hours after the initial contact, a so-called 'half squadron patrol', led by 3 SAS Squadron commander Major Vance Khan, arrived under cover of darkness to rescue the patrol. US forces had judged the situation too dire to send in helicopters to extract them.

The official Defence briefing said, 'Upon reaching the area of the contact, they were engaged by the same hostile elements. As night fell they fought their way through to a rendezvous with the first group. Again the hostile groups attempted to move behind the second force and to destroy them before they could escape. The Australians were able to conduct a safe rendezvous and disengage from the contact and withdraw back to a safe area without casualties. The marry-up and withdrawal was assisted by very effective close air support from US Air Force AC130 aircraft.'

As Khan's force withdrew from the valley with the patrol, the AC130 crew reported enemy activity off to their left flank and requested permission to engage the enemy with their considerable fire power.

Major Khan refused, saying his men were not under threat.

The patrol escaped from the valley without casualties.

The troops and their commanding officers were convinced that those firing at the patrol had been Taliban or al Qaeda. According to the initial official Defence briefing on the incident given in Canberra on 17 May 2002, 'The Australians were where they were supposed to be, doing what they were supposed to be doing and doing it well.'

But one of the diggers had disobeyed an order and souvenired an Afghan hat and weapon from a body on the battlefield.

The entire patrol was subjected to disciplinary action due to allegations made following the heat of battle.

The five patrol members were segregated but remained in the squadron. Following an investigation, the second-in-command was 'Returned to Unit' (sent home to Perth). The patrol commander went on to conduct a further patrol before requesting to Return to Unit. The three remaining members stayed in Afghanistan to complete further patrols. However, when they were in Kuwait on their way home to Australia with the squadron, they were issued with a 'Notice to Show Cause' why they should remain in the SASR. The soldier who had disobeyed a lawful order and taken souvenirs from the battlefield was sent back to Perth.

The patrol commander was subsequently moved to another squadron, but left the SAS soon afterwards.

Ultimately the so-called 'fog of war', in which everyone involved in a particular combat incident has a different recollection of events, meant that the full truth might never be established.

Chapter 18

THE EVIL EYE OF THE GOAT

The tinkle of bells sounded like an alarm to the patrol commander, Sergeant George. A herd of goats and their herder were wandering towards his observation post.

George and his patrol thought they had built the ideal hide, high on a mountain side in northern Afghanistan. They had checked it from every angle, reckoned it looked just like all the other camel-thorn bushes in the vicinity, and rated it a top-shelf OP.

The diggers hadn't done a bad job of individual blending into the environment either: smelling like the locals was not difficult for 37-year-old George and his patrol, due to the lack of opportunities to bathe. 'The Americans called us "street folk" or "the unwashed",' he says. But the sparse ground cover made concealing six Australian blokes a much greater challenge.

George had realised that the lack of cover for his men would be an occupational hazard when he first set foot on the baking earth of the Mars-like landscape. Arriving at the old Russian air base at Bagram, north of Kabul, in August 2002, his first thought had been, 'Where the hell am I going to hide here?' For soldiers trained largely in the Australian bush and the lush jungles of Papua New Guinea, Afghanistan's barren mountains were a nightmare.

As George recalls, 'My first impression of it was that the terrain was unbelievable. In order to do the sort of roles and tasks that we're designed for, I thought, "This is going to be quite difficult."'

And difficult it was proving to be as the goats on the mountain side moved closer and closer, seeking out whatever morsels they could find in the nearly food-free environment. What George hadn't known when he chose the hide was that camel-thorn bush, a leafless plant with thin thorns as long as a man's finger, was high on the list of goat favourites.

George's patrol had completed a full day of covert observation from their hide and they were feeling pretty good about themselves when they heard the bells. The six soldiers were laid out in a defensive posture as the goats grazed nearby.

The SAS troopers were secreted in a place where water had miraculously run down a hill and cut a recess into the rock with a lip further down. 'Looking back up at it you'd see the rock wall and then back up past the hill. We could almost be higher than it and behind it but not be seen because of the slope of the terrain,' says George. 'We had one full day in there undetected, and it was a good day. We got tonnes of reporting, we saw as much movement and stuff as we could on the area that we were interested in. We couldn't be seen from above or below, so I was pretty satisfied with that, and our escape routes were fair, but we had a good amount of fire power and the air cover was always there.'

Showing just how effective their position was, a local goat herder — armed with the mandatory AK47 assault rifle — had earlier moved within 10 metres of the OP without seeing the patrol. Also reassuring to the men was the fact that locals would be unlikely to graze their animals in an area littered by land mines.

During the day goats had simply wandered around the intruders, making what George describes as their 'merry way across the Afghan landscape'. Eventually, though, the new herd zeroed in on the hide and began to devour the patrol's only cover: the delicious camel-thorn.

George also briefly wondered whether goats were attracted to the smell of human urine.

'So we were hiding in this magnificent hide with goats all around. I don't know whether you've ever seen a goat's eyes close up, but they're quite evil-looking because their pupils are elongated, horizontally, with one vertical slash in between. I know, because we had a goat sitting right there with us. We were trying to hit them with things, throw rocks and even hiss at them to shoo them away, because we really didn't want the herder to come in as well, [but] eventually he did.'

The startled goatherd got the shock of his life when several heavily armed, unwashed Australian soldiers literally popped up out of the ground pointing a variety of weapons at him.

'It was like on the movies,' George recalls, 'you know when he's seen you, it dawned on him that we were sitting there. So we just stood up, said, "G'day", and gave him a biscuit. We got out and had a good look at our hide as well, what it looked like in the daylight, and it was quite a good hide — at least, up until the point he walked on it.'

One patrol member, Harry, was the self-appointed language expert. Most of the blokes reckoned they were 'carrying their language' — in other words, their weapons — but Harry was genuinely interested in languages, according to George.

'He tried a few things with [the goatherd] and none of them really worked, so we smiled and nodded and gave him another biscuit. He looked either sheepish or friendly or whatever and he moved off virtually within ten minutes because I don't think he wanted to hang around with us. Seeing as we were blown, I tried to keep our numbers down as much as possible so he wouldn't know how many of us there were. So maybe three of us came out and had a look at him, sat and ... just got up on high positions and watched what he was doing.'

The local man perched up on a higher bit of ground and watched the patrol. He lit a fire and started cooking, and sat there for a good three hours.

The patrol had a resupply planned for that evening, when it was due to rendezvous with a nearby vehicle-mounted patrol.

'We made a show of moving up to a position so that he could see us moving away,' says George. 'There was nowhere to hide any more and I'd rather them see us go away.'

But George managed to convince his command that the patrol should be reinserted on a neighbouring hill so that it could keep up its observation task. 'They'd seen us come out, so therefore we should be able to slide straight back in somewhere else and continue with the task, and [we] would probably see more because they'd figure we'd gone, perhaps.'

So the SAS soldiers hitched a ride on an LRPV to the second hill, as far away as they could get from the place where they had been compromised. And not only that — they were dropped off a fair way from their objective and it took them days to reach the spot.

It was a small group carrying very heavy packs; for security of movement, they split into two: 'One lot would work up while the others covered,' George says, 'and then we'd go solid cover and the others would move up and so we'd caterpillar our way up. But at least we had some form of security of movement, rather than just all head down with packs thinking, "Fuck, this is heavy." And indeed it worked well.'

On the second night the patrol was moving up a hill when a loud shot rang out from the valley floor. The round, probably from a Mauser hunting rifle, ripped through the rear half of the patrol, narrowly missing Harry the linguist. George's initial reaction was that one of his men — probably his sniper, Gibbo — had accidentally let one rip.

'I was fuming and sitting up on top as they are making their way back up to us, about to rip Gibbo a couple of arseholes for doing that. "What the fuck's going on, who was that?" "It wasn't us!" they said and they were quite agitated, fuckin' angry, really.'

The patrol stopped and George looked at the valley below. He spotted the culprit: a local who must have heard a noise and fired randomly in their direction. The man was about 300 metres away and moving in a low, grassy patch at the edge of the hill.

'I don't think he did see us, I think he heard us,' George says. 'It's very hard to get up those rocky slopes without slipping on a rock or something. He must have heard something like a rock slip ... watched, maybe heard some more, because there were two groups moving, and thought, "Fuck, this is either wolves or bandits or something", and quite accurately, given that he couldn't see as it was very dark, just ripped off a round up the hill, in among us. I'm thinking to myself, "What have we got, what are we going to do?" Because those guys were angry and I think they wanted a piece of his arse! But obviously we don't just go ripping out and tearing everyone apart.'

The rest of the patrol trained their weapons on the lone ranger.

'That was quite humorous, because everyone's just looking at him, thinking, "Well, what are you going to do now?" So we had him, we could see him, we watched him, and his gun was back on his back and he was walking around again. So, yeah, we could have toasted him, but in my heart I couldn't do that. I was looking, thinking, "Okay, he's not really posing a threat to us any more, he's let a round off and maybe he's staked his claim to his land or whatever he's doing." So I thought, "Fuck it, we'll leave him be." And I'm glad we did, in retrospect. I don't think he knew what he was shooting at, because he was just nonchalantly walking around. He wasn't running back to wherever it was he came from. So he'd just shot at whatever he'd heard up on the hill.'

Once in their hide, the patrol established a routine of covertly watching a small village of about five buildings going about its business, with women drawing water, two families moving around. 'We watched them move their goats off and we were satisfied that they weren't really awake to what we were doing,' says George.

'The next evening we moved back up onto the hill to conduct our task again, and the fuckin' goat-bell noise is there again. So we had a decent look and I figured it was this same bloke, same guy, sitting there with his goats at night, which is unusual in itself. I can understand if he went up on the hill to have a look around, but why he took his goats is beyond me. I don't know — I'm not a great Afghan goat scholar.

'I thought, "Okay, fuck, we can't go on the hill", and we were going to head off back to our hiding spot. He ripped off another round, but it was in a different direction. So I don't know if he was just some madman who loved shooting his rifle for the sake of it, but it wasn't at all towards us.'

They watched the local man for two hours, then he suddenly got up and started moving towards the patrol's OP.

'And old Harry, my erstwhile linguist who was the bloke who was probably the closest to being shot, just said, "Why don't we just 40 mill this bloke? Put a few grenades on him or something?" "Well, if he gets to this point we will! Harry, chill out, man. Just watch him and see what he does." And fortunately off he went. The next morning we were in our nice little LUP there, relaxing, thinking, "What the hell are we going to do? We can't do our task!"

'And we were going to get picked up in the afternoon of that day, so we were a bit disappointed that we couldn't just get in, sit down and do what we wanted to do [i.e. observe the area], because it was so difficult to [execute] that task given what's moving and the fact that you can't hide. And this fucker turned up on the hill again! He's on the hill opposite us and moving down through the saddle towards us.'

George then realised that 'this guy's a nightmare that will never go away'. It was obvious to the soldiers that the local was just strolling, but he was coming towards them, and he had his goats with him. So rather than let the Afghani get too close, surprise him and risk a hostile reaction, George decided to go out early and greet the man.

George and Harry walked up towards the local and tried not to laugh at the shock written all over his face when he realised what he'd been shooting at.

'You could just see him thinking, "Fuck!" And he started shouting back down the hill. I said to Harry, who was on the other side, probably about 50 metres from me, "Harry, say something to him, mate! Chill him out!" Harry was racing to think of something to say and he finally blurted out, "*Shaa geeza*". I said, "What is that, Harry?" and his interpretation — which I don't think was correct anyway — was "Nice goat!"'

The Afghan shooter was not impressed by the compliment — he wanted nothing to do with the SAS troops. He took off down the hill, and later that day the patrol was extracted.

By this stage it seemed as though goats could prove to be an SAS bugaboo. Well before these incidents, various trials had been conducted to find a suitable goat repellent — they had even tried imported Siberian tiger shit — but because of the lack of natural predators of goats, nothing seemed to work.

'We had five goats in the compound at Bagram and they were seen actually eating the [tiger shit]!' says George. 'Bushes were sprayed with it and then devoured by the goats. Nothing worked.'

Sergeant George had been desperate to get to Afghanistan, to test his skills. Determined to be in on the action, he had to call in a lot of favours to get the tour of duty. The snag that initially prevented his selection was that he was a specialist water operator and there would be no call for those skills in the mountains of Afghanistan. So he got himself on a free-fall parachuting course. Seventy jumps later, he still did not feel 100 per cent comfortable in the air, but he managed to get posted to 2 SAS Squadron for second rotation in the Afghanistan operations.

There was a good reason for George's reluctance to leave solid ground: he had been on board the third helicopter during the 1996 Black Hawk tragedy, and had been awarded a commendation from the Chief of Defence Force for his actions on that terrible night.

'I remember my first parachute jump, it scared the absolute shit out of me just because you're falling to earth and it's noisy, there's so much to think about, so many things to do and it's so different,' he says now.

He'd had a near-death experience on another jump when he was leading a team on a free-fall exercise.

'I was activating my canopy the lowest so I could lead them in, and everyone's higher than me and I activated at 3000 feet, which isn't really that high, and I had nothing. So I had to get it off my back and get it to function and by the time I had control of my canopy it was 1500 feet. I suppose the parallels are that once you step out of a plane, you're going to hit the ground one way or another. Even though it's short and it's not as arduous and hard as water ops, the risk element in free fall is enormous and a lot of the factors can make things go wrong. If you activate it on an angle, you've got all this equipment that those lines are going to go past and can catch up, so [you] have to be very good at falling and be squared away. It takes a lot of practice.'

Even before the Black Hawk crash, helicopters made George nervous. 'Helicopters scare the shit out of me,' he admits. 'Once you're up there, you've got to come down. Hopefully it's in a manner that you've planned to.'

That trepidation wasn't helped during one night mission in Afghanistan, on board a US special forces Chinook helicopter. The machine was bristling with weapons including mini-guns and Mag 58 machine guns, but no one had told the Aussies that the weapons had to be warmed up because of the freezing conditions.

'It was a reasonably long flight, and we were sitting in the back of the aircraft, just relaxing, when all hell broke loose, these two mini-guns and two Mag 58s just started ripping. We're all thinking, "What the fuck's going on?" And the Yanks told us, "Just siddown, siddown — it's just what they do."'

When he rejoined 2 SAS Squadron after a stint on other duties, George had been impressed by the new kit they had been given since East Timor. The latest weapons, communications gear and training all combined to generate high morale and a very positive attitude. 'We've even got a psych attached to the unit now and I suppose people might think that's as a result of going off on all these operations, [that] we might be all fucked up, coming back. But really I think he's here because when things kick off and people don't go, they really have to go and see old Mike and wail and scratch and carry on.'

In addition to the challenges of the locals and their animals, SAS patrols in Afghanistan faced the usual issues confronted by a group of healthy young men pretty much living on top of one another. George recalled his chook — his signaller — having the patrol's first operational wank. 'In close proximity to all of us and no one had a clue that he'd just pulled himself! And he was very proud of himself.'

Morale was always on the minds of troop and patrol commanders, especially during long and arduous patrols. Often they couldn't use their hexamine solid fuel stoves or the chemical heaters in the US ration packs because of the odour, so warm food became a real luxury. On one occasion George was showing his pack to some Americans and they laughed at his hexamine stove.

'Well, how do you guys heat food?' he asked them. The answer was simple: 'We just call in the helos.'

Transport to and from the area of operations was often a challenge for the foot patrols. George recalled one mission where they were supposed to be inserted by chopper, but the weather closed in and made it impossible. The American special forces commander had hired a number of brightly decorated locals' trucks — known as 'jingle trucks' because of the chains hanging from them — as alternative transport, so the SAS patrol was inserted using one of the trucks.

'We got the USSF guys to give us a bit of security on the move and they took us in. Unfortunately we ended up 3 kilometres away from where we wanted to be, so we had the liability of quite a mountainous trek to get in there.'

That trek turned into a tough, three-day march, made tougher because of the weight of their packs which, including water, came to around 70 kilograms each.

'We just moved consistently all through the night in order to get to the objective that we'd been given. And it was quite taxing — the blokes were fairly rooted, but at least they could lay up all day and relax as much as [they could].'

George was also concerned about the bloke driving the truck. 'The fellow who drove the jingle truck was an Afghani goatherd type, I didn't know who he was. Obviously he was in the employ of the Americans, but you don't know where [the locals'] loyalties lie — it wasn't part of our plan. So, having been dropped off, we moved off in the opposite direction that we were going to be going, just for him, so that if he was going to be reporting he'd say, "I dropped off some silly Australians and they moved off in that direction."'

hexamine solid fuel stoves or the chemical heaters in the US ration packs because of the odour, so warm food became a real luxury. On one occasion George was showing his pack to some Americans and they laughed at his hexamine stove.

'Well, how do you guys heat food?' he asked them. The answer was simple: 'We just call in the helos.'

Transport to and from the area of operations was often a challenge for the foot patrols. George recalled one mission where they were supposed to be inserted by chopper, but the weather closed in and made it impossible. The American special forces commander had hired a number of brightly decorated locals' trucks — known as 'jingle trucks' because of the chains hanging from them — as alternative transport, so the SAS patrol was inserted using one of the trucks.

'We got the USSF guys to give us a bit of security on the move and they took us in. Unfortunately we ended up 3 kilometres away from where we wanted to be, so we had the liability of quite a mountainous trek to get in there.'

That trek turned into a tough, three-day march, made tougher because of the weight of their packs which, including water, came to around 70 kilograms each.

'We just moved consistently all through the night in order to get to the objective that we'd been given. And it was quite taxing — the blokes were fairly rooted, but at least they could lay up all day and relax as much as [they could].'

George was also concerned about the bloke driving the truck. 'The fellow who drove the jingle truck was an Afghani goatherd type, I didn't know who he was. Obviously he was in the employ of the Americans, but you don't know where [the locals'] loyalties lie — it wasn't part of our plan. So, having been dropped off, we moved off in the opposite direction that we were going to be going, just for him, so that if he was going to be reporting he'd say, "I dropped off some silly Australians and they moved off in that direction."'

George says that morale in a patrol is largely personality driven. 'There might have been two guys in my patrol who didn't like each other. Not openly or hostilely, but you can observe that, you can see it quite clearly that if people are going to be abrasive in any respect, it's easy to pick up. So we'd always keep those guys apart wherever possible. I wouldn't say it would ever have come to a flash point in our patrol. I know in some patrols — or even with some people, some people I just can't handle or tolerate — we'll always do our job, but you think, "Fuck! This is just torture, I really don't want to work with this guy."'

His own patrol at that time, he says, was 'a really good set of blokes'. The group included several 'retreads' — experienced SAS members who had left and subsequently rejoined the regiment to be in on the action. George's patrol scout, Peter, was one of them. He had done selection at the same time as George, but because of his time out he was ranked as a junior soldier, with experience way beyond his ranking. 'So we were very lucky in that respect,' says George.

Peter had a wide range of skills, as he also led the way in keeping his patrol commander in line with some well-timed banter and piss-taking. A perfect opportunity arose one day when George asked Peter to get him a meal.

'In one of those LUPs I was really quite starving, and the rations — you'd get, maybe, biscuits in the morning, maybe a meal satchel of whatever type in the middle of the day, and a brew in the evening with maybe some more biscuits. And that was your lot because that's all you could carry.'

Peter presented him with his main meal: a satchel of mashed potato from one of the American MRE packs. 'It was hideous, and I was looking at it thinking, "What the fuck!" And I couldn't even heat it up, because we couldn't cook — and the amount of joy that gave them, to see me suffer like that, was remarkable,' says George.

Humour was a constant tool for boosting morale. 'Even when someone's walking near you, there's a lot of times you just sit there biting your fingers because of the stupid looks on people's faces, or to find a suitable goat repellent — they had even tried imported Siberian tiger shit — but because of the lack of natural predators of goats, nothing seemed to work.

'We had five goats in the compound at Bagram and they were seen actually eating the [tiger shit]!' says George. 'Bushes were sprayed with it and then devoured by the goats. Nothing worked.'

Sergeant George had been desperate to get to Afghanistan, to test his skills. Determined to be in on the action, he had to call in a lot of favours to get the tour of duty. The snag that initially prevented his selection was that he was a specialist water operator and there would be no call for those skills in the mountains of Afghanistan. So he got himself on a free-fall parachuting course. Seventy jumps later, he still did not feel 100 per cent comfortable in the air, but he managed to get posted to 2 SAS Squadron for second rotation in the Afghanistan operations.

There was a good reason for George's reluctance to leave solid ground: he had been on board the third helicopter during the 1996 Black Hawk tragedy, and had been awarded a commendation from the Chief of Defence Force for his actions on that terrible night.

'I remember my first parachute jump, it scared the absolute shit out of me just because you're falling to earth and it's noisy, there's so much to think about, so many things to do and it's so different,' he says now.

He'd had a near-death experience on another jump when he was leading a team on a free-fall exercise.

'I was activating my canopy the lowest so I could lead them in, and everyone's higher than me and I activated at 3000 feet, which isn't really that high, and I had nothing. So I had to get it off my back and get it to function and by the time I had control of my canopy it was 1500 feet. I suppose the parallels are that once you step out of a plane, you're going to hit the ground one way or another. Even though it's short and it's not as arduous and hard as water ops, the risk element in free fall is enormous and a lot of the factors can make things go wrong. If you activate it on an angle, you've got all this equipment that those lines are going to go past and can catch up, so [you] have to be very good at falling and be squared away. It takes a lot of practice.'

Even before the Black Hawk crash, helicopters made George nervous. 'Helicopters scare the shit out of me,' he admits. 'Once you're up there, you've got to come down. Hopefully it's in a manner that you've planned to.'

That trepidation wasn't helped during one night mission in Afghanistan, on board a US special forces Chinook helicopter. The machine was bristling with weapons including mini-guns and Mag 58 machine guns, but no one had told the Aussies that the weapons had to be warmed up because of the freezing conditions.

'It was a reasonably long flight, and we were sitting in the back of the aircraft, just relaxing, when all hell broke loose, these two mini-guns and two Mag 58s just started ripping. We're all thinking, "What the fuck's going on?" And the Yanks told us, "Just siddown, siddown — it's just what they do."'

When he rejoined 2 SAS Squadron after a stint on other duties, George had been impressed by the new kit they had been given since East Timor. The latest weapons, communications gear and training all combined to generate high morale and a very positive attitude. 'We've even got a psych attached to the unit now and I suppose people might think that's as a result of going off on all these operations, [that] we might be all fucked up, coming back. But really I think he's here because when things kick off and people don't go, they really have to go and see old Mike and wail and scratch and carry on.'

In addition to the challenges of the locals and their animals, SAS patrols in Afghanistan faced the usual issues confronted by a group of healthy young men pretty much living on top of one another. George recalled his chook — his signaller — having the patrol's first operational wank. 'In close proximity to all of us and no one had a clue that he'd just pulled himself! And he was very proud of himself.'

Morale was always on the minds of troop and patrol commanders, especially during long and arduous patrols. Often they couldn't use their someone farts, or whatever it is that happens that's just remarkably funny. It seems to just magnify the humour of things, being in that sort of situation.'

Motivation was sharpened on 12 October 2002, when news came through that many Australians had been killed by terrorists in the holiday resort of Bali. The Indonesian island is a particular favourite with Perth residents because of its proximity to the city, and many SAS soldiers had holidayed there.

According to George, the bombing provided the SAS men in Afghanistan with a fresh emphasis on what they were doing and why they were fighting the war against terrorism.

'We were out on patrol when we heard about the Bali bombing, and people were angry and more determined, I'd say, to get on with doing what they were doing. On the same night that it occurred, we were hearing media reports from that little bearded fellow that they've locked up [Jemaah Islamiyah leader Abu Bakar Bashir], saying, "It can't be us, it's the Australians and the Americans". This made us more mad at the way they operate, and increased our resolve to get hold of them and fix it. It gave us more feeling that what we were doing should be done and done as well as we [could].'

Warrant Officer Macca spent three months in Afghanistan. 'The squadron actually deployed there in August of 2002 and I went in September of 2002 and came back in December. The reason for that was [that] I was away doing a mountain warfare instructor's course and joined the squadron three weeks after they deployed there. I flew into the country, spent a few days basically acclimatising, and then I went straight out and took over a patrol.'

That patrol ended up being out for nearly two months, the longest patrol of the Afghanistan campaign. The season was summer going into winter, so when Macca first arrived there were still days of plus 40°C, but as the long patrol progressed the men experienced temperatures of minus 14°C overnight.

'We were travelling around the villages, gathering whatever intelligence we could, hearts-and-minds work,' says Macca, 'and just getting into our AOs [areas of operation] and finding out what was there, where people were going, where they were coming from, if we could find ways that the Taliban or al Qaeda people were supposedly coming in and out of Afghanistan, all that sort of stuff. Trying to find possible weapons caches, that sort of thing.'

Maintaining morale became a serious challenge on that long patrol. While it could not compare with the longest SAS patrol on record — 89 days, led by Sergeant Arch Foxley in Borneo in 1965 — it was an extreme patrol in the context of modern military operations.

Macca found it difficult to manage the men's morale for such an extended period — eating from the ration packs for so long, and being on edge twenty-four hours a day with only broken sleep, was not easy.

'It's quite demanding and it does wear them down,' he says now.

Macca began to notice the strain around the 32-day mark. The soldiers were not used to patrolling in populated places, and their area of operations at that time was quite crowded with locals who were all curious. They could find no privacy wherever they went and whatever they did — often they couldn't even go for a wash without attracting a crowd.

'You could pull up on a hill somewhere and try and get into some bush to hide, and a hundred locals turn up to watch you, and they even want to follow you down to watch you have a crap to see what you do. And ... it wears pretty thin on the blokes after a while.'

Apart from the curiosity, some of the locals were hostile towards the Coalition forces, although that was offset by some very friendly welcomes once the Afghanis realised the SAS soldiers were Australian like cricketer Steve Waugh. On one occasion Macca went into the house of a village headman and saw a large poster of Perth on the wall. He discovered that the family had decided that the SAS Regiment's home city was the second most favourite place where they wanted to live on the whole planet, just from this one picture.

'One of them had found [the poster] in a travel agent in Kabul. They were aspiring to find out how they could get to live there. It took a bit to convince them that we were actually from there.

'I have to say, though, that in most cases, when they found out that [we were] Australian and where [we] came from, they were totally open and relaxed with us and more than willing to sit down with us and tell us most things.'

Even so, towards the end of the long patrol the tolerance of the troops for the locals had worn very thin.

'You could stop at a river and work the roster out, and everyone would get in and have a bath, and the next thing you know, about twenty of the locals [are] just sitting there! No matter what you did to try to get them away to stop looking at you bathing, they'd run round and try to find somewhere else to come and look at you. In most cases, who cares, but after a while the guys were going, "Come on, we just want to be left alone for a while."'

Strategies for dealing with ebbing morale are not easy to find in the limited environment of wartime patrols. Macca kept a close eye on the blokes; if he sensed that someone was having a low period, he would go and talk to them or switch their duties for a bit of variation.

'An example of that is, usually you had the same driver and the same gunner on each vehicle. Well, just try and swap them around to make sure they get a bit of variety into what they're doing each day.

'If I went into the villages to talk to the village heads, I would take different blokes in with me, and then what I'd do is sometimes show them what I'm doing, say, "Okay, when we go in, you talk to the village heads for me", and I would just sit there and monitor what they're doing and keep an eye on them. Do something different. They're running around with weapons all the time, [so] you can't say, "Oh, just ignore it." A bloke's got a weapon — you've got to watch him.'

When he joined the long patrol, Macca thought it might last twenty-one days. 'The only sort of break was when we got to go into one of the forward operating bases down at Khost. We were there for a day or two and that was a little bit of down time, re-equip the vehicles, get all the rations back up to standard, refuel, re-arm, whatever we needed to do, and then, *whssht*, straight back out again.' They were also resupplied by air on three occasions.

The patrol worked in two different areas of operation, with the vehicles often 40 kilometres apart. They did 'marry up' regularly for certain tasks, and that also boosted the troops' spirits.

The patrol ended with a long drive from the Pakistan border south of Kabul back to Bagram, which provided the troops with some interesting insights into the various cultures of Afghanistan. But, all things considered, Macca reckons the 52-day patrol was far too long. His view is supported by that of the SAS commanding officer at the time, Gus Gilmore, who said that anyone who has done long patrols knows that by about the fourth week, effectiveness begins to wane.

'You can only push so far and be highly effective. I think in terms of the SAS patrol, they could continue for much, much longer but their effectiveness at some stage would get to the threshold where it becomes cost-neutral and you'd really need to pull them out.'

But he says that the reasons for leaving such a patrol in Afghanistan out for so long would have been sound and based on issues such as the lack of a replacement patrol, or specialist knowledge of a certain area. Such issues would have had to be balanced carefully with the morale question.

'I think also what might have happened,' Gilmore continues, 'was that they got a very good local knowledge in that particular area and, based on potentially withdrawing our commitment to Afghanistan — it might have been around that time or not — there was just benefit in not upsetting the general response of the locals in the area by putting someone new in for a period of days or weeks.

'I suspect it was perceived by the squadron commander that they hadn't quite reached that point [of needing to be removed] and therefore, in terms of priorities, he could afford to extend them to that point while also undertaking a couple of other high-priority Coalition-type tasks.'

The long patrol moved in a very large, high-priority area of operations, a long way from their base at Bagram and close to the Pakistan border. Small American outposts to the north and south of the AO were being regularly rocketed by al Qaeda, and American commander Major General Vines regarded the SAS patrol as vital to his battle plan.

According to Gilmore, the high-quality intelligence the patrol provided often featured in Vines's daily operational briefing. 'The effectiveness of this single, small patrol was such that Major General Vines expressed real concern to me on several occasions when I advised him of the requirement to extract the patrol to allow for our withdrawal from Afghanistan.'

When Macca and his patrol returned to Bagram, Vines deployed almost an entire battalion, comprising several hundred troops, into the area. Macca and his men didn't get much rest: they were ordered out on another patrol after just three days off. And after that final job, they had to pack up all the vehicles and gear and travel to Kuwait. They stripped down and scrubbed all the cars for quarantine purposes before returning to Australia.

Chapter 19

THE BRIDGE TO IRAQ

Many of the Australian SAS soldiers posted to Afghanistan had worked with US special forces units prior to the mission, either on exchange or on exercises. Few, however, had experienced a full-blown operational deployment where the might of America's war machine was focused on a new enemy.

The sheer scale of it hit Sergeant George the moment he walked down the ramp of the C-130 Hercules at Bagram air base in August 2002. Giant C-17 transport planes, Apache attack helicopters, A10 Thunderbolt close-support aircraft, lethal AC130 Spectre gunships and a myriad of other aircraft were coming and going at a great rate.

'Seeing all those resources was remarkable,' George says now.

The US military operates on a scale that mesmerises outsiders and members of other military forces, and at Bagram it was at its dazzling best. In addition to the hardware and the incredible level of close air support the US provided, the Australians had to get used to American army food and a much more formal approach to military matters. Even in the long queues in the mess tents — where the food was mostly reheated after being flown in fresh from Germany — the US soldiers were much more formal than the Aussies were used to.

It was not easy for the Australians to keep a straight face when an American soldier — carrying a tray laden with such delights as hamburger patties or a frozen cream cheese bagel and the mandatory chocolate ice cream or Oreo bar — blurted out a crisp 'Yes sir, no sir' in response to an inquiry about the weather.

George also found the sight of the Americans strolling around in pressed uniforms saluting one another quite unusual. 'I wouldn't say we got in trouble, but I think we irked them no end because it became "No, no, sir, you can't do that" and all this sort of business when we're thinking, "No worries, mate, we'll just get on with what we're doing."'

The diggers often felt that they were bucking the system with their casual approach, but also that some of the Americans thought that was pretty cool.

Throughout his tour of duty, George had difficulty understanding why the Americans did not take full advantage of the advanced military equipment that their country produced. 'We did a number of jobs with American units and I talked to them at length about that,' he says.

On one occasion, some US soldiers asked the Aussies to show them their equipment. 'We were showing them the equipment, equipment that they've designed, and we're saying, "We use it like this", and they're saying, "Gee, that's a good idea", and we're saying, "Well, fuck me! You guys made this stuff, not us."'

George says that some of the Americans found it difficult to understand the way the Australian SAS patrols set out to smell like the locals, as part of blending into the environment.

'We . . . didn't shower at all. The Americans called us "street folk" or "the unwashed" — I can't remember, they had a name for us.'

While the Australians were in absolute awe of the scale and might of Uncle Sam's military, the Americans in turn were amazed by the Australian and British tradition of long-range patrolling in small, self-contained groups. According to many senior American officers, the Australians are world's best at that type of patrolling, and they were astonished by the ability of the SAS patrols to be away from base for weeks on end without regular resupply. This capacity did not exist to any extent in the US military.

There were other niche skills that the Australians were able to bring to the fight. George's last job in Afghanistan involved a pesky but fairly primitive enemy rocket launcher.

Every night the US bases were getting rockets fired into them, and 'they were poorly aimed — they just lie these things on sticks and light them and off they go. But they're still 120 mm rockets and would do damage if they hit anything. So the Americans decided they'd had a gutful of it and they wanted to eradicate them, so we came in with two virtually hunter–killer teams. My scout — who had been given a big 50 cal sniper rifle, was the happiest I'd ever seen him, despite the fact that he had to lug the thing around.'

The patrol did the maths, worked out where the rocket launcher was probably based and moved into the area to put eyes on the target.

'We just went in to overwatch the occupied area for about four or five days,' says George, 'and while we were there, not a single rocket!'

On another occasion the Americans got wind of a high-value target who was supposed to be moving through a particular area.

'It was going to be difficult for them because it was a vehicle interdiction ambush [meaning that a vehicle needed to be stopped and those on it taken into custody]. They had anti-armour weapons, but they wanted to have a discrete capability of stopping a car without killing everyone in it. If you put an 84 anti-tank weapon into it, you've toasted everyone, and we had a 50 cal sniper rifle, which they didn't, and they wanted it. But to get it they had to have us.'

To move into position for the ambush, the SAS patrol had to traverse a large snow-capped mountain. The lessons of the earlier SAS rotations had been learnt by now, so George and his men were well equipped with quality cold-weather gear. They carried their patrol packs and their puffy suits because they knew it would be below zero up on the mountain.

'The Yanks were looking at us, [saying] "What are these mad fucking Aussies doing?" because we had our packs on. It was only an in–out sort of task but in our packs was all our [cold-]weather gear, because we knew on top of the hill it was going to be fucking freezing cold, because we could see snow on it.'

The Americans all wore light gear and were carrying an array of weapons.

George continues: 'You sweat like hell going up a hill, but when you sit on top of the hill you freeze almost to death because it was minus 20, we had a little wind-chill fucking reader. Halfway up the hill Simmo, the patrol chook, said, "Jeez, I'm glad we've done the patrols we've done", because they were all foot-mounted, all heavy packs over rugged terrain. In an hour we were sitting happily on top of the hill in our puff-gear that we'd brought out of our packs while [the Americans] sat shivering and really, really suffering. So I was happy with the method in which we operated, and the state of the blokes was really satisfying.'

The 50 calibre sniper rifle proved a valuable weapon in Afghanistan, where a new long-range record was set by a Canadian soldier. Using a McMillan 50 calibre, he killed an al Qaeda fighter walking along a road in the Shahi Khot valley, from a distance of 2430 metres. The shot broke the 35-year-old record of 2250 metres set in Vietnam.

George and his men were deeply impressed by the professionalism of the US special-operations forces. They had come to prominence during the 1993 Somalia crisis, when they lost six men, including two snipers, Randy Shughart and Gary Gordon, who were posthumously awarded the Medal of Honor after they died trying to save the crew of a downed Black Hawk helicopter. The profile of the US special forces was raised again during the Afghanistan campaign, when their members were filmed during a number of high-profile actions, including the assassination attempt on President Hamid Karzai — whom they were protecting — in Kabul in September 2002.

George was amazed by the US special forces' ability to call in and coordinate air power and other assets. 'Their ability to pull in a massive amount of coordination on lots of working parts is outstanding, it's unbelievable. I think it would take us a long time, because we don't use the assets and so on. The proficiency and professionalism of their operators is quite awesome. They're very sure and very capable blokes. But then they're different again to us, they're mainly direct action tasks, not sustained stay-and-watch patrol sort of fellows.'

The biggest lesson George took away from Afghanistan was the need to constantly fall back on the basics of operational training, even to the point of insisting on his men wearing their camouflage gear regardless of the environment they were in.

'I made them cam up all the time and they'd think, "We're sitting in the middle of a fucking desert!" It may sound like a small thing, but anything you do to break up your outline is going to be of value, and it's something that they harp onto us all the time — and I think it's true — is that concentrating on the basic level of operational training is the thing that's going to sustain us or keep us ahead of the game. I know that in some ways they think I was a bit anal in that respect, [but] I think it's something you can never ignore. And I think it's the thing that has held us in good stead over some time.'

As a patrol commander, George was acutely aware that his responsibility was to return from every patrol with the same number of men as he set out with: 'I think, retrospectively, I've done harder exercises in Australia, because of the demand and the requirement to maintain absolute standards. I think the way we train is really well suited to doing operations, because obviously when you get on operations you can't always do things that way [you would on exercises]. You might have to just slide left, slide right, but in order to be able to make a decision on whether I can do this or can't to achieve my aim, you need to have a really good base level of standards — not only understanding, but actual practice of what the blokes do. And I found it was easy to make decisions on ops based on the way we train here [in Perth], which was so rigorous, so demanding. I wouldn't say people get crucified, but you've certainly got to account for yourself if you've done something that is not the way we should be doing it.'

Captain Neil, who has had years of experience working with the Americans, believes the US made a quantum leap forward as a result of their experiences in Afghanistan. 'It's really been a crucible of fire that's formed a lot of the guys now in the US armed forces. And they've come up with a lot of good techniques and invaluable lessons, even for Australia.'

Duncan Lewis also argues that the campaign marked a turning point for the role of Australian special forces in joint operations. 'We've now moved from being what I might describe as fringe elements of the joint fight into being a major and significant player in the joint fight. Now, we're still small by comparison to the large maritime, land and air forces, but we are an essential and central part of all of that.

'Afghanistan, in particular, was a very good example of where this new connection between special operations and air power came together. It's a very interesting professional development.'

A key part of that was getting 'eyes on the target', so that commanders could be as near to certain that the target would be hit. 'Is that particular individual in the car or is he in that building or is he in that particular copse of trees or whatever? And it's very difficult at times to tell that using technical means. So eyes on the target are quite important, and that also has helped us.'

Just as helpful was the extraordinary amount of work the SAS men put in with the local tribal leaders, in order to gain a valuable understanding of the community dynamics.

Overall, some salient lessons were learnt from the Afghanistan campaign, both positive and negative.

One major headache for the SAS task group was the dreaded '2000-mile screwdriver' — the name soldiers give to the perceived interference from higher command and others up the food chain back in Australia.

As Operations Officer in Afghanistan, Pete Tinley was directly in the firing line and felt that the interference was often 'pretty raw', especially when he was sitting in his command post at minus 5 or 10°C fielding emails from Army Office in Canberra. It was worst when an incident occurred or something related to the SAS was reported in the media.

General Cosgrove says that commanders try very hard to modulate the 2000-mile screwdriver. But, like it or not, a young patrol commander may perform a tactical action with strategic consequences that could rebound up the line, so 'from time to time you have got to use the screwdriver. Troops will always complain [but] we do try to give them a decent directive, let them go, trust them, watch carefully and keep the requests down to just the essentials.'

Nonetheless, the field soldiers' feelings about the screwdriver would be incorporated into the planning for Iraq.

There was another lesson learnt about operational arrangements, which were complex in Afghanistan. The diggers were under the tactical command of the American commander, James Mattis, but national command in Australia also had to be obeyed. In other words: nothing could be done without a tick from two bosses.

The lack of special forces expertise in the higher command chain was another source of frustration, as was the 'peacetime mentality' in many of the headquarters, according to Pete Tinley.

'You'd ring up someone else around the place — "Oh well, they've gone for the day." "They've gone for the day! Well, we haven't, we're still here!"'

Duncan Lewis says that the quest for information was a huge management issue for military officers, as the traditional steps in the command chain were being compressed. 'As a result of the compression, you'll get a lot of the traditionalists who'll be saying, "Well, hang on, there's interference going on, there's a lack of responsiveness" or, "Things aren't going right". But I've got to say that they are, in my view, the dreamers … This is the reality, that's what's happening now, and you'd better get on board.'

The war in Afghanistan did a great deal to reinforce the Australia–US military alliance. Relationships with the Americans flourished at most levels. Despite the odd cultural difference and close-run blue-on-blue incident, the alliance provided a real opportunity for hundreds of Australian special forces soldiers to work alongside their US counterparts.

Warrant Officer Steve recalls one incident after the rout at the start of Anaconda. '[The Americans] had nothing but praise for us, and especially after that first mortar barrage, there was myself and one other guy helping two of their guys pull out these bloody mortar base plates in the midst of this mortar barrage. We knew if we left them then they weren't ours and they would fall into the hands of the enemy.

'I remember the commander came up said, "Gee, Steve, it was good to see you and your Aussies hung around those mortar base plates." We were also picking up locals and throwing them on the roof of our 110 Land Rover.'

Lieutenant Colonel Rick took over command of the Australian task group in Afghanistan in July 2002. Earmarked at that time as the next commanding officer of the SASR, he was widely regarded as a broad strategic thinker and a 'fantastic bloke' by soldiers of all ranks.

Rick describes Afghanistan as having been a 'very ambiguous' environment. 'We really didn't know who was who and the call on the guys [was] to just go out there and interface with the population in what was a very dangerous environment. And, certainly, the Russians experienced that in that same sort of area, in the eastern part, on the border. It's a notorious zone — where not to be. And again the guys applied themselves to that . . . and produced a very, very good result. And you can sense that just by talking to the locals . . . I got to see the guys in their true colours and they were very, very impressive.'

Rick believes that was why the SAS achieved such an incredibly good result, out of all proportion to their size. 'Little teams going around, they can do the work of a thousand men.'

One thing the Aussies had in common with the locals near the Pakistan border was cricket.

'They were all cricket mad in Pakistan and the influence was coming into that area,' Rick explains, 'whereas further down that wasn't the case. So a few of them knew Australians and [that] Steve Waugh was a great cricketer and it was quite amusing.'

Prime Minister John Howard received a first-hand assessment of the SAS in Afghanistan from the US Commander in Chief, President George W Bush, during the APEC leaders' meeting in Shanghai in October 2001.

'We were talking about the operation,' says Mr Howard, 'and he was thanking me for our involvement and he just said, out of the blue, "I hear that your SAS are fantastic", or words to that effect. I naturally agreed with him. He would have spoken in very approving terms of our SAS on several occasions during the operation in Iraq. He did, of course, make special references publicly to Andrew Russell, the SAS soldier who lost his life, in that address he gave in the Rose Garden [at the White House] on the first anniversary of the September 11 attack.

'Our conversations, of necessity, were not so much about the performance of individual units but, obviously, about the broad policy. [Bush] clearly had a view about [the SAS] which was informed, not by discussions with me, but informed by discussions presumably with his own military.'

By late 2002, when the Afghanistan operation was winding down, the issue on everyone's mind was: *Will we be going to Iraq?* The Australian SAS men were monitoring the media avidly. They were very conscious of the vital niche role, as long-range patrollers, that they had cemented in the Coalition order of battle. The diggers regarded every job in Afghanistan, no matter how insignificant, as a golden opportunity to impress the Americans, whose generals were already on the public record praising the work of the SAS and hoping that they would be alongside US forces if Iraq were invaded.

Says Sergeant George now: 'I must admit [that] when we were leaving Afghanistan, there was a lot of brouhaha about what was going on in Iraq. George Bush was waving his flag and we honestly thought we were going to be going directly from Afghanistan. We were horribly disappointed.'

Some of the men in 2 SAS Squadron started placing bets on whether they would go back to Perth or move on to the Middle East to build up for Iraq. They felt they were right on top of their game, and 'we were absolutely chomping at the bit,' says George. 'I mean, everyone was happy to be going home to see their families, but it was a shame that we couldn't have just rolled on. You build up and you get into that operational flow and you're good to go. If we went to do it again we'd have to build up and get back into the flow again.'

That operational flow included very close bonds with men from the US Air Force's Special Tactics Squadrons (STS), whose job it had been to provide a link between the SAS patrols and the US air assets that the Australians called on for close air support or strikes against targets throughout the Afghanistan campaign.

The Americans forged strong ties with the diggers and in later campaigns there was strong competition within the STS to try to join up with the Aussies on operations. The Americans blended into the patrols they were attached to and worked as part of the team, eating, sleeping, fighting, laughing and crying right alongside the Australians. It also meant doing their share of duty on the weapons systems used by the patrol.

One of the controllers working with the SAS was named Airman of the Year for 2001 for his work in Afghanistan while he was attached to Matt Boulliaut's patrol during Anaconda. Several of the blokes ran into him after they'd all left Afghanistan and he was very grateful, telling them that what he had achieved had been due to the SAS crew he had worked with.

Trooper John describes his STS airman as 'a twenty-three year old who looked about twelve', and who, with the help of the patrol, underwent a traditional initiation into Australian culture. 'He was a really nice bloke,' says John, 'but he didn't really know how to swear very well. We taught him how to swear in Australian and he loved it, and all the rest of his crew swear now as well.'

The swearing and other cultural lessons would continue in the desert of western Iraq just a few months later.

According to official figures from the Department of Defence, two rotations of approximately 150 men from Campbell Barracks served in Afghanistan, comprising an initial deployment and two rotations.

The initial deployment left Australia on 22 October 2001 and returned on 4 April 2002. The first rotation left on 28 March and returned on 30 August. The second rotation left Australia at the end of July and returned on 17 December.

Seven SAS men were decorated. Lieutenant Colonel Rowan Tink and Lieutenant Colonel Peter 'Gus' Gilmore both received the US Bronze Star; Gilmore was also awarded the Distinguished Service Cross, as was Sergeant Matthew Boulliaut. Signalman Martin 'Jock' Wallace was awarded the Medal for Gallantry; Major Dan McDaniel was awarded the Distinguished Service Medal; and Warrant Officer Class Two Mark Kelly was awarded the Medal of the Order of Australia in the Military Division.

The whole SAS Regiment received a Meritorious Unit Citation for outstanding contribution during Operation Slipper in Afghanistan.

IRAQ

Chapter 20

THE HARD SELL

Many sets of eyes had been poring over maps of Iraq during 2002. On 29 January 2002, US President George W Bush used his State of the Union address to label Iraq part of the 'axis of evil'. The US, he said, 'will not permit the world's most dangerous regimes to threaten us with the world's most destructive weapons'.

By June 2002, when Bush announced his new defence doctrine of pre-emptive strikes, secret contingency planning for a possible Australian deployment to Iraq was under way. The prime minister, John Howard, called it 'prudent planning', and that became the catch phrase for the Australian approach.

In September, Brigadier Maurie McNarn — who would become the Australian commander in the Middle East — led a team to US Central Command in Tampa, Florida, to dovetail with the American war planners. With him was Lieutenant Colonel Mark Smethurst, a former SAS squadron commander, and representatives from all three services. Their job was to find out where Australian forces might fit into a potential US-led operation in Iraq. They drew up a list of possible options, including special forces, naval and air force elements. Those options were then placed in 'compartments', ahead of the political decision-making, on a 'no commitment' basis.

It became apparent early on that special forces and the Air Force would be the key contributors if Australia were to commit. The RAAF's role would be somewhat limited because of the lack of self-protection on its F/A-18 Hornet fighters, but the SAS could be fully engaged and would provide the best bang-for-buck ratio.

Links between the SAS and US Central Command had been established in the lead-up to Afghanistan by the then Commander of the Special Forces, Brigadier Duncan Lewis.

'It's true to say that, when we came to do the Iraq operation, it was more slick, in that sense, than Afghanistan because we'd been through it before,' says Lewis now.

In November 2002, Colonel Mike Hindmarsh — a former commanding officer of SASR who was spending a year at the Royal College of Defence Studies in London — got a phone call. He was to go straight to Qatar to join an overarching exercise being run by the head of US Central Command, General Tommy Franks. Afterwards he went back to the UK and collected his family before returning home for the final phase of planning. Hindmarsh was promoted to Brigadier and appointed to the pivotal position of Australian Commander of the Special Forces Task Group for the Iraq mission. He was one of three component commanders (the others were Navy and Air Force). His job was to act as a buffer between higher command and the SAS operational commander, Lieutenant Colonel Rick, alleviating some of the pressure of the notorious 2000-mile screwdriver on the commander in the field.

'Iraq was on such a bigger scale than Afghanistan ... It was necessary,' Hindmarsh says now. 'What you don't want to happen is ... the pressure from higher going into the back of the head of the tactical commander. In Afghanistan, to a certain extent, that happened ... and I think that was probably distracting. They should have had the freedom just to focus on what they were there to do and run the tactical side of it.'

Meanwhile, a regimental team led by SAS Commanding Officer Lieutenant Colonel Gus Gilmore and SAS Operations Officer Pete Tinley travelled to America to join a planning team for a stint of hard bargaining. Gilmore then left the SAS team in Tinley's hands. They worked 18-hour days planning operations for the strategically vital western part of Iraq.

The SAS was now part of the US-led Task Force Dagger, which

comprised about 4500 people, including Coalition special forces, air force and army aviation elements.

The Australians were under the command of a US special forces colonel who had worked with the Northern Alliance early in the Afghanistan campaign.

'He was a great guy,' says Tinley. 'He understood what we had contributed in Afghanistan, and I've got to say [that] the support we got and the jobs we got in western Iraq were largely delivered by the goodwill that we'd developed in Afghanistan.'

The SAS developed a plan to capture western Iraq and, specifically, to prevent the Iraqis from launching Scuds — long-range theatre ballistic missiles — at neighbouring states, particularly Israel.

Saddam Hussein had fired Scuds into Israel and Kuwait during the first Gulf War and had also used chemical weapons against the Kurds during the 1980s. It was widely expected that, if attacked again, Israel would retaliate with nuclear warheads.

As Tinley recalls, 'It sharpened us up altogether, because we didn't want to be at Ground Zero, that's for sure, because we knew a nuclear response was always a possibility. God help us if it ever got to that.'

While the Israeli message was devastatingly clear, the position on whether or not Saddam still had any Scuds was not so straightforward. The US intelligence community thought Saddam had about twelve mobile Scud launchers hidden away. The SAS mission would be to deny him the use of those launchers. Saddam's alleged weapons of mass destruction (WMD) were the primary reason used by the Howard government and the Bush administration to justify Australian involvement. But the lack of accurate, contemporary intelligence on WMD would become the single biggest military and political flaw of the war.

The uncertainty of intelligence was nothing new to Mike Hindmarsh. 'I know how difficult it is to comprehensively determine one way or another whether people have got this or that. Intelligence is not foolproof. We're in the intelligence game — we know this for a fact! We weren't certain whether there were going to be any [WMD] there, nor were we certain that there wouldn't be some. We're always in the game of assuming worst case ... So the way we conducted the operation tactically was on the assumption that there would be stuff there.'

Pete Tinley knew that Iraq would require different capabilities, because it would be a different war to Afghanistan. 'The threat level was a lot higher, it was a lot more conventional, there was a greater capacity to do some damage to us. So a lot of our planning was changed.'

The Australians settled into tough, three-cornered negotiations with the British and the Americans to establish who would do what and where inside Iraq. The Australians wanted the middle sector, which included a long stretch of the main six-lane highway between Baghdad and Jordan, and about 9000 square kilometres of enemy territory which was a good match for the Australian capability.

The planners had to tread a fine line to make certain that Australia's mission had nothing to do with 'regime change' — namely the ousting of Saddam Hussein and his enemies.

Regime change and high-value human targets such as Saddam and his sons were at the core of the US war plan, but the Howard government wanted to distance itself from the policy for domestic political reasons, to dilute opposition to the war. Later, when no WMD were found, the government shifted its political ground and hammered home the regime-change line with a terse and predictable, 'Would you prefer it if Saddam were still in power?'

'The effect was the same,' says Tinley, 'but it was very, very important that we didn't have [a mission] that talked about toppling regimes.'

Mike Hindmarsh explains further: '[The Australian mission] was purely denying Iraqis within our AO the capacity to launch Scuds or WMD to neighbouring countries, essentially. There was no mention of "And furthermore, exercise regime change".'

Hindmarsh says that, for reasons of sovereignty and control, it was vital to ensure that Australian assets would be under the national command of Australia at all times, in an Australian area of operations and with a mission determined by Australia that was in accordance with the whole Coalition mission for the Western Desert.

Back in the United States, the SAS planning team covered every aspect from logistics support to insertion methods and air cover. Their biggest difficulty was the lack of a definite commitment from the Australian government.

'It was all just "prudent planning",' says Pete Tinley, 'and it was pretty tough when you were trying to work that far away. Only a very small number of people were allowed to look at it in Canberra.'

The government's hesitation also made it difficult to negotiate an Australian area of operations. 'It was basically [about] who was bringing the most resources, and we were being honest about it and were saying, "Oh, we don't know what we're coming with. Oh, by the way, we don't know whether we're coming!" Which is a very difficult position to negotiate from, but then we just had to fight it on our own merits.'

The fact that the Aussies got on very well with the American planners helped a great deal. So did the clowning of one of Tinley's signallers, who did an excellent impersonation of the Australian personality Steve Irwin, a.k.a. the Crocodile Hunter.

'When they were at loggerheads you'd send the signaller in first and he'd do his Steve Irwin impersonation, going, "Crikey, what's going on here?" And the Americans love the Crocodile Hunter ... so they'd all fall off their chairs laughing ... It broke the tension, and more often than not we were [then] able to provide some sort of brokerage to come in with an alternate view.'

Tinley was very conscious that it was not the planning team's job to tell the boys in the squadron how to fight. 'I was just putting those things in place that would allow them to work it out.'

The horse trading went on for weeks.

Fortunately, the Australians were working with the Green Berets from the US Fifth Special Forces Group, with whom they had worked closely in Afghanistan. Their close relationship dated back to the Vietnam War. And the Green Berets knew exactly what the Aussies were capable of in terms of long-range desert operations in a highly risky environment, hundreds of kilometres from help.

Towards the end of the negotiations Gus Gilmore flew to America for a commanders' meeting. He was able to cut through the lack of resolution and nail down the result. The Aussies got what they wanted.

Pete Tinley arrived back in Perth in late December, and after a few days off with his family, he was back on deck for the final phase. By early January 2003, the regiment received fairly direct guidance that the Iraq mission would be on. It was time to join up the dots — and Operation Falconer was born.

According to Mike Hindmarsh, when the 'compartments' were finally opened there was a period of 'furious catch-up football' so that wider units could get up to speed with the planning teams.

'It's when the units drill down and start looking at the detail that the rubber really hits the road,' he says. 'It's the most important phase of the planning. And that happened quite late because it was all compartmented, you know. You'll find January [2003] was a bloody furious month, January and February, trying to catch up with the detail.'

In mid-January a commanders' meeting was held at Swanbourne near Perth, where plans were revealed for an Australian task group of about 550 people. It would include special forces, Army aviation, Air Force, intelligence and logistics personnel.

Tinley says now, 'I outlined the plan for them as we had it, which was pretty definite at that time, the areas of operation and how we would do it and the resources and command and control, the bits and pieces that go with it. And that was the first time those commanders had ever seen it. The day after, we started deploying.'

Trooper John, a veteran of both East Timor and Afghanistan, had been home for about a year when the news came that 1 SAS Squadron was being given the thumbs up to go to Iraq. He was ecstatic — he and his mates in the unit had been desperately trying to read the tea leaves for months.

'You go through in your mind the reasons for and against your squadron and in the end we're going, "Oh yeah, it's got to be us!" with a little bit of hope in our hearts that it does [have] to be us, but you don't know. And all you do is . . . just wait and hope. And when we found out it was us, it was "Outstanding!" and "Let's not rub it into everyone else too much!"'

From that point on 1 SAS Squadron's reputation as the 'lucky' squadron was assured. For its members, it was the beginning of a whirlwind of preparation.

'We're always on this short notice to move,' says John, 'we're always ready to go somewhere and do something, but once you're given the green light you can start going to those one-per-centers that make a difference between normal soldiers and special soldiers. You go, "Right, what's Iraq look like? What's the ground like? What are we working against? Who's in charge? What are we going to do over there? Which area do we work?" All of that stuff.

'[B]ecause our vehicles had gone from Afghanistan, where they'd got a hiding, we knew they'd been getting refits and things like that [but we were wondering] will they be ready in time? Will they be up to standard? Will we have to make changes? Do they have new equipment on them that we need to learn about? Every soldier goes, "Right, this is what I've got to start thinking about." And you don't have time to be prancing around. You start focusing really in deep on what you're doing.'

There was a huge amount of preparation to be done in the Middle East, including the construction of a green-fields — brand new — staging base at a desert location close to the Iraqi border. The squadron also had to establish their own headquarters and help the Americans set up a special forces headquarters.

At the same time, the command rotation at SAS clicked over and Gus Gilmore moved to Canberra, to be replaced by Lieutenant Colonel Rick, who had brought the troops home from Afghanistan. Pete Tinley was his deputy commander.

Rick thought the broad plan for the SAS in Iraq was very good. He knew he had the right troops and equipment to do the job; more importantly, the men understood both the job and the commander's intent.

As the task force commander, Rick was based at the forward command centre outside Iraq and liaised directly with the SAS commander on the ground, Major Paul. There were a number of planning groups, and Rick engaged directly with commanders at every level.

'We could adjust the plan so that everyone was comfortable with their part in it, right from the early stages,' Rick explains. And the situation would continue to be 'extremely dynamic'.

There were times when Rick longed to be going across with his men to confront the unknown, but he knew that the best place for him was in the operations centre inside the headquarters, where he had access to all the right communications and information.

'Of course I wanted to be out there!' he admits. 'But my job was to position myself in the best place to exercise my span of responsibilities across the task group, and to trust my subordinates on the ground to implement the plan.'

The tactical plan had followed a logical course to a point where a decision had to be made as to whether the SAS would fight in small patrols, to maximise the number of eyes on the ground, or go in with a bigger force and greater fire power.

The Iraqi special forces would be desperate to bag an SAS patrol, as they had done in Gulf War I with the ill-fated British SAS 'Bravo Two Zero' patrol. For that reason, together with the old military adage that you should never fight the last war, the Australian SAS opted for a bigger force with close air support. The Australians' rehearsals in America had refined the practice of calling in the air support very quickly. Speed would also be of the essence on the ground from the moment they crossed the border.

The diggers were glad to have a decent lead-up time, as Trooper John explains: 'It makes a difference to us because you can start acclimatising, which can save lives, and you can start planning things and working things out. So we did all of our initial build-up, everything's working for us, everything's right. Then they tried to give us a bit of leave so that you've got time with your family. And then ... we left [Perth] and went somewhere else and got to acclimatise and do training and get vehicles ready and all that sort of stuff.'

Primarily a water operator, John was also qualified in vehicle-mounted operations.

'All of our Afghanistan veterans were squared away with vehicles, but we had new guys into the squadron since then. So we had to change focus and get them to understand the drills and how we used vehicles ... Things like that are second nature to people who've done it before in Afghanistan and have done vehicle-mounted drills, but if you haven't done it before you need to learn it. And we had to bring them up to speed in a fairly quick sort of time.'

The men used every minute of that lead-up time in the Middle East, because 'when you're planning to invade a country, a month isn't a long time. But you can choose plans and then throw them away, choose better ones and make adjustments and things like this. Because we had a month, everything worked in well, gelled in together, we could plan.'

Every trooper was involved in discussing the details. As Mike Hindmarsh explains: 'Often it's the case that the lowest-ranked trooper of SAS will reveal something that ... you didn't think of at a higher scoping level or you assume or pay lip service to. And when you ask yourself, "Well, does that really work?" it's quite often the digger that will be asking those sort of questions. That's the great plus of the Australian system — everyone gets involved with the planning.'

For Troop Commander Captain Quentin, the planning period was long, intense and at times frustrating, but he knew the benefits were great. 'As things change you have to war-game everything again and the process is fairly detailed. It enables you to foresee as many unforeseen circumstances as possible, and you've already thought through in your mind what will happen.'

Before crossing the border, some of the men discussed with Pete Tinley and amongst themselves the moral aspects of pre-emption and of invading someone else's country. The discussions usually finished at the same point: they were in a volunteer force, they could walk away, but when they'd enlisted they had committed to going wherever the government sent them, to do whatever job it wanted them to do.

'I know that that entails a whole bunch of risk, but that's it,' Tinley says. 'So it came back to your higher professional commitment to the country.'

With anti-war demonstrations escalating at home, it was also not clear how much support the troops would receive from the Australian people. Captain Quentin worried about that then, and says now, 'That was one of my concerns for our guys — that when we got back we would get spat at, like they did in Vietnam. But I think it was handled quite well amongst Labor and Liberal [in that] the politics were separated from the role of the soldier, which was important.'

For his part, Rick was very conscious of the burden of command. 'As a commander it's obviously an enormous amount of responsibility for the people and the mission to be successful. You've got people's lives on both sides of the fence that you're responsible for. And, yeah, it weighs on you. The stakes were high but I knew that I had done everything I could to make sure that we could be successful, to achieve our mission and minimise any loss of human life ... War is a dangerous business. We were ready — then we were into the lap of the gods.'

Finally, the planning and the last-minute rehearsals were over.

'Then we got the guys back together,' Rick recounts, 'and got them all together in the hangar and, yeah, just had a good old command chat to them.'

He spoke to the men about the importance of the mission, emphasising that they had the confidence and support of the nation, 'that they're to do themselves and their families and the regiment proud, and just keep reinforcing the fact that they are the best troops for the job, and believe in yourself, believe in the mission and get on with it.

'And you know, there were some hearts in mouths at that time, there's no doubt about that, but everyone understood the mission right from the day we left [Swanbourne] and they had plenty of time to think about it. It's really just that last coach's chat before they go out on the ground.'

Then it was time to pre-position themselves at the border and wait for the green light.

'I did another quick trip just before they went across, to see them,' says Rick, 'came back to the command centre, gave them the word and then, "Okay, let's get on with it."'

Chapter 21

THE INVASION

It felt a bit like running onto the paddock for a Saturday afternoon footy game.

The American National Guardsmen who had dug out the anti-tank berms — large earth banks built by the Iraqis to prevent an invasion — stood aside and cheered the Aussies across the border.

'Give it to 'em, boys!' they yelled as the SAS LRPVs crossed over and sped into the pitch-black Iraqi night.

It was on. For the first time since Gallipoli almost ninety years before, an Australian force was at the head of a military invasion.

Patrol Commander Shane was feeling a bit tense as they passed an American flag on the first berm before being waved in by the Guardsmen. 'Well, gee, we're in the country, what's going to happen now?' he thought.

To Trooper John, it felt like an exercise: 'We just did it.'

Squadron Commander Major Paul felt excited, with a touch of trepidation. This was his first operational command. His main thought was, 'I wish I had a camera.' His lasting impression, as they rolled over the berm, was of an American soldier standing there with his Kevlar on and holding his pennant with two flags. One was an American flag and the other was like a triangle.

'This is very like bloody running on the paddock,' he thought. 'Shit, here we go.'

Paul gave the lads a bit of a rev, making sure they were very clear on what they needed to do. Then it all became very cold and professional, and all his training kicked in.

He had a plan, and he was confident in the plan and in the blokes.

The men had been close to the Iraqi border for two days, waiting for word from Canberra that the mission was a goer. As they had been in the region for a month preparing for the job, when the word finally came to kick off Operation Iraqi Freedom they were ready.

At 2 p.m. on Tuesday, 18 March 2003, Prime Minister John Howard rose in the House of Representatives in Canberra and announced the government's decision to commit troops to the campaign in Iraq. It was 7 a.m. in Baghdad. As Colonel John Mansell from Special Operations Command told a media briefing on 9 May 2003, the Australian troops entered Iraq during the first period of darkness after the government's announcement. The exact time they crossed the border has never been made public.

The first obstacles the troops encountered were the anti-tank berms and trenches that virtually surrounded the country. Designed to slow or stop an armoured invasion force, the 5- to 10-metre-high earthen wall berms might also have stopped an SAS LRPV. Before the invasion began, various methods of dealing with them had been tested, including bombing them from the air, blowing them up or digging them out by hand. The latter was considered most prudent, so the US National Guardsmen were flown in to dig an access track for the Aussies and the other Coalition special forces.

After a month of intensive training and acclimatising, the squadron had been placed on stand-by and told to drive to a staging point about 10 kilometres from the border.

As Shane recalls, 'It was quite amazing — we drove all night to get there and then during the day we could see, coming over the hill, these Americans everywhere in their Humvees with their cam nets still up. We saw them all sitting around there and thought, "Oh yeah, this is fair enough, going in in a big convoy with them." The plan was to go in the convoy, get to the border, split [up] and then go and do what we have to do and they'll go and do what they have to do.'

During the two-day wait, word spread that the Iraqis had deployed Hind attack helicopters to the area. The Mi-24 Hind was the first Russian-built attack helicopter. It could carry an enormous amount of weaponry plus eight troops, and is considered deadly to ground troops. The possibility of its presence made the SAS troops understandably nervous.

Troop Commander Captain Zan was feeling a little anxious as his LRPV negotiated the roughly hewn track through the first high berm and entered the 400 metres or so of no-man's-land before crossing a second berm which was much smaller.

'There were Iraqi border positions, but there was no opposition when we went across. We didn't know what there would be. There were plans to deal with [the enemy] and it was probably envisaged as a dangerous part when you actually cross into the other country. It's easy to get split, especially at a choke-point like that. They'd sited it well but it turned out incident-free.'

The troops were prepared for battle as soon as they crossed the berms. The invasion route had been well planned so that they would weave into the country, staying well clear of known enemy positions.

About 45 minutes — or 30 kilometres — after they crossed the border, they ran headlong into an Iraqi convoy, which included a bus full of soldiers. The night was moonless and very dark, so their night-vision gear gave the diggers an immediate advantage.

'I don't know what they were doing,' Zan says now. 'They weren't patrolling. I mean, they weren't geared to fight — their weapons weren't with them in their hands. The weapons — a lot of the equipment — was stored in the trucks and they were heading north. We were heading east and, just by pure fluke in the middle of the night, two convoys travelling blacked out, we hit 'em straight on. Couldn't have timed it more perfectly.'

This was the first ground contact of the Iraq war and it happened very quickly. There was no time to waste, as the force was due to be a long way inside Iraq by daybreak.

'We basically chased them down and disarmed them,' says Trooper John, 'and blew up vehicles and did all of the good stuff that we got trained to do, and it was almost like a race to see who was first to get the job done. It was interesting.

'I think [the Iraqis] were in shock because they realised something bad was going on, and they were hightailing it away from us and then basically they couldn't outrun us, and we neutralised that vehicle and the individuals, and that was it — they were basically fixed up and let walk, but they didn't have their transport or any of their ammunition or anything.'

John thought the vehicles looked as if they were travelling from a range to a base. 'A busload of guys with all their weapons and then following them up was a shitload more ammunition and weapons. It was like they'd been down to the range and picked up some extra stores and were going home.'

Shane couldn't believe that the Australian force could run into an enemy convoy in the middle of the desert, in the middle of the night, just 45 minutes into the country.

'Everyone was going, "What? This is the middle of the desert! And there's a few buses and trucks coming at us!" I think they surprised us and we surprised them. They didn't know what was going on, and all of a sudden it comes on the radio, "Stop those vehicles!" and the vehicles just bolted and went straight through us, through the middle of our formation. And so I sort of turned around and thought, "Well, we can't fire, 'cos we can't fire into our guys. Hopefully the other SAS guys will", and they did. They fired into them and stopped the vehicles.'

Captain Zan thought the most important thing about the first contact was that everything went to plan, and that put everyone at ease.

'Getting a contact like that, which was, for us, fairly safe — a few shots were fired and we had to react quickly, you know, and all these vehicles suddenly racing round trying to cover them. They tried to escape, they did a bit of a starburst, so we had to round them up.'

Everyone suddenly became more relaxed after the contact. The fact that a few of them had already fired weapons at work so soon after crossing the border gave everybody a lot more confidence.

Zan felt that, overall, it hadn't gone too badly. 'We could have done it better, but I think everyone ran over in their minds, "Oh, if that happens again, I'll do this, I'll do that."'

Everyone — from the drivers to the gunners, the communicators and the commanders — had had to make a few quick decisions.

Says Zan, 'When you're travelling along in vehicles and you've got to jump out and deal with POWs, you suddenly realise that you've got to be able to jump out straightaway, especially if you're connected with communications sets to the vehicles. I needed to jump out; I couldn't do it quite so quickly. So, from that second on, I reconfigured my gear so I could jump out immediately. So from that point of view it was pretty good for us. It cost us about an hour, but the boss [Major Paul] was right onto us the whole time — "It's got to be quick, got to be quick" — and just pushed us through it.'

The Iraqis were scared, so after treating the wounded, the diggers gave them some blankets and water and sent them off into the desert.

'These weren't crack troops,' says Zan, 'they were guys, they were just blokes. They may have even been deserting themselves, travelling like that — they weren't on a road.'

The diggers knew that there were many different forces within the Iraqi military. It was obvious to SAS troop commander Captain Quentin that some of them probably didn't even want to be there, while others were there under protest. 'Some were there because a guy was holding a pistol to his head and saying he would shoot his family, and we hit some of those guys in the border guard units. We just took the weapons off them and said, "Look, the war's over, just go home", and they weren't arguing, they were pretty happy to go home.'

Some didn't know where home was, or where they were, or even where the road was, because they had simply been put in a truck, driven somewhere and told to stay there.

'So we realised that there were different types of forces,' says Quentin, 'and with each one we were basically waiting for them to act before we reacted, to a certain extent.'

The soldiers on the ground weren't the only ones with anxiety issues to deal with. Back at Coalition headquarters in Qatar, a neighbouring Arab state, Brigadier Mike Hindmarsh was watching the action on a screen. Tracking technology allowed him to count the vehicles and see that they were all moving as soon as the contact was over.

It was all happening in real time. As General Cosgrove said in August 2003, 'My commander at the time in the Middle East, Brigadier [Maurie] McNarn, could read intelligence reports from our Defence intelligence agencies back in Australia seconds after they were lodged. We could digest his account of senior Coalition commanders' meetings in the region immediately after they had occurred.

'Our special forces could send us data including images from enemy territory. We could send them, from any level of command, anything from military orders to the rugby scores.

'We also had the opportunity to use networked technology on the ground for the first time in the guise of a blue force tracker — a sort of GPS system for the troops to enable them to be seen in headquarters on map displays as moving symbols showing their progress and their safety.'

'I was bloody concerned,' Hindmarsh says now of that first contact. 'We all were. This was serious shit. I remember having this discussion with others that ... "We expect to lose people here". These guys were going into harm's way. The enemy, quite clearly ... weren't stupid. They would have learnt from the previous Gulf War what we were likely to be doing, and the intelligence reports that we received indicated that that was the case.'

With powerful, highly mobile and mechanised enemy forces based at Ar Ramadi, to the east of the Australian area of operations, and elsewhere, there was always the possibility of a contact with well-armed and trained hunter–killer Republican Guard or Fedayeen units whose job it was to find and destroy Coalition special forces.

It was early morning back in Canberra when Mike Hindmarsh became aware that General Peter Cosgrove was about to brief the prime minister about the start of the war.

'[Cosgrove] wanted to go in with news, good or bad, so we were getting pushed for information at that point.'

Initially the squadron was going to insert by air. The final plan involved a couple of troops driving across the border and travelling into position on the first night, while another troop was inserted by US helicopters deep behind enemy lines, after flying 600 kilometres from the SAS staging base outside Iraq. That troop of Australian SAS soldiers was the closest Coalition force to Baghdad for the first 96 hours of the war.

For father of two Sergeant Peter D, this was an intense and sleepless period. After flying in on American Chinooks, the fear of capture was always in the back of his mind. His thoughts often went to his wife and two kids back in Perth, but no SAS soldier carries photos of his loved ones into battle. The men are 'sterile' except for their military identification plate — the dog tag — that they wear around their neck; 'if they were captured, something like a photo could be used against a soldier during any subsequent interrogation.'

A troop's first job was to lie up in a clandestine fashion for four days, watching and reporting everything they saw. They did observe missile launches, but only of surface-to-air weapons. 'Any hint of forces moving to launch and we were in a position to call in air strikes or destroy it ourselves,' says Peter D.

As Major Paul's headquarters element, made up of about a dozen men, and Captains Quentin and Zan's troops proceeded in on the ground, A troop and its vehicles were moving forward in the Chinook helicopters. This was a tense time. The weather had been terrible, with serious dust storms; the Iraqis had plenty of ground-to-air missiles deployed; US helicopters were crashing; and, to top it off, the refuelling nozzle on one of the helicopters carrying the Aussies deep behind enemy lines was damaged, so they had to abort.

'Despite this, we all had the old fingers crossed and legs and toes and everything else that it would all go according to plan,' says Hindmarsh.

Special Forces commander Brigadier Duncan Lewis, who was based at his Sydney headquarters at the time, said it was an 'extremely sobering' moment when the call came to invade Iraq. 'I got a message from the CDF [Chief of Defence Force, Peter Cosgrove] that it was good to go,' he says. 'But the command chain at that point was down through Maurie McNarn, so the message was passed then officially down through his chain.

'I passed it on to Mike Hindmarsh, who was my deputy that was [on the ground]. I spoke with the commanding officer of the unit on the telephone just to see that all was set, all was good. And then of course begins the wait. And we only had to wait a short time ... before the first contact.'

The incident really set Lewis's mind racing, because he had not expected a contact quite so soon. He had thought they might have been able to get through the first line without being sprung.

'So from that time on — and the first contact was successfully resolved — it was very quick, it was very clinical, everything went exactly as one would have hoped.'

In Qatar, Mike Hindmarsh was not quite as surprised as his boss that the first contact had happened so soon. 'No, no, we were pleasantly surprised it hadn't been earlier, to be honest. I mean, they had to punch through the border, the ground elements, and we expected a bit of a shit-fight there, but they got through undetected, did really a fantastic job, actually, to get through undetected ... [We] thought there would be contacts much earlier than there were. So we weren't really surprised when it did happen.'

Thanks to the technology available to him in Qatar, Hindmarsh was able to provide almost-live briefings to his higher command without having to annoy the operational commander, SAS CO Lieutenant Colonel Rick, who was monitoring the operation from his headquarters at the forward staging base.

'I didn't need to ring him and say, "What's going on, Rick, what's happening with that contact?"'

Instead, Hindmarsh told his staff, 'Just go away and tell me how many vehicles — count the number of vehicles and tell me whether they're still bloody moving!' And tell him they did. 'That was one of the big achievements,' Hindmarsh continues. 'I'm conscious of this, being a previous commander, that you always have people above you wanting to know what the hell's going on, and I can understand why they want to know — there's a very good reason. But as long as we can buffer the tactical level [keep the interference to a minimum] — and I think we achieved that on this operation.'

Back in Canberra, Army chief Lieutenant General Peter Leahy was confident that the Special Forces Task Group had been given the time and the logistical support to complete their mission. But in the command bunker at Defence headquarters in the offices in the Canberra suburb of Russell, he was tense as the force crossed the border. Then came the news: 'There's been a contact!'

'Oh, shit,' he said.

It was another few hours before the word came through: 'It's okay. They're all moving!'

General Leahy said it was clear that once they had got past any formed defences — which were known to be slight — the Coalition's mobility would kick in. And then, 'They're going to keep people off balance, they'll be moving all the time, they'll do long distances by night.'

The early indications were that the Iraqis appeared to be using the tactics from the last Gulf War, during which the allied special forces operated on foot. Consequently 'they didn't anticipate that [we'd] be so mobile and ... so agile.'

★　★　★

Once the first contact was over, the troops drove all night to reach their first major objective on the so-called Scud Line, the area from which Iraqi Scud missiles had the range to hit Israel. The SAS aimed to reach the location without encountering enemy troop concentrations along the way.

Says Patrol Commander Shane, 'There were a lot of battalions, a lot of enemy locations, and we would bypass them because it wasn't our job to take them on. Our job was just to find these locations, so we weren't trying to get any biffs or anything, we were just sort of trying to find these things. The first couple of days that's all we did, check these locations out.'

The troops drove all night, using night-vision gear to find their way across the moonless desertscape. Morning arrived and one troop set off on a reconnaissance mission, while another searched for a location to lay a cache of weapons. The two troops and the headquarters element met up later that day. None of them had had any sleep.

Mike Hindmarsh sent between fifteen and twenty emails on the first night of the war, updating his military masters back in Australia. 'You couldn't really relax ... I was up all night, [but] I wasn't the only one — the poor buggers in the field were up for the next seven nights straight. But the first night we were up all night.'

A feeling of relief washed over Hindmarsh when he heard that the patrols were in their hides. And thanks to exhaustive planning, there had been no blue-on-blue incidents involving Australians.

'The Task Group had planned in minute detail leading up to this, with our Coalition counterparts, so it worked extremely well. They'd war-gamed it and the whole thing just happened. It worked a treat.'

The only question mark hung over the troop and its insertion using US helicopters.

'We'd also had reports that another insertion, one of the American insertions, had gone awry, and one of the helos had crashed in a bloody dust storm, so all this information was coming back in the evening. Once we got the word that the ground-based gentlemen [and] the

259

vehicles were in their hide, and the helo insertion … had also successfully managed to get into a hide before first light, that's when we could start to relax a little bit. But that was only temporarily, of course.'

For the men behind enemy lines there would be no rest or relaxation for many days. While one troop stayed silent and watched for four days at one end of the AO, another couple of troops were making plenty of noise at the other, trying to unmask Saddam Hussein's Scuds.

The first day set the pattern: surveillance; night clearance of a target; couple of hours' recovery time; more surveillance; then a day clearance, all the time telling the locals, 'The war is over, go back to your families'.

It would be more than six weeks before the Aussies could do the same.

Chapter 22

GAME ON

The first planned SAS attack on an Iraqi target happened on the second night of the war, when one of the troops identified a military communications post. It was a suspected control node and hiding place for Scud missiles.

The men were ordered to get into their nuclear, biological and chemical warfare suits. As it turned out, they weren't needed, but they provided some extra relief from the cold desert night.

The plan called for the troop to raid the place, have a good look around and destroy any military hardware, while another troop stayed on the perimeter providing cover.

Sergeant Shane, a veteran of East Timor and Afghanistan, was second in command of his patrol, and remembers the night well. 'We started rolling forward and it's really hard to see, 'cos they had guards up in the posts and we couldn't see the command and they had bright lights and we had NVGs on. So we just crept up and slowly see what's going on.

'All of a sudden firing broke out and we were copping 40-mill [grenade rounds] behind us and you could hear some of the shrapnel hitting the back of the car.'

He started shouting, 'They're firing 40 mill at us, the buggers, they've got 40 mill, they're firing 40 mill at us!'

He soon realised that the ammunition was coming from one of the other SAS patrols. 'They were in a bit of a stoush up in the top part, they were flying 40 mill over their heads and nearly hitting us! So we were nearly hit by our own guys.'

Shane jumped on the radio, instructing others to 'Look out for this strobe [light], watch this strobe, do not fire at this strobe!' It worked.

Then he ran over to the patrol commander and said, 'We are in the wrong spot!'

Vehicles starting tearing out of the facility and the men were ordered to stop them. Through their thermal imagers they could clearly see the vehicle hot spots, such as the engine block.

'We just sat there firing at these vehicles 300 metres away,' says Shane, 'shooting and stopping these vehicles.'

Despite the Australians' technology and weapons, two vehicles managed to escape in the direction of an Iraqi military stronghold which was visible in the distance. Troop Commander Captain Zan was watching the fleeing vehicles through his night-vision gear. The bigger of the two was a truck.

Says Zan, 'You could actually see the 50-cal rounds hitting the back — it was like a Mog and the back tray was down — and the vehicle kept going and the gunner had his 50 cal on it the whole time. So it was a good lesson learnt there, that just because you've got a 50 cal on your vehicle, you can't necessarily stop vehicles travelling at 60 ks an hour. It's hard to simulate that in training, so we'd done that by night, which was good.'

The troops managed to stop one vehicle, but the second escaped and, on fire, sped off towards the town. Enemy wounded were treated and prisoners told to go home.

The mission was a great success. American air support from A10 Thunderbolts destroyed the facility. It turned out to be the key Iraqi communications centre for the entire Western Desert region, and its destruction was a major blow for Saddam Hussein's regime.

The SAS men kept moving. One troop stayed south of the main highway and another travelled on the north side. For a time they could see each other as well as communicate by radio. While one was moving, the other was watching.

The next day they raided a second, smaller communications facility close to the highway and captured a few ragtag Iraqi conscripts. Patrol medic and gunner Trooper John was busy processing three prisoners. When he pushed them against a wall and gave them a smoke, they thought they were about to be executed. 'Once they realised they weren't going to be dying that day, they were pretty happy,' he remembers.

Suddenly, six Iraqi sports utility vehicles (SUVs) arrived on the scene. The word was obviously out: the Aussies were now top on the list of Saddam's most wanted. The diggers knew there would be Special Republican Guard or Fedayeen hunter–killer teams out searching for Coalition special forces troops.

It was Trooper John's job to operate his vehicle's 50 calibre machine gun, Javelin anti-armour missile and the sniper rifle. The young digger stood with his mates and watched the SUVs pull up about 3 kilometres down the road. The vehicles were armed with Russian-made 12.7-calibre heavy machine guns and rocket-propelled grenades.

The communications facility was located in a slight bowl with a couple of small hills off to one side, a wide-open plain on the other and a road down the centre. Off in the distance on the plain was a large Bedouin tent.

As the SAS men moved to defensive positions, more SUVs pulled into the Iraqi formation, which had moved forward to within about 2000 metres of the Aussies. By this stage enemy fighters had fanned out from the vehicles and were firing on the Australian position.

Troop commander Captain Quentin, whose boyish appearance masks a hardened military mind, ordered the vehicles back to a position where their weapons were out-ranging the enemy. The diggers began the fightback from behind some high ground.

'We were going, "Cheeky buggers, they're getting out!" And sure enough, they were getting out to get in a firing position and that's when they started shooting,' says John. '"They're shooting at us! How dare they, cheeky little buggers!"'

The sides were evenly matched: the Iraqis had the SAS troops on their toes, their rounds spraying up dirt around the diggers. The retur fire from the Aussies was more accurate and effective, but neither side was giving any quarter.

'We knew [Iraqi] special forces were out there, and out to get us, and these were them,' continues John. 'They were aggressive, well trained, knew what they were doing, had drills down and started firing, then RPGs started going off and we were basically in contact. It was a good contact; it was going well for both sides at that stage. Our rounds had a little more projection, we had a bit better sort of fire power, but the ground fire from them was effective and it was keeping us on our toes. It wasn't like a one-way firefight.

'I thought they were moving to do a left-flanker on us and these cars were racing around to come out behind where we'd moved our vehicles. And that's when I decided to use the Javelin.'

The SAS had been equipped with the US-built Javelin anti-armour missile for the Iraq campaign. The 'shoot and forget' missile was designed to take out heavy armour at distances of up to 2.5 kilometres. The weapon has two attack modes, direct or top, the latter used to attack tanks from above where they are most vulnerable. It had never been fired in anger by an Australian soldier before.

John attached the command launch unit (CLU) to the launch tube, jumped off the vehicle and, lugging the 22-kilogram weapon, ran behind some cover to prepare to fire.

'I got a good target picture on one of these cars and then, just due to the ground, the picture became shit,' he says.

He then glanced over to where the enemy rounds were falling in between himself and his vehicle and thought, 'I don't want to go there!' But that was his only option, and he was conscious of the dirt spattering around his legs from the impact of enemy fire. He tried to make himself very small, and got the sight picture on the car. Then he yelled out, 'I'm firing now!'

John had been trained to use the weapon on a simulator, rather like a video game. 'You don't have to fire a live one,' he explains. 'And it's set up that you're doing things against tanks and all this sort of stuff, and when I got into the thing and put it on, it's almost like I'm back playing video games as a kid — or, in my case, as an adult. Playing a video game, getting it locked on, make sure everything's all right, and you want it to work and you want it to be no room for error.'

He went through the routine he had learnt in training. 'The little things inside are called recticles and you make sure that the recticle's right and then, "Yep, it's right, fire it", and as soon as you fire it you come back to, "Shit, there's rounds around me and stuff's going on, grab the thing and — in my case — get back to that car!"'

As soon as John had fired the Javelin he indeed ran back for the car. Suddenly everything went quiet, and he heard, 'Yee-hah!' Then a big cheer went up. 'And I looked and, yeah, the car's a flaming mess and it was great, and then I turned back and ran to the car. Firing continued and at that stage [the enemy] started deciding not to go against us any more and cut their losses.'

The troops later worked out that the reason the target image had blurred was because of the speed of the Iraqi SUV. John estimated that it had been travelling at between 50 and 60 kilometres per hour, going from his left to his right.

Once the driver realised what was happening, he would have had just a momentary view of a trail of smoke heading his way. He started to do U-turn but it was too late. The machine-gun operator saw the missile coming and jumped off, but the soldiers inside didn't; in an instant the vehicle flipped onto its back.

The Iraqis gathered their wounded and moved back to the communications facility, where they continued to engage the Aussies. By this stage John was back behind his 50 calibre machine gun as the SAS vehicles launched an assault on the enemy.

'I'm on the 50 cal firing at this individual that's firing and setting up stuff on the right-hand side of this compound that we'd just cleared. As I'm lining him up, one of the guys in the other cars is yelling out, "John, four fingers right", and I started giggling like a schoolgirl because he's only got four fingers and I'm going, "Of course it's four fingers right."'

The diggers realised the enemy force was trying to set up a mortar line and was being resupplied from a road behind the facility. When an army truck pulled up, it was time to call in some 'air'. A US ground attack aircraft soon arrived on the scene and, as John says now, 'That was the end of that.'

The fight had lasted about two and a half hours and had exposed a problem the Aussies would encounter several times during the campaign.

The Iraqis had transported their wounded off the battlefield and to the Bedouin tent off to one side. 'We couldn't do anything then because of the Bedouin tent and civilians,' says John. 'But ... a car would come back out by itself — just out of our reach — swing by, pick up one guy and go back to the tent.'

They found these Iraqi troops to be highly professional and committed. 'They were looking after each other as professional soldiers would and ... they were well trained and aggressive, and even after they'd been smacked down, they were still happy to have another go.'

The Iraqis' conduct on the battlefield was not the only thing to impress the Australians. When the SAS troops examined the destroyed car they found a lot of equipment they had not expected, including night-vision gear, which was a huge surprise as no intelligence briefing had mentioned enemy night-vision gear; anti-aircraft weapons; a 7.62 mm machine gun; sniper rifles; and the mandatory AK47 assault rifles.

A key part of the SAS function is to gather intelligence, so when they sent back a detailed report of the firefight and its aftermath, which included information on the Iraqis' high-tech kit, it changed the face of the campaign. The crucial lesson for the diggers was that you cannot rely 100 per cent on what you are told before the battle begins.

The SAS was also completely sold on the merits of the Javelin missile, even at $150 000 a throw. John says that the weapon altered the dynamic of the fight from being an even contest to the Australians dominating the battle space. His own reaction immediately afterwards had been, 'Right, this is a great piece of kit and we're keeping it. And let's get a replacement rocket.'

As for his feelings about the enemy fighters who were inside the vehicle when the missile hit, he says, 'I was . . . ecstatic that I'd got to do my job. And to do it well. And these guys weren't there to play Tiddlywinks — they were trying to kill me and my patrol . . . . At that stage I'd been in for fourteen years and been in a lot of different conflicts and operations and jobs, and so I'[d] done a lot of different stuff. And that was like a culmination point, to do something so big in such a way to change the battlefield and then, after it, to be able to give all that information over to help the Coalition. Basically, it was a big moment for my career, for me.'

With typical understatement, Captain Quentin describes the contact as 'fairly significant': 'That was probably the heaviest one that we had as a troop . . . That was probably the largest . . . there was a lot of fire from RPGs, and indirect fire and heavy machine-gun fire kicking up the dirt around us. However, the difference between our fire going back, I think, was that it was a little bit more accurate — we had good sighting systems and zeroed weapons and had a little bit of extra range as well. But the guys did well.'

The real difference was that the Iraqis were hitting the ground and the Aussies were hitting them. 'Looking at those guys compared with the [Iraqi] border guard units, these guys were highly trained, [they were] older soldiers and with a lot of training as well — fighting back into the killing ground to pick up their fallen guys, and the way in which, basically, as soon as they saw us, everyone fanned out either side. There were . . . five or six guys on each vehicle fanned out in an extended line, and within thirty seconds pretty much everyone and all those vehicles were returning fire at us.'

When it was over the men moved up to the 'smoked' vehicle and took some photos to show the higher-ups the type of vehicle involved and the extent of the damage. 'When we got back I thought, "Yeah wouldn't mind a copy of that."'

The first major contact of the war had been a remarkable success. It had given the troops confidence in themselves and their weapons, especially the Javelin, and it had provided vital intelligence about the enemy which would be useful for the entire Coalition.

When the troop met up with the rest of the squadron after the battle, Trooper John was the centre of attention: everyone wanted to know what it was like to record a kill with the Javelin.

'I said, "Oh yeah, [I'm] pretty happy", and in hindsight I was going, "Yeah, it's pretty hairy, in future I'd like to have a few more people around", [that] sort of stuff, but it's only in hindsight you can think that.'

The boss, Major Paul, was so impressed that he made John put everyone through another training session on the weapon. That meant having someone supporting the Javelin operator: 'I set the trainer [missile] up and had to run everyone through it again,' says Paul, 'and then I'd run guys who hadn't used it, or been trained in how to use it, and set it up in case it was needed later on.'

That meant all patrol members could load and fire the weapon if necessary. These skills would prove vital the very next day when a troop got into a major firefight with another Iraqi special forces unit.

Again the focus of the battle would be on the gunner, but this time it was not just the Javelin that got a guernsey but the suite of weapons carried on an SAS vehicle.

In addition to their personal weapons, usually M16 or M4 carbines, the LRPV was equipped with a 7.62 mm sniper rifle, which is accurate to beyond 2000 metres; a 50 calibre machine gun, Mag 58 machine gun, Mark 19 grenade launcher and an 84 mm rocket launcher, plus the Javelin missile. Each soldier was familiar with more than one weapons system, but only the gunner was intimately involved with all of them.

Another Trooper John in the squadron — who would become famous as 'Trooper X' — is a typical slow-talking and laid-back

Queenslander. The 36-year-old, a real bushie, had a considered approach to life and soldiering that was about to be put to the test.

On 24 March 2003, Trooper X and his patrol were conducting a clearance and observation of an enemy position close to Highway One, between the Jordanian border and Baghdad. All of a sudden they were confronted by an enemy force of fifteen men in two SUVs. The troop commander ordered the SAS men to engage, and Trooper X tried to launch a Javelin from about 2000 metres. The first round failed to fire, but eventually he took out both vehicles with the deadly shoulder-fired weapon.

'The fact we could engage them at 2000 metres was quite shocking to the enemy,' he says now.

The battle intensified, and Trooper X had fired about 200 rounds from the 50 cal when he noticed an enemy mortar base plate being set up about 250 metres away. He grabbed his 7.62 mm sniper rifle and, with little thought for his own safety, lined up the enemy mortar tube in his sight. He fired and hit the tube just as a mortar round misfired in the spout. The soldier heard bullets whizzing and cracking around him, mortars were landing behind him, and RPGs were bursting above and in front of the vehicles.

'They were a threat and they had to be neutralised,' he says matter-of-factly. 'No doubt they were trying to kill us.'

By now, enemy were dying, surrendering and fleeing the battlefield, and some were even trying to lure the Aussies in for the kill. The troops later recovered a weapon with a white flag attached that had a bullet hole and powder burns on it.

This would be Trooper X's heaviest contact of the war, with 200 50 calibre rounds, two Javelins and two sniper rounds fired. Almost all of them hit their mark. For his actions, he was awarded the Medal for Gallantry under the name Trooper X, as all serving SAS soldiers are not normally identified by name. To his mates he became 'Trooper X-rated'.

Trooper X's citation focuses on the fact that he was exposed to enemy fire throughout the action. 'Everyone was exposed,' he says. 'It's a bit hard not to be in open vehicles.' With typical humility, he says every man in the troop did his job perfectly: 'Any of the other blokes would have done exactly the same thing. That is not false modesty; it's just a fact.'

During this battle, the SAS soldiers accounted for the much larger force of more than 100 enemy without sustaining even a scratch. Squadron Commander Paul did not know exactly how many enemy were killed but believes there were 'quite a few'. 'If they decided to fight us, they paid the supreme sacrifice,' he says now.

For the quietly spoken father of two, originally from Albury in New South Wales, the first battles of the campaign ran like clockwork. 'I was able to survey the battlefield, the troop commanders and patrol commanders were able to survey the battlefield, and say, "Righto, fellas, direct your energy and focus onto that." And they'd go and do it. The guys are so highly trained and smart [that] you don't have to micromanage it.'

All he had to say was, 'Righto … destroy, neutralise!' and they would go and do it. 'And they do it in accordance with the laws of armed conflict. For me as a boss, as a commander, it was easy. I only had to set about the tactics and the manoeuvre of it. And of course, [ask the question] "What was going to be the effect of us doing that, what was the enemy going to do, so where do I need to place myself?"'

They always had a situation where, when one action was occurring, another element of the squadron was poised to support it. 'That's how we moved,' explains Paul. 'We didn't just bum along and shoot everything up; it was all very deliberate. We knew pretty much what we were doing, and on any given day one troop would be here [and] another would be there.'

The only unknown was how the enemy would react — how would the reality compare with the Australians' expectations? Says Paul, 'We assessed that Saddam would have moved on from '91, and we assessed that there were going to be these SUVs with these smart, special forces type enemies after us out there, because we knew … we were high-value targets. If they could achieve getting one of us, as they did with the Brits [in 1991], and put them on TV or something like that, it would [have been] a real victory for the enemy.

'I thought they might regroup and fight after that first action and subsequent actions. The effect was that they knew *we* were out there, but they didn't know *what* was out there. One day they'd see two cars and the next day they'd see fifteen cars moving at high speed out to the east, and then after lunch here'd be eight cars moving around out to the west. We were completely chaotic, in the enemy's eyes.'

Eventually the Australians pushed most of the enemy hunter–killer units north.

In conclusion, Paul says, 'We had learnt a lot of lessons from [the contacts] and sent them up into our American and UK guys, and one of the guys came back and said, "Thanks very much for all those reports because you probably saved our bacon in a lot of instances."'

Deception was a key tactic of the SAS troops. They would observe by day with enemy eyes on them and then that night they would move to a new location. Part of the deception strategy was to make the enemy think there were more of them than there really were. It was a bit like a judo match, where the aim is to unbalance your opponent rather than bash away at his head.

'We saturated all their senses,' says Paul, 'all their visual senses, their electronic senses we destroyed, a lot of their communications systems were destroyed. They'd see something out there and then, "Oh, by the way, we're getting hit from the rear". It's the old David and Goliath — we were a very small force and we unhinged them. There were nearly 200 people in and around Kilometre 160 [so named because it is 160 kilometres from Baghdad] and we were a smaller force.'

With each successful job the men, especially the new members, grew in confidence — 'it's not until you actually get under fire and see how people react under stress that you realise it's all coming together,' says Paul.

Despite this, Major Paul describes the initial contact as a 'bit stilted': 'We had guys — eyes like mad cats, I guess — out there looking at what was going on. We dealt with that. We had this action the second night we were in there — it was very successful, and we started recognising the effectiveness of our weapons systems.'

By the time the Javelin was used for the first time, he could see that they were really starting to get in the groove. The men knew how to employ their weapons systems well under fire and they were composed. On the other hand: 'The enemy, they weren't composed. They started to engage us at the maximum effective range of their weapons systems. Which was silly, you know — they had nowhere to go. All we had to do was reverse a little bit, get into some high ground, take our time, assess the ground, keep cool, calm and collected, and then engage them with our weapons systems. Our weapons outmatched them every time. So it was good.'

The SAS advantage was more than simply better technology and air-power superiority, though; it was the quality of the men and their ability to keep thinking.

'It's like a game of chess. It's how you move — set all your pieces up, okay. Good, okay, *whack*. Otherwise, if you don't take that time, it's going to be a long, drawn-out fight, you're just bouncing from one bad idea to the next. And that was the key with the guys. Each man could look around [and say], "Okay, that's over there, there's a better fire position over here, move. Engage."'

Fatigue was a major issue for the squadron during the first week. After 48 hours of constant movement fuelled by adrenaline, the men were exhausted and drained, especially the drivers who had been driving all night using night-vision gear, in itself tiring due to the concentration required.

As Sergeant Shane recalls, 'I remember as we were driving along and as the sun's coming up, you're starting to hallucinate and see things, and nodding off as you're driving, and we're saying to the boss, "We need to stop, it's going to get dangerous if we get in a stoush now, people aren't going to be effective, so we're better off resting."

'The boss is in the same boat as everyone — he's tired and trying to find the right spot and chasing the bare ground there. But we stopped — we finally found a spot where there are some old earthworks — and as we stopped we could see in the distance what we thought were some artillery pieces.'

The boss ordered a patrol to move up and see what it was all about, but when it turned out to just be some more earthworks, the men knew they had to rest.

'We thought, "This is just ridiculous", and we went back and said, "Let's get some sleep."'

After 72 hours on the go, some patrol commanders and the troop commander, Captain Zan, had to be told bluntly to go and get some sleep.

They camouflaged the vehicles as best they could and Shane had just nodded off in his sleeping bag for the first time in three days when voices yelled, 'Tanks! Tanks! There are tanks coming!'

As the soldiers knew that elements of Iraq's 10th Armoured Brigade were in the area, they were very worried about encountering tanks. So the Australians fled the scene, positioned for an ambush and got the Javelins ready to fire, but no tanks eventuated. To this day the troops are not sure whether there were tanks out there or not. However, the incident forced the Javelin operators to have their weapons prepared to fire at all times. Even in their sleeping bags, they would be ready to just sit up and fire.

'I think we pushed their endurance to the limit,' says Zan, 'but it didn't become an issue. We didn't not do anything because we had to stop and sleep.

'A couple of nights we wanted to have more sleep, but because of the ground we just couldn't stop where we wanted to, and we had to continue ... [with] Bedouin moving over there by night, you'd get woken up — just these little factors, so I guess if you were planning it again you'd need to add in fudge for sleep. But at the same time, the first seventy-two hours of operations — not only this kind of operations, but with a battalion or whatever — you're not going to get much sleep. It's just a fact of warfare: it's intense, and you're not going to get much sleep, and you've just got to deal with it.'

Regardless, by the fourth night, when he fell asleep while writing a message, Captain Zan realised he needed to have a proper rest, and he slept for two hours straight.

Some of the older hands of the regiment believe that having the squadron commander on the ground and in the thick of the action throughout the Iraq campaign was crucial to its success. Because of the completely different nature of the job in Afghanistan, the headquarters had only occasionally deployed on operations.

During 42 days of operations in Iraq the SAS had twenty-four reportable contacts, most of which occurred in the first nine days. The squadron headquarters were either involved or close by for many of them.

Squadron Sergeant Major Warrant Officer Steve, a wily and mischievous senior soldier, remained by Major Paul's side throughout the operation. He says now that, for such a young man, his boss has a 'fucking brilliant' tactical mind: 'From the time we crossed the border it was agreed the headquarters were going to be out there for the whole period of time, until we had done what we had to do, like secured the area, and we didn't know how long that was going to take.

'When you're screaming across the desert and you look back and you've got a whole squadron in vehicles, it's quite an impressive sight.'

Chapter 23

OUT OF THE BLUE

The blue uniforms stood out in stark contrast to the khaki summer kit worn by the diggers. On the parade ground on a crisp June day at SAS headquarters at Swanbourne near Perth, the flamboyant US Air Force (USAF) dress rig brought a touch of Uncle Sam to a very Australian parade.

The 1 SAS Squadron was on parade before the Governor-General and the prime minister; they were to be presented with the military's highest group honour, the Unit Citation for Gallantry, for their daring deeds during the Iraq war.

Australia's top soldiers don't much like parades or the drill practice they entail. But in accordance with the SAS ethos of striving for excellence in all things, they marched in perfect unison before national leaders, military top brass, family, friends and quite a few 'old and bold' ex-SAS soldiers.

Four American airmen also marched that day as members of 1 SAS Squadron and as honorary Aussies, their mateship forged forever on the battlefields of Afghanistan and Iraq.

A key part of the Iraq operation was calling in US air strikes against the enemy and preventing air strikes against friendly forces. In the first two weeks of the war, SAS patrols directed more than 46 000 kilograms of high explosives onto hostile targets in western Iraq. Most of those strikes were physically called in by a liaison officer from the USAF's Special Tactics Squadron (STS) who was attached to an SAS troop.

Mercifully, not a single friendly fire incident involving Australians occurred during the Iraq campaign, but the risk of such a disaster was uppermost in the mind of Special Operations Commander Major General Duncan Lewis.

'I spoke to the squadron before they left and I said to them on the tarmac before they took off, "The greatest single threat you're going to face in this operation is blue air … your single largest threat, more than any enemy ground force, will be your own air [support] because it's just the way of things,"' he said.

The SAS enjoys very close links with US special forces units, including the STS, thanks not only to operational experience in places such as Afghanistan and Iraq, but also to extensive exchange programs. Squadron Commander Major Paul was embedded with a US task force during Afghanistan, and his boss, SAS commander Lieutenant Colonel Rick, had recently commanded the task force in Afghanistan and also spent two years at the US Marine Corps Command and Staff College in Quantico, Virginia. The experiences gave the two men a great understanding of the American way of thinking and working.

Two of the four Americans who worked with the squadron in Iraq had already been with the regiment in Afghanistan. Working with the Australians was regarded as a plum job amongst the Americans and there was always strong competition for slots with the SAS.

The Australians regarded the STS boys as a great force multiplier and a sound insurance policy against friendly fire incidents. As Rick explains: 'They gave me and, I know, all the guys on the ground, as well as the Americans and the pilots, a lot more confidence that they could support us and prevent any sort of casualties occurring. They talked the language, literally, and that's their job.'

The liaison officer principle had been enforced on every Coalition operation, as having an experienced person working with the partner forces both saved lives and enhanced operational effectiveness. In Iraq the principle was so well understood that the STS men fitted straight into the SAS troops and patrols. In addition, there had been enough lead-up time before Iraq to rehearse or war-game most aspects, including the air war.

The most crucial element of using the close air support was not hitting the target; it was to avoid your own people. During a high-tempo war, when crews on the ground and in the air were on edge and tired, it became even more important. Not only did the USAF STS men fight as fully fledged members of the SAS patrol to which they were attached, but they ensured that, before they released their bombs or opened fire, the American pilots knew exactly what the target was and precisely where the SAS units were.

Despite all the rehearsals and all the planning, it was an Australian soldier who called in the first air strike of the Iraq war when the dedicated American communications gear failed at the critical moment. That was another first for the diggers of 1 SAS Squadron in Iraq.

The STS airmen had joined the squadron just ten days before the curtain went up in Iraq. The Australians were very confident of the Americans' ability to fit in and get the job done. The Americans had missed a lot of the build-up training, but the diggers took them under their wings and got them up to speed on everything from pack weights to operating the weapons on an LRPV.

'We were working with American Air Force, these [STS] guys are American Air Force, [so] their accent even helps!' says Paul. 'An Australian accent talking to a pilot at the heights they were doing — with so many things going on, the passage of information needs to be clear. They know the capabilities of the aircraft better than ... we do, they know which buttons to press and how to get aircraft quicker than ... we would, so it was handy.'

It was also handy for the American airmen to become members of the SAS team. Each one had to be able to drive the vehicle, sit in the turret and operate the 50 calibre machine gun, or fire the Mag 58 gun or the grenade launcher.

Paul continues: 'Manpower was a little bit limited in those areas, so that's how we used them. Otherwise they would have just sat in the back manning a radio, and they could have been doing so many other things. They're key specialists who need to be able to plug in — they don't need to be able to do everything we do, but they need the core skills, which are weapons handling, conducting a little bit of surveillance, doing picquet sentry — basic soldier skills.'

The Americans were as keen as mustard to work with the Aussies and, says Paul, were accordingly very enthusiastic. 'They were pretty much self-motivated, self-controlled sort of guys, and their skills with communications systems were fantastic, and they augmented our communications architecture as well, because they had different links to what we had.

'Eric would go off to a side and send a sitrep [situation report] back to his chain of command, so we had some dual chains going there as well, and in preparing for deliberate action onto a target, I'd say, "Eric, this is what I want to do", show him on a map; he'd deal with the target reports, deal with the detailed planning for how many bombs would be required in support of this operation; he'd make sure the aircraft was going to be on station and would have the correct overlap for refuel and all that sort of stuff. At no time did I have to worry about it — I'd identify a target either on a map or I'd physically point to it and say, "Neutralise that, mate, so I can manoeuvre our ground forces", and he did it, just like that. Sensational.

'He'd say, "Can you give me a grid?" And I'd work out the grid, or he'd get out the laser range-finder and vector onto the target, and I'd say, "How long?" and he'd give me a time frame and he was pretty much always there. And he would go through the array of weapons systems that were available to him and he'd recommend the best one and we'd go for it from there.'

'Eric' was Technical Sergeant Eric from the Special Operations Air Force Command, one of 350 men in the USAF who are part of US special forces. He was talking directly with the US pilots and their command chain. As he describes: 'If he's over the top of me, let me start talking to him now, or if he's in another country, just tell him to get here as fast as the thing will carry him. Basically I just tell them my situation, how badly we need [air support] and it's for them to decide, because if somebody else is in a worse situation than us, of course they're going to get it first. They basically have to figure out who's going to best help us. So they give me an idea how long it's going to take and I just get ready for them, and hopefully by the time they get there, I'm all set.'

Eric was appreciative of the efforts the SAS men had made to fully inform him and his colleagues about the vehicles and weapons after their late arrival at the FOB.

'The guys I was with every day were taking me out, making sure I was up to speed, giving me a quick train-up on things I didn't know; walking me through the vehicles, walking me through the plan, emergency procedures — pretty much anything I had a question about, they're more than willing and took the time that they had to spend with me, so even the short period I had with them, I felt comfortable with them by the time I went out.'

Once inside Iraq, if the Americans weren't operating their radios in the rear of the vehicles, their most common job was manning the turret and the 50 cal, or, occasionally, the Mark 19 grenade launcher.

One thing the Americans didn't get to operate was the Javelin missile. 'They wanted that all for themselves!' says Eric. 'Besides, you can't really practise on those except on a simulator. It's a lot of money to be throwing around.'

The Americans had no qualms about placing their lives in the hands of the SAS soldiers, because, as Eric says, 'I knew exactly what I was there to do and I could do it, and I knew why they were there, because of how good they are — so I knew they were going to take care of me.'

Apart from making sure his targeting information was 100 per cent accurate, Eric's most important task was liaising with his boss, either a troop commander or Major Paul, to make sure he knew exactly where all the SAS men and vehicles were at all times.

'I gotta keep an eye on them to make sure I don't do any kind of fratricide or collateral damage to any of our guys or any other people in the area. And that is a big thing with the vehicle-mounted. With the foot patrol you're a small group and you're all together — for the most part you're normally all together — whereas vehicles can be all over the place. So you've really got to be on top of your game to know where everybody is.'

Thanks to modern battlefield communications, the STS men were in constant contact with the troops and patrols. The US pilots played a vital role as well, as they made it their business to study all Coalition vehicles, and even to go out and have a look at them, to make sure they knew exactly what they looked like.

'Any chance I had, I'd have one of them double-check,' says Eric, 'just to make sure that I was looking at the right thing and stuff I was sending off was right. So, that way, two eyes checking out the same thing, two brains looking at it, it's a lot easier to catch something that might have gone wrong.

'Even when we were just driving around, I'd just have the sat comm [satellite communications] on, listening so I'd know what's going on above.'

Despite all the precautions taken during the Iraq campaign, Eric and an SAS troop narrowly avoided a friendly fire incident when they were targeted by an aircraft during a mission to destroy an Iraqi facility. Eric 'just jumped on the radio and told them, "Hey, just hang on a moment, reconfirm what you saw, and the coordinates!" And it was us, sure enough — he thought it was the bad guys.'

Friendly fire was a continual risk during the high-intensity air-power conflict in Iraq. 'You're going to have planes flying overhead a lot in this type of situation — whereas one flight flies over and they leave, I'm not worried about it; if they start circling we get on the radio and we call them directly, [saying] "You're looking at us, we're friendlies."'

Eric's comrades Technical Sergeant Ian and Staff Sergeant Clint also worked with 2 SAS Squadron in Afghanistan. Ian first met the SAS in Kuwait in 1998 during Operation Desert Thunder, when several STS operators were attached to Australian and Kiwi SAS patrols.

'I was very impressed with them, [they were] very professional,' says

Ian. 'We had seen some of the things they were doing — if we got into a firefight then they were the ones we wanted coming to help us out.'

Both Clint and Ian went to Afghanistan and joined an SAS patrol almost as soon as they arrived. Another STS man was a member of the longest Aussie patrol in Afghanistan.

Ian continues: 'Some of our guys had worked with the squadrons previously in the war, so we'd talked to some of them and heard the stories, that they did a lot of good work, like during Anaconda [in Afghanistan]. So when they asked for volunteers to go work with them, we couldn't have volunteered fast enough. There was a little bit of wrestling and fighting to see who got to go.'

Clint says that the good thing about working with the SAS guys was the fact that the Americans were welcomed as soon as they arrived. 'They just welcome you right in, and the next thing you know, they're hounding you just like anyone else, giving you shit. Constantly, but it's cool.'

The Americans' job while attached to 1 SAS was designated as command and control integrating air and ground forces on the battlefield. They handled all the airspace matters, whether they were to do with fighters and bombers or air-traffic control and resupply.

The STS men had to be familiar with all aircraft types, including Air Force, Army, Marines, Navy and Coalition. 'We have to be able to work with pretty much anybody,' Eric says.

He reveals that it takes about two years to qualify as an STS operator. Volunteers are put through an intensive selection course which includes weapons, parachuting, diving, air-traffic control, survival and tactics, before they join a team. Part of their training is conducted with special forces units, so they know exactly what to expect when they get posted to an operational unit like 1 SAS.

'We actually go to the experts and let them teach us.'

One of the biggest early barriers for the Americans working with the diggers was coming to grips with the bad language and slang terms used by the Aussies.

'In the US military we get a little bit colourful as well,' Ian admits. 'But there's a few words that I picked up from the boys that I get in trouble with at home with the ladies — they don't like a certain word. Every once in a while when something isn't going my way, I say, "Come on, you fucking cunt", and if there's women around, it's not pretty. "What did you say?" "I said, I'd like to go hunting!"'

Clint says that another interesting word was 'root' — 'Give her a root, that's like pigs going at it for us!'

When Clint and Ian went out for their first night duty, they were told they had picquet duty from such and such a time. Their response: 'Picquet? What the fuck is that — picquet?'

'It's guard duty.'

'Oh! Okay! Why do you call it "picquet"?'

Another alien word was 'brew', the diggers' slang term for a cup of tea or coffee. Australian soldiers brew up at every opportunity, but the Americans thought they were talking about booze.

As Ian recalls: 'When I went to meet the commander the first time he said, "Hey, let's go back here and have a brew." I'm thinking of beer. "Sweet! I'm hardly here one minute and I'm already drinking!" And he was like, "Coffee?" and I'm [thinking], "Where's the brew?"'

Then there was 'having a feed'. The Americans thought they were talking about cattle. Not to mention '"Back to the rear" or "Throw your thongs on!" "Thongs? Sick! Fucking weirdos!"'

And there was 'mate' and 'singlets' and 'jumpers'. It was an entirely new language to the Americans.

One cultural aspect the Yanks were very familiar with was taking the mickey out of your mates. The Americans fitted in well on that score. 'We do that as well in our job,' says Ian, 'so coming in we were kind of quiet at first, trying to see how things were going, but now I give these guys just as much shit as they give me.'

Another reason why the Americans were so fond of working with the Aussies was the regimental culture of sharing. The strict SAS creed was to share the load. So if one man had 50 kilograms of gear and another had 100, they split it and carried 75 kilograms each. The Americans were used to lugging around up to 100 kilograms, most of which was radio gear, so the sharing concept was a real blessing.

As Ian describes it, 'Any time we dismounted with these guys, all packs got weighed — they're all within a pound or two of each other. That way it's equal across the board. Some Coalition teams I've worked with, I'm carrying 180 pounds, they're carrying 80 pounds. Try and get them to carry some of it and they say, "It's yours".'

By comparison with the foot patrols they were used to, the vehicle-mounted operations in Iraq were a dream. So it was no wonder there was an excess of STS volunteers to work with the SAS in Iraq. Ian was one of them. 'Our 2IC of the squadron came out and said, "Hey, we need three guys to go with the Australians — you guys [have] got to leave in five days." I . . . said, "I'm goin'."'

For Clint, thoughts of Australia had never gone beyond vacations, beaches and the Great Barrier Reef. 'The other good thing is that a lot of our guys do know a good bit of military history, so . . . just the SAS alone, the fact of knowing it's that unit, a lot of the guys know what they've done in the past. It's not something we were going to get thrown into where we're going to have to watch our backs the whole time.'

The STS men — who had all volunteered for Iraq while still in Afghanistan — also knew that, because the patrols were vehicle-mounted, they would be able to live a lot better than on foot patrols. This was where Australia's favourite spread came in.

'We got introduced to the old Vegemite,' says Ian. Clint's take on it was, 'Vegemite — I need to pick some of that up, actually . . . [I] took a while to turn to that.' Ian was never persuaded. 'It's an acquired taste. They still haven't turned me!'

In terms of field rations, it was the age-old story: the Americans preferred the Australians', but the SAS troops thought Uncle Sam's good old MREs were the way to go. The Australian freeze-dried packs and the savoury crackers and Vegemite were the clinchers for the Americans. In addition, the ability of the Australians to brew up a thermos of piping hot tea with sweetened condensed milk for the men on night picquet duty was a revelation.

'Every day, just before dark we'd make up a thermos for the picquet that night,' says Ian, 'make up a good tea brew, with the creamer and sweetened condensed milk — that was another thing that we kinda got used to. You don't really get a whole lot of that in the States. So we could keep warm on the picquet at night.'

Another thing that made the Americans really envious of their Coalition partners was their clothing and webbing. 'They had a lot better stuff,' say the STS men.

The Australians still enjoyed the major cold-weather gear advantage they had picked up in Afghanistan, and their puffy thermal jackets were the envy of their American mates during the cold desert nights. According to Ian, 'They'll save you, especially on one of the open LRPVs when you're driving down the road.'

Another huge positive as far as the Americans were concerned was the type of vehicle used by the SAS — they found the LRPV to be a far superior vehicle to the American-built Humvee. The power, six-wheel drive and storage space amazed the Americans.

'You get in the thing, and it's literally built to store everything,' says Eric. 'Whereas [with] our vehicles it's more like you have to find a spot to store. It just looks like . . . every time they've gone out they've learnt something, and something's got changed on the vehicle when they came back. You can put so much stuff on the vehicle.'

'And the Hummer's a good vehicle,' adds Ian, 'it's a really good vehicle. But when you see something like this! You see a lot of it is just organisation . . . You can get a lot of stuff in there but it's still readily accessible, whereas in the Hummer you can get a lot of stuff in it but if you need something that's on the bottom, you've got to take everything out to get to it.'

For Ian, there was a comfort issue as well. 'You can take a lot more of the niceties, a lot more of the warmies, whereas when you do the dismounted patrol the amount of equipment that we carry, you're really limited on the niceties that you can carry.'

In general, for the STS men, Iraq was a very different job to Afghanistan. In Iraq their role was immediate and vital to the success of the mission. Air power took centre stage in Iraq, whether it was cruise missiles destroying palaces in Baghdad or A10 Thunderbolts taking out a communications tower identified by an SAS patrol.

'I'd say for us, being on the leading edge of the battle, especially right at the beginning, that we did have a lot more air support than we did in Afghanistan,' Ian says. 'Just because it was a more defined battle for us, rather than in Afghanistan where it's kind of hit or miss — you may go an entire 100-day rotation in Afghanistan and never get shot at. So you really don't have much of a call to call for the close air. Every once in a while we'd get something in for recce or whatnot, but we were definitely a lot busier in Iraq.'

For Clint, the operation presented a different challenge. He was with the patrols that were deployed by helicopter deep behind enemy lines, and that meant severe weight restrictions and some hard decisions about what to take and what to leave behind. 'There was a lot more kit that we couldn't take. Some of the kit, like our laser designators for laser-guided bombs, I couldn't take it because of the restrictions. They sent it out later, but there were a lot of issues there at the beginning, where they had to get waivers to allow them to take that much weight in the helos. And, as I say, it was going to be two weeks before we got resupplied, so ... we really had to sit there and go, "Oh yeah, I can have this stuff sent out later — what do I need? What's the minimum I can get away with?" We had to really look at that.'

The bottom line for the STS operators was their total confidence in the ability of the SAS soldiers. They knew that if things turned ugly, the Aussies would fight to save them.

'We do work with a lot of other coalitions,' says Ian, 'and some of them are really good at what they do, and some of them are not so good at what they do. I was talking to one of the [SAS] guys after Iraq and told him [about] some of the coalitions we've worked with and some of the scary things that they do and this and that, and one of the guys said,

"You can have that job! I wouldn't want to go out and work with these guys." Because you don't know, if you get into something, if they're going to fight to save you. Whereas when we worked with the SAS guys, you knew that these guys would fight to save me just like I would fight to save them. That made a lot of difference.'

The three STS men were also deeply honoured to be included in the Unit Citation for Gallantry. It was the first time the award had been made, and it was the first time American personnel had been accorded such an honour. They will only be allowed to wear the ribbon at certain functions, but the honour will stay with them always.

'I was really kinda taken by surprise when I heard that they were going to include us,' says Ian, 'and really honoured, actually, to be recognised. Just how big of a deal it is, and being the first Yanks to ever be awarded anything from the Australian military, and this award, being the first time it's ever been awarded — it's just really big for us.'

Chapter 24

WHITE LINE FEVER

It might have been North Africa in 1942. The soldier standing in the middle of the desert highway wearing shorts, a bush hat and rolled-up shirtsleeves could only have been an Aussie.

Unlike his forebears, though, he was not fighting German and Italian armoured divisions. He was on the lookout for the Coalition's most wanted man, Saddam Hussein, and other Iraqi luminaries who were trying to flee their fallen country.

As a carload of Australian journalists approached the SAS checkpoint on the way to Baghdad in mid-April 2003, the digger trained his M4 carbine on the driver, signalling for him to slow down.

The Australian troops had a no-nonsense reputation with the mainly Jordanian drivers who ply Iraq's Highway One, charging US$1000 or more for the journey to or from Baghdad in their GMC V8 station wagons. The Aussies were determined to avoid suicide bombers, so [they] had a strict policy of dealing with all vehicles at a distance until they were cleared to proceed. Slowing down doesn't come easy to the carefree — some might say careless — drivers whose livelihood depends on speed. It is nothing for these low-flying highway pilots to make a boiling cup of tea on their laps as the speedometer nudges 170 kilometres per hour. Apart from bandits and the occasional war, the biggest risk on the drive from Amman in Jordan to Baghdad is a high-speed puncture and almost certain death.

As the media vehicle crawled through the checkpoint, several LRPVs were parked off to the side and a number of Iraqi vehicles were being searched and their occupants questioned by the Australian troops.

Windows down, the newsmen — Mark Willacy, Trevor Bormann and Louie Eroglu from the ABC and myself from News Limited — tried to engage the SAS trooper in conversation.

'No comment', came the thick Aussie accent in reply.

'Get rid of them, Filthy!' a commander barked from a vehicle off to the side. At least, that's what the journalists thought he said. My subsequent news item quoting this immortal line caused extreme amusement among the men of 1 SAS Squadron. 'Filthy' became an international man of mystery. According to Troop Commander Quentin, his nickname wasn't 'Filthy' but something close to it. The trooper's true identity — along with the reason why the mistake caused such mirth — remains a closely guarded regimental secret.

The highway, which is the main supply route between Baghdad, Jordan and Syria, is a beautiful piece of road, and it was Iraq's lifeline during twelve years of United Nations sanctions. Built with British expertise, the six-lane motorway runs almost gun-barrel straight for hundreds of kilometres across Iraq's Western Desert. A few hundred metres off to one side runs another, less impressive road used exclusively by oil tankers. Flyovers mark the turn-offs to towns or intersecting roads, and numerous bridges ford the many wadis that cut through the barren landscape.

For six weeks during March and April 2003, Australia's SAS 'owned' hundreds of kilometres of Iraq's highways, including Highway One. The bridges had provided ideal hiding places for Saddam's mobile Scud launchers, which had used the road during the 1991 Gulf War, when several were fired into nearby countries including Israel and Kuwait.

The SAS also used the wadis and bridges to good effect. Some of the most intense battles of their campaign were fought along or close to the highway, and many of the early targets were Iraqi military communications or command posts built nearby. The two SAS troops that drove into Iraq on day one of the war began setting up snap vehicle checkpoints almost as soon as they hit the bitumen. They would set up a roadblock and stop, search and send vehicles on their way. Then the soldiers would disappear into the desert, only to turn up the next day somewhere up or down the road.

In between they would watch the highway using their high-tech scopes and binoculars from clandestine OPs on hilltops well back from the road. They observed everything, from trucks and buses going towards Baghdad to media vehicles — or, at least, vehicles with 'TV' signs on their roof and sides — fleeing towards the Jordanian or Syrian borders.

'That was our biggest problem there, everyone putting "TV" or "Media" on their car,' says Patrol Commander Shane. 'Everyone put it on their car and you're pulling up families and they had "TV" written on their car. Some had "VT" on it, backwards!'

Highway One was also a vital channel for the Bedouin tribes who tend their struggling flocks of sheep along its length. With military vehicles travelling up and down the highway and Bedouin at every turn, it didn't take long before the SAS was compromised and Iraqi special forces killer squads were sent out from the Republican Guard stronghold at nearby Ar Ramadi to hunt them down.

Sergeant Shane describes driving down the highway as an 'amazing' experience. 'The cars were coming at us, and some of them were military and they would flash their lights at us ... they must have thought we were on their side.

'Before they knew it we had 'em on the ground and were searching them, taking their weapons off them and their uniforms and telling them to get out of there — rack off. We couldn't do anything else.'

Many of the vehicles they stopped simply resumed their journey in the direction of Jordan or Syria.

The diggers were especially on the lookout for dark-coloured Mercedes Benz or BMW saloons, which were the carriages of choice for senior Ba'ath Party figures and wealthy Saddam cronies.

Captain Quentin's troop received word that a high-speed convoy of just such vehicles was heading his way and he was told to intercept the convoy and check it out. What he didn't know was that one of the cars contained a very irate Russian ambassador to Iraq, whose convoy had been shot up (allegedly by the Americans) the day before. Several of his staff had been wounded and the vehicles were badly damaged.

'They were all in black Mercedes Benz or black BMWs,' says Quentin, 'and anyone driving that type of car was suspect because that's pretty much the type of car the Ba'ath Party were driving around in, not in jingle trucks and beaten-up cars.

'There was a convoy of these cars heading fast — at a high rate of knots — heading west, and another troop who couldn't get to the road saw it and rang it through to us. We moved onto the road to intercept it.

'The Russian ambassador was there; he spoke a little bit of English and he was pretty upset that we'd stopped him, but he was pretty happy that we didn't shoot him.'

The envoy, who was one of the last foreign diplomats to leave Baghdad, called the US headquarters on his satellite phone to give his liaison officer an earful about being stopped again. There were a couple of wounded in the cars and after the shooting the more serious cases had been taken to a hospital closer to Baghdad.

Quentin continues: 'We offered them medical support, we offered to call in a helo to cas evac [casualty evacuate] the guys that were there, and we also checked out the vehicles to see how many bullet holes were in them. It was just small arms.

'It was a good little scenario where we were just trying to ease the tensions of the guys and offer them as much as we could, saying that we would organise for an escort, and air escort just so that they could get out. And I think his response was, "I think we've already had enough of your hospitality!" So I said, "Okay, no worries!"'

The Russian handed the young SAS officer his phone so he could talk to the American liaison officer, who told Quentin to let them go and thanked him for a job well done.

'It gave us a few brownie points with the Russians and the Yanks. It was a good experience and I think anyone here, given that same opportunity, would have done exactly the same thing. I was just lucky to get the run. Very lucky, in fact.'

Lady Luck continued to smile on the youthful captain's troop, which had more than its share of action and adventure during the six-week campaign. On 11 April they intercepted a bus and two cars containing fifty Iraqi Fedayeen and Ba'ath Party members, carrying about US$600 000 in cash stashed in bags, tissue boxes and shirt boxes. They also found weapons, radios and gas masks, and documents offering a $5000 reward to anyone who killed a US soldier.

'The money was accounted for, documented and handed over with the detainees,' Quentin says. As for the Iraqis: it was a general rule that the Australians did not detain prisoners, and most of the dozens of people they captured were sent on their way. On occasions when they did come across someone they suspected offered good intelligence, the detainee was immediately passed to other elements of the Coalition.

After the battle where Trooper 'X-rated' won his Medal for Gallantry, Captain Zan found himself responsible for the only officer taken prisoner by 1 SAS Squadron. He happened to be a lieutenant colonel and, under the Geneva Conventions, officers were to be separated from other ranks and placed in the care of a fellow officer.

'Suddenly I was in charge of looking after this officer, and so there was a line of fifteen or so enemy on the ground with the blokes looking after them and then, off to the side, was me by myself looking after this enemy lieutenant colonel! Not an ideal situation, but that was the way it turned out. And I specifically remember it was tricky at the time — I had to talk on the radio and the boss was still a couple of bounds back [quite a distance away] looking after the rear and trying to talk to some planes.

'And this lieutenant colonel reached into his pocket — even though he was on the ground, hands out waiting to be searched, [he] went to reach into his pocket and I didn't know what he was reaching for. So I think he just saw it in my eyes that if he was going to reach into his pocket, I'd be forced to shoot him.'

The Australian officer clicked up the dust cover on his weapon, which sounds like the safety catch being released. At that point the Iraqi chose discretion over valour and moved his hand away.

'He stopped, fortunately, and then when we did get to search him [we found] he had two little hand grenades in his pocket. So I don't know whether he was going for the hand grenades to try to detonate them, or to indicate to me, "Look, I've got hand grenades in my pocket", and trying to do the rightie and hand them up.'

The diggers noticed a big difference in disposition between the various military prisoners they captured. Some were obviously fearless, battle-hardened veterans who looked at their captors with arrogance and contempt. 'Whereas other guys,' says Quentin, 'I think some of them actually pissed themselves, they were scared as ... [they] just sort of looked at you as if, "What's going to happen?" But we let most of them go. Again, we weren't out there to catch Iraqi soldiers. We were out there for a specific mission.'

Still, for the diggers, it was odd to be in a fight to the death with enemy soldiers one minute and relieving them of their weapons and letting them go the next.

The hardened prisoners with the red tabs of the Republican Guard on their uniforms also had a mission. With memories of Bravo Two Zero — the infamous British SAS patrol captured during the 1991 Gulf War — in their minds, their mission was clear: capture a Coalition special forces soldier to show the world Saddam was really in charge.

The regime's obsession with special forces was on display in Baghdad when Saddam's mouthpiece, Mohammed Saeed al Sahaf (nicknamed 'Comical Ali' and 'Baghdad Bob' in the media), announced that enemy special forces troops had been sighted in downtown Baghdad and were being hunted down. The remaining media at the Palestine Hotel were even treated to a direct-action clearance by Iraqi troops of a reed bed alongside the Tigris River directly in front of the hotel. They set fire to part of it, but no 'enemy' troops were ever found. That is not to say there weren't Coalition special forces troops in

Baghdad during the war; in fact, there almost certainly were. But Saddam's men never found them.

Another disturbing factor for the Australian SAS men as they cleared up and down the highways was the busloads of men heading into Baghdad from neighbouring countries. Always all male and of military age, it was obvious to the diggers that at least some of them were coming to join the fight.

Jihadists — holy warriors — from across the Arab world had descended on Baghdad prior to the start of the war. Jordanian-born al Qaeda mastermind Abu Musab al Zarqawi had also planted his terror cells in Iraq so that they would be ready to sprout once Saddam lost the war. Hard-core Islamic extremists were commonplace in Baghdad as war approached, their ice-cold eyes flickering with contempt for any Westerner they met in a lift or on the street.

For the Australian soldiers, it was galling to watch dozens of young men with one thing on their minds speeding to Baghdad in air-conditioned coaches.

'They all had short haircuts,' recalls Quentin, 'and about a bag of stuff between them, some with military uniforms in amongst their bags and with their passports sequentially numbered.'

Some said they were going to Baghdad to support their families, but the diggers were certain they were going to support the dying Saddam regime.

'They would tell us they were going in to see if their families were all right and stuff like that,' says Sergeant Shane, 'but I think also reports came through that buses were put on for free to get them inside. But there was nothing we could do about it. Which was frustrating on our behalf, because we were thinking, "If these people are going in as fighters and soldiers, it would be nice to stop them here" — but we couldn't. They didn't really do anything wrong.'

At about this time, US Defence Secretary Donald Rumsfeld issued a blunt and very public threat to neighbouring countries, especially Syria, telling them to cease sending their young men across the border.

From day four onwards, and following some well-earnt sleep, the SAS troops cleared along the highway — one troop on the road and the other off to the side — up to the point known as Kilometre 160. On one occasion as they watched an Iraqi position, two Iraqi SUVs with heavy machine guns in the back drove out to observation posts, intent on finding the SAS. At this point Major Paul decided to call in an air strike on the enemy position.

'So we rang up and got some female pilot, and she dropped a few bombs anyway down on that,' Shane recalls. 'I think it was only three bombs we dropped on them at that time, and the plane took off — it was starting to get low on fuel, I think.'

His patrol stayed in the OP for the rest of the night, and the next day they observed several hundred Iraqis milling around the command post.

'We thought, "This is like a gold mine, all this enemy and stuff around there."' But Shane and his men were worried that if they themselves were spotted, the Iraqis might be able to flank them, so they asked for another air strike to try to split the enemy force. At about the same time another troop was contacted — engaged by the enemy — so the aircraft were diverted to them.

Eventually the aircraft came back to Shane's patrol, but by that stage the Iraqis were dug in and the pilots couldn't find them.

One of the A10 pilots decided to take a closer look, and as he got close to the ground the Iraqis opened up with small arms.

'So his mate behind him whacked them with a couple of bombs,' says Shane.

Soon after, the SAS patrols pulled back from Kilometre 160 to plan an assault. That day, a huge sandstorm blew in and all air and ground activity ceased as the diggers, who could barely see a metre ahead, took cover as best they could from the incessant blast of the granules.

The following day, a number of aircraft turned up and spent the day picking off targets at Kilometre 160. It was, however, still too dusty for the Aussies to provide accurate damage reports, so the next day the Americans decided to drop Joint Direct Attack Munitions (JDAMs) onto the hapless Iraqis. These 2000 pound laser-guided weapons can be dropped from up to 25 kilometres from the target and are specifically designed for use in adverse weather conditions. They can also include a hard-target penetrator, allowing them to blast through reinforced concrete.

'So we stood back and they dropped twelve JDAMs on the place,' says Shane. 'We were about 4 or 5 ks away, but you could feel the heat from where we were.'

When the diggers moved in later they found the Iraqis had probably used the cover of the sandstorm to fly the coop.

By the middle of the first week of the war the men were wary about setting up roadblocks and checkpoints. Word had come through about the use of a suicide bomber at a Coalition checkpoint down south in Basra, so the troops approached every vehicle with great caution.

Shane describes the procedure: 'We would put two people in the middle of the road, basically, and they were just pointing guns at people and saying, "Stop!" and hopefully stopping them at 20 to 30 metres away, get 'em out of the car before they even came close to anyone. So that's the best you could do to counter that. If they kept going we were just going to shoot, which happened a few times. There's a few [times], the cars came out, and whether it was language barrier or whatever I dunno. We had some linguists with us, but they just kept driving and driving. At that stage you're worried about the bombs going off so we just shot at the vehicles' engines and they stopped real quick.

'If it is a bomb, you don't want them in the middle of your checkpoint, so you want to stop them at a distance. That was our first major concern — stopping the vehicles, giving them a cursory search. If we think they need a bigger search we pull 'em in, if not we let them go.'

They had to shoot the tyres out of one vehicle whose driver refused to stop as the car headed towards Baghdad; when it was searched they found it contained al Qaeda material, including computer disks.

Sergeant Shane says that the Iraq operation was just like one long patrol for the SAS.

'We got resupplied by air and that was it, we kept pushing on and did what we had to do.'

They had no problems with the American aircraft, but that didn't stop them from looking skywards every time they heard an aircraft and hoping they had all their identifiers switched on so the pilots knew they were friendly.

For Squadron Sergeant Major Steve, one of the biggest challenges was organising aerial resupply. The second 'resup' of the war consisted of thirteen bundles and was the biggest aerial supply drop to Australian forces since World War II.

During the war-game phase of the planning the SAS estimated that resupplies would be required at about 9 and 16 days. Those estimates were based on extensive consultations between Steve and the commanders and senior soldiers as to how much fuel, water, ammunition and food they would use under 'normal' circumstances. But because 'normal' was so hard to define, and due to the intense level of activity — including twenty-two contacts in the first week — the first drop was brought forward to 7 days out.

The resupplies were pre-planned, down to the last detail, at the FOB. Steve said he spoke to all the troop sergeants and asked them what else they needed in terms of batteries, chocolate bars or other luxury items such as cigars. As in Afghanistan, even some of the profoundly committed nonsmokers took up cigar smoking during the war.

'It was a daily occurrence that you'd look around and fuckin' every bloke had a cigar in his mouth,' Steve recalls. 'I remember for one resupply I ordered 300 cigars. Only cheap cigars. The troop sergeant would say, "Oh yeah, I need fifty fucking cigars for my guys." Even the medic . . . we had in our car — he never smoked in his life — said, "Oh fuckin' disgusting", by about week three he had a cigar in his mouth. You could see him fuckin' sitting up there puffing away. It was just a bit of a luxury.'

The habit began during their lead-up time in the FOB base when the American store sold sweet-tasting cigars. Inside enemy territory, Steve reckoned that smoking became a way of passing the time between contacts.

However, ammunition was their most pressing need after the first few busy days, especially the bigger stuff such as Javelin rockets, 40 mill and Mark 19 rounds.

For the resupply drop, a location was selected and the squadron group pushed down there to collect the loot. The drops took place about an hour before first light, when the Hercules transports would sweep in low and fast over the drop zone and kick all the bundles out. The bundles consisted of wooden pallets with a cardboard base, wrapped in plastic. Once they hit terra firma, Steve and his men would go in and cut them open, then distribute the contents.

The different bundles were colour-coded so the men knew exactly what was where once they hit the ground.

Says Steve, 'I'd unstrap the fuel first with a couple of the other guys and we'd essentially just set up a fuckin' petrol station. We'd put in the hand pumps, call the vehicles down. We had the whole squadron resupplied in record time.'

Steve's final job would be to stack all the rubbish and surplus items in a large pile, place the parachutes over the top, throw on some diesel and . . . *whoof!*

He got some bizarre requests for goods and for the biggest — the 14 days drop — some of the men ordered fresh underpants. Some bright spark back at the FOB threw in hundreds of pairs of Army boxer shorts instead.

'So essentially I think I burnt about 1000 pair of boxer shorts in one of the piles of fucked stuff! But, yeah, obviously the priorities were water, food, ammunition, and then the MEIs [mission essential items] come after that, and then, if there was any room, the luxuries.'

The luxury items requested included fresh fruit, cans of Coca-Cola, Mars bars and, on one occasion, a special order for fifty Cuban cigars.

The MEIs, which included replacement radios — especially after the big sandstorm — night-vision gear, compasses, GPS, batteries and weapons, all took priority over the luxuries.

When it was over and he had lit the fires, Steve would make a final sweep of the area to double-check that nothing of value had been left behind.

'Unfortunately a lot of the shit we probably could have left for the Bedouin, but we didn't know that the enemy could have got it either, so we burnt it all.'

One important item that almost didn't make it into the history books was the 1 SAS Squadron flag which Steve ordered on the second drop for the class photograph. The shot shows about twenty-five SAS LRPVs lined up in the desert with the squadron flag flying proudly alongside the Australian and US flags.

'I'd asked for the squadron flag to be put in with the resupply. So I took the resupply, secured it, opened it up, brought the squadron down and I couldn't find the flag. "Fuck! I can't believe they fucked up the flag!"'

Just as they were pulling the parachutes over the piles to torch them, he noticed a yellow envelope taped to one of the bundles. Steve opened it up and there was the flag. So he said to the boss, 'Well, let's get a fuckin' photo here.' The image would later appear in newspapers around Australia.

Back at the FOB, Major Neil had organised a trade with some Americans: Aussie ration packs for boxes of Oreo chocolate biscuits. Some wives had sent over coffee bags, and the Oreos went very nicely with a good cup of coffee.

'The next resupply I didn't drop any Oreos in — I didn't have any — and I got the signal back, "Where are the Oreos, you fucker?"'

Neil says that the types of requests also provided a hint as to the state of morale on the ground. 'You always get, "Send me an inflatable doll" or something. There's always some bullshit. The trouble is, sometimes they could be serious and sometimes they may not be. But it's a sign they're still maintaining their sense of humour.'

The urge for fresh food is strongest when soldiers are away from their base.

For Captain Zan and his troop, on one occasion it meant paying some locals to head into town to buy them some kebabs.

They were at a pump station on the highway where the Bedouin would go to get water. After having a 'birdbath' and filling up their own water supplies, they gave the locals some cash and asked them to get fresh food.

'They brought back these kebabs which were ... I think they were goat or lamb, with some naan and pickled cucumber, and they were disgusting,' Zan remembers. 'The naan bread wasn't bad, but you could taste the gas on it. [They'd] just cooked this stuff over a naked gas flame, not through metal, and it tasted like gas and I think everyone had the shits for about 24 hours after eating it. But still, it was fresh food, sort of.'

When, on day eleven of the war, Saddam's Ministry of Information expelled a South African journalist, Bonny Schoonakker, and myself from Baghdad, we became unwitting witnesses to some of the damage the SAS men were inflicting in the Australian area of operations.

As we were zooming along the highway towards the Jordanian border, we passed one bombed bus with Syrian registration on a bridge that had been hit by an air strike close to Kilometre 160. There was no evidence of any bloodshed, and the fate of the passengers was a mystery, although there were reports of ten Syrians being killed in one hit.

We also passed numerous destroyed Iraqi armoured vehicles and SUVs, not realising that many of these were the handiwork of the Australian SAS. Quite a few of the bridges along the highway had been hit by Coalition air strikes, but the purpose of the damage was unclear, as most had large holes in them but were still passable. Unlike in a jungle or a complex urban environment, those that weren't able to be used simply required us to make a minor detour off the tarmac.

Little did we know that a huge air strike on a facility close to Ar Rutba which was being carried out as we passed was also almost certainly called in by my fellow Australians.

It later transpired that the troops watched the progress of our GMC as it sped towards Jordan in convoy with a French news team heading for Syria. It was on the way back in, ten days later, that we met 'Filthy', whose classic digger shorts, it turned out, were not strictly Army issue.

According to Major Neil, the men had been dropped a complete new set of camouflage clothing because the previous lot had all been ruined in rain and a mudstorm. 'You'd have hoped they wouldn't cut the legs off their trousers, but they sort of had to, really,' he says.

One of the most frustrating things for the men about being on the road and watching the traffic going to and from Baghdad was not being able to duck into the fabled city themselves.

They had a definite point on the road that they were not allowed to pass because it was outside their area of operations, and no amount of pleading would change the mind of the senior commanders in Canberra.

Defence chief General Peter Cosgrove says that at one stage the men were very close to their eastern boundary and were trying to find an excuse to go over it.

'Just a little bit?' they would ask.

'No, don't go over the boundary,' the general told them.

Cosgrove says now that 'for a number of reasons I didn't want them to go over the boundary. That eastern boundary was very important.'

When he visited the squadron in Iraq, Army chief Lieutenant General Peter Leahy was also confronted with pleas of 'What's next?' and 'Can't we go to Baghdad?'

'There were some of those sorts of discussions,' says Leahy, 'because Baghdad was still going off and I think there was a sense, "Okay, we're ready for that, we want to get in there as well." And we were sort of trying to dampen them down a bit.'

For Captain Zan and his men, it was quite frustrating: 'We always wanted to push further east towards the Euphrates. We did get some extensions, but maybe not as far as we would have liked ... In hindsight it's probably a good idea — we weren't fitted for driving around an urban area, we were fitted for the desert.'

The squadron did eventually reach the Euphrates at a town called Baghdadi, close to the defining objective of their mission, the al Asad air base. But none of the diggers crossed the ancient river into the fertile valley of the Tigris and Euphrates rivers, known to students the world over as the cradle of civilisation.

Chapter 25

MIGS AND THE TEMPLE OF DOOM

Having secured a large chunk of Iraq's Western Desert, 1 SAS Squadron turned its attention north, to the massive al Asad air base.

Iraq's largest air force base had always been an objective, but not before the squadron had cleared the Scud line and neutralised Saddam's command and control facilities along their patch of the country's main highway. This was achieved by early April 2003, and while one troop stayed on highway patrol duty, the others and the headquarters moved northwards.

Al Asad is about 200 kilometres west of Baghdad and 80 kilometres north of the highway close to the Euphrates River. It was the jewel in the crown of the Australian mission in Iraq.

About 20 kilometres south of the base were the Kubaysah cement works. Built to service the air base, its vast concrete runways and the surrounding area, the works loomed out of the desert, dominating the flat landscape.

As he observed the structure through his high-powered telescope, squadron commander Major Paul thought it reminded him of the 'temple of doom' from the Indiana Jones movie of the same name. For the next 48 hours the SAS officer, known for his aggressive command style and brilliant tactical mind, pondered how he would clear the works, which stood between his force and al Asad. He didn't want to destroy the facility — which would be important for Iraq's post-war rebuilding phase — or kill anyone if he could avoid it, but he wanted to capture and clear the huge plant that offered plenty of potential as a Scud or WMD hiding place. On one side of the works were the ten-storey-high production towers resembling blast furnaces, and at the other end was a nest of silos for storing the cement. The plant itself was surrounded by compounds containing trucks, workshops and raw materials.

As they moved closer, the diggers saw armed enemy soldiers mingling with civilian factory workers. By this stage the squadron had been in Iraq for close to three weeks, and the men had become familiar with the landscape and the tactics of the enemy. From their observations, and due to the isolated location, they judged that this enemy force was unlikely to consist of hard-core Republican Guard soldiers.

And they were right.

A guard post was located just south of the main approach road to the cement works, so the first objective was to capture that post and gain as much information as they could from the occupants. The shocked Iraqis were duly picked up by an SAS patrol and questioned by an Arabic speaker. They revealed that there were about forty people inside the plant including a small number of armed guards carrying light machine guns and assault rifles.

Rather than risk any collateral damage, Major Paul decided to try to frighten the enemy into submission. In order to do this, he says, 'A show of force was required.'

As the SAS moved towards the works, Major Paul ordered two vehicles around to the rear to cover the only exit from the facility. A four-vehicle assault formation then drove towards the main entry gates as Coalition aircraft circled high overhead. The cars stopped about 800 metres out, just clear of the effective range of the enemy weapons that had been revealed to them by the detainees. Two patrols pushed forward on either side of the road and Major Paul ordered the Iraqi detainees up to the gates with an unambiguous message for those inside: 'Come out or the place will be destroyed in 30 minutes.'

During this particular mission, the diggers had been appalled by how badly the Iraqi military treated its own troops, particularly the conscripts. At one outpost near al Asad, Sergeant Shane's patrol had found an old man inside some berms surrounding an olive grove. The terrified veteran told the diggers that he had been tortured and left in the middle of nowhere, without food, to guard the olive trees.

'They'd left no food with him — he'd been eating grass, living off grass, poor old fellow. He's practically crying when he's talking to us and we felt really sorry for this poor guy, and he ripped his shirt open going, "I hate Saddam's guts" and pointing to himself. We just left him a couple of boxes of rations and gave him some smokes; I think he wanted some smokes. That was the big thing, when we went in we carried cartons and cartons of smokes. When we came across a Bedouin we gave them a couple — it was a big icebreaker, a few smokes — [then] sat down and had a meal with them. Anyway, this poor guy, we just felt so sorry for him.'

The patrol later stopped a suspicious car close by; after disarming its uniformed and well-fed occupants, they were on the verge of commandeering the vehicle and giving it to the old Iraqi to drive out of there.

'Then I thought, "We'd better not start knocking cars off!" The old Robin Hood thing — trying to do the right thing — but you know how it'd turn around and bite you on the bum.'

As he was considering how best to encourage the enemy at the cement works to yield peacefully, Major Paul recalled an incident near Adelaide, some years earlier, when RAAF F-111 strike jets had shattered several glasshouses when they broke the sound barrier, creating sonic booms.

'I had never actually heard the sound barrier broken, but had seen it on the news,' he says, and he thought a similar noisy effect right above the cement works would probably be all that was required to create the desired outcome — namely, to clear the place of enemy while leaving the plant intact. 'It was my assessment that the aircraft would not be in danger.'

Meanwhile, only a small number of civilian workers had opted to join the capitulation, and time was running short.

As luck would have it, the USAF STS specialist attached to Major Paul's headquarters, Technical Sergeant Eric, had used a sonic boom effect during the Afghanistan campaign as a scare tactic. 'It was a show of force, almost crowd control,' Eric says, 'trying to get some people away from us.'

Eric hadn't applied it in a tactical sense, but he was clear on Major Paul's intention. 'Basically just letting them know, "Okay, this one's free, the next one's going to hurt a little more if you don't come out."'

The two men hatched a plan to call in an F-14 fighter and have it fly low and fast over the works, breaking the sound barrier and creating a sonic boom directly over the top of the high towers. Major Paul describes the genesis of the idea: 'Eric and I, we were bouncing ideas off each other, and we wanted to create an effect ... and, you know, just chewing the fat between the two of us, that's what we came up with.'

They sought and received permission to execute their audacious plan from well up the US chain of command, but the first American pilot Eric spoke to reported that he was unable to do the job because his aircraft was carrying too many heavy bombs to do the job safely, plus he was low on fuel. Then suddenly over the airwaves came the voice of an enthusiastic volunteer: 'Yeah, but I sure can!'

The Top Gun pilot's first run was too slow and high to create the main effect. Despite this, the SAS men at the back of the factory reported white flags starting to appear. On his second pass, the American F-14 pilot got it spot on. The boom crashed out precisely over the top of the towers and the shockwave stirred up plenty of cement dust and broke several windows.

As Eric recalls, 'He shook the entire place, and a lot of the guys I was with thought he actually dropped on us, because it was — I mean, it was perfect, and it sounded exactly like a bomb going off. And it was funny to watch almost everybody come out of the compound with their hands up.'

The pilot was keen to come back for another run, but they sent him up to start keeping an eye on things. At that point the SAS troops at the rear of the factory observed a lot of armed men scurrying into bunkers located around the facility. Meanwhile, people from the nearby town had driven out to see what was going on, but bolted as soon as they saw the Australian vehicles.

A number of workers gathered near the front gates, throwing down weapons and putting their hands up. The squadron interpreter went forward and told them that the men in the bunkers had fifteen minutes to surrender or else. And they did.

After a 90-minute operation the SAS had captured the factory and taken about forty prisoners without firing a single shot. Major Paul met the manager, who escorted the soldiers through the plant, and two hours later it had been cleared.

In one of those odd wartime encounters, the two men from vastly different cultures and occupations sat down and had a cup of tea together. The Iraqi asked the young Aussie officer if it would be okay for him to continue production, because the local economy depended on the cement works.

'It was in their interest to get the economy moving so I said, "Go for it." I told him that we would be in the area and would keep an eye on things. Once they realised we were not there to destroy everything, they were quite supportive.'

From the cement works it was just a 20-kilometre drive to al Asad air base. The base had already been extensively bombed by Coalition aircraft. According to US intelligence, there were just two Russian-built MiG fighters at the base and not much else.

It was 9 April 2003, just 20 days into the war, when the SAS first laid eyes on the base. Al Asad is a massive facility with a perimeter that is 14 kilometres long by 7 kilometres wide.

By that time 1 SAS Squadron was dominant in its area of operations and was growing in confidence. They had reports that their

Coalition partners, particularly British SBS patrols north of the Euphrates towards the Syrian border, were being frequently attacked.

'We thought, "The fight's still on here",' says Paul. 'We were then told that we could push; we were waiting for a boundary clearance heading up to al Asad. We knew that the UK were having some good fights up to the north, [so] we thought, "Al Asad's going to be an interesting fight."'

The Aussies wanted to use the airport to either stage their return home or move somewhere else, but the original plan was for the SAS to simply a look at the air base and then start degrading its combat capability.

'It wasn't until the first troop got up there and they started to degrade the base that they realised there weren't too many people there,' says Paul.

In fact, there were about 100 armed men in the facility — and most of them appeared to be looters. The biggest shock, however, was the discovery of a vast stockpile of weapons on the base. Instead of two Migs they found fifty-seven aircraft; several were operational. The collection comprised three new-generation Mig 25 Foxbats, a Mig 29, dozens of old Mig 21s, helicopters, 100 surface-to-air missile systems including the state-of-the-art French-built Roland weapon, and almost 8 million kilograms of high explosives (bombs and other ammunition). There was also an underground command bunker and tunnels containing biological and chemical warfare equipment and antidotes, plus a centre for training in the handling of WMD. The diggers also found vats of what they first thought was mustard gas.

The SAS squadron had hit the jackpot, and it was only because their eyes were on the ground that they picked up the extent of the weapons treasure-trove. After all, intelligence had indicated that there were just two operational Migs at the base.

Not for the first time, the Australians had to deal with the discrepancies caused by the Americans' reliance on their technical capabilities and the hard reality of what the soldiers were witnessing on the ground.

Says Pete Tinley, 'For ten years the Iraqis had learnt how to hide things, which in itself, I think, at some point fuelled [the Americans'] belief that there were WMD.'

In the meantime, the SAS men had set about employing their tried and tested art of deception to convince those occupying the base that they were a much bigger force. They executed this, says Major Paul, 'using snipers and effective, well-placed, well-aimed shots in the vicinity of the enemy that were in there, and [we] created that effect that we were a larger force than we were, and we took it in two days.'

There were still enemy forces on the base and looters around the barracks. The main infrastructure was on low ground, but the airstrip was on the high ground.

'We'd secured the high ground,' says Paul, 'and told the lads to apply fire in the vicinity of the people who were down there. And, you know, a shot would land between their legs [from 800 metres] and they realised, "Holy shit! There's some accurate fire coming here!" And you could see the effect was immediate. They'd run and jump [in]to their cars; as they were trying to drive off . . . rounds would be engaged to the front of them to make sure they kept going, or behind them to make sure they kept going.'

In addition to the sniping and deception, the diggers called in air strikes using RAAF F/A-18 Hornets equipped with 500- and 2000-pound precision-guided bombs to destroy key areas and some aircraft. Under their rules of engagement the Australians could have killed some of the enemy, but Major Paul says there was no need to do that to achieve the task. And, he emphasises, the SAS was not into body counts: 'That's the difference between poorly trained troops and well-trained troops — it's the effect that you're trying to achieve to do the mission. If we had needed to kill them, they would have been killed. But I didn't need to kill them to achieve my aim.

'But be in no doubt — if you want to fight, I'll fight. But if you want to give up and run away and cower in your cell, well, I'm happy with that too. Because we weren't there to destroy Iraq — we were there to liberate as well.

'That's the other thing: we could have destroyed all the aircraft there and everything, but we knew at a point it would just wreak havoc in the country, because they needed to get on their feet.

'The lads knew George Bush's intent, the prime minister's intent, and it wasn't to unleash horror. And I think we got a great deal of respect out of it as well, the way we treated our prisoners, the Iraqi people — the Australian soldiers, fair, firm and professional. They walk away with that. It's gaining the respect from your enemy, I guess.'

During the first day at al Asad, the SAS engaged in a number of small battles as some of the looters decided to take them on over their booty. In one case the enemy engaged them with a four-barrelled 50 calibre anti-aircraft weapon. They had another quick stoush with six Iraqi military who were trying to clear out the armoury.

As the first day at al Asad drew to a close, Major Paul did something he never thought he would do as an SAS officer — he gave what he thinks were the first set of defensive orders ever issued in the history of the regiment.

The SAS was digging in.

He chose his vital high ground — the airport control tower and its surrounds — and issued his orders, telling Eric to get an American AC130 Spectre gunship on station for the night and ordering his men to fortify their defensive positions.

'We got in a position where we could fight come nightfall, because we were very close to Baghdadi, and what the hell was in Baghdadi? We knew that all the people who used to be on the base knew how to get back onto the base.'

Baghdadi is an ancient town of mud huts and date palms on the banks of the crystal-clear Euphrates, just a few kilometres from al Asad.

'It wasn't until probably two nights later, when we were reinforced with a platoon of commandos [from the Holsworthy, NSW-based

4RAR Commando], that we really started to know the base — we had all our positions well established so we could fight if required.'

Paul says that the SAS doesn't normally dig gun pits and fight a defensive battle — that's a job for the infantry.

'We're mobile troops, we're very offensive in our nature. When we're doing SR [special reconnaissance] and we get contacted, we'll return fire and then withdraw.

'This time we were going to hunker down and we were going to fight a defensive battle, you know. The boys had established defensive positions on the high ground, had sited their guns in, were drawing up range cards so they knew what ranges would suit certain things and how to do reference points and all that sort of stuff. So it was a defensive routine — we weren't going to run away, we were going to set in and fight.'

By the time the Commandos were flown in on Australian Army Chinook helicopters, the SAS had secured and cleared about two-thirds of the base. But, says Paul, 'we hadn't cleared the entire base, so we had to put our nodes where guys could observe the dead ground so we didn't get caught by surprise or anything like that. And we had to pick areas where, if someone was going to assault us, we could fight and engage them to the maximum range with our weapons systems.'

The SAS and Commandos repaired one of the bomb-pocked runways using equipment either hot-wired on the base or borrowed from the cement works with the manager's blessing. The first aircraft to land was a C-130 Hercules from 36 Squadron based at Richmond near Sydney, New South Wales.

In addition to the Commandos, the Quick Reaction Force that flew in from the FOB included a troop from the Australian Incident Response Regiment, experts in nuclear, biological and chemical weapons. They also had mechanics to work on the SAS vehicles, which had started to show the strain after three weeks of nonstop operations.

Once the Commandos arrived, 1 SAS Squadron began conducting hearts-and-minds patrols into Baghdadi to win over the locals, and to keep them away from the base.

At its peak, the Australian force on the ground at al Asad included about 200 special forces personnel. It was the largest ever gathering of Australian special forces troops in an operational location. There were also RAAF aircrews flying in and out in C-130s and the Hornet fighters patrolling the skies above. Two Hornets provided a fly-past on 25 April during the Anzac Day service at the base.

In the early stages of assault on al Asad, Major Paul had requested a troop to reinforce his force. But Captain Quentin and his band of merry men were too busy. They were involved in an event of enormous strategic significance: overseeing, with their American comrades, the historic capitulation of the Western Desert on the highway close to Ar Ramadi.

The main US force invading from Kuwait in the south had done a right turn into Baghdad before they got to Ar Ramadi, and the city remained strategically important because it was where most of Iraq's powerful sheikhs had gathered. There was even a rumour that Saddam Hussein might be there.

The sheikhs began to make contact with Quentin's troop, which was the closest Coalition force to the town. A power vacuum had developed and the tribal leaders were jockeying for post-Saddam positions.

'Whoever came in with the Coalition forces, side by side with the Coalition, would become the power base,' says Quentin. 'So every sheikh under the sun came out and would try to speak to us and tell us where there were IEDs [improvised explosive devices] and tell us where the weapons were, so it was a great source of intelligence for us to pass back.

'The trouble was, each sheikh didn't want to be seen dobbing in the other sheikh, so there were all these different sheikhs and we'd have them hidden behind cars and in dead ground [an area away from the others], and another one would turn up and he'd finger-point through the car onto this, with his shamargh up against his eyes with only his eyes showing.

'They'd all be pointing out each other, so our troop interpreter and myself were walking around speaking to each of these guys, trying to work out what information they had and who we could benefit from and all sorts of stuff. At the same time worrying about vehicle-borne IEDs and guys and normal traffic flow that was starting to increase now that most of the bombing from the Americans had slowed down.'

Then a key figure from the former regime, a general who was in charge of the Western Desert, came out and offered to capitulate.

'Then the Yanks came forward and they basically facilitated the capitulation of the Western Desert — this general's in charge of the Western Desert, one third of Iraq,' Quentin says. 'Because we'd been there and we knew who ... the key players [were], we basically handed over all the information to them and they then flew a high-ranking officer from the Yanks in, set up a big table and they had the embedded media turn up, and they videoed the capitulation of the Western Desert. So that was a highlight of the trip.'

It was a historic moment for the United States of America. But behind the scenes it was the young, deceptively baby-faced SAS Captain Quentin, a Queensland country boy, who for that brief moment was probably the most pivotal Australian in Iraq and, possibly, the Middle East.

Chapter 26

GOING HOME

The squadron spent three weeks at al Asad before patrolling back the way they had come, out of Iraq to their forward operating base in a neighbouring country on the first leg of the long journey home to Perth.

Once the air base was secured and the 4RAR Commando troops were in position, providing an outer cordon, the SAS men spent time maintaining and repairing equipment, patrolling out into the local area, fixing the runways where precision-guided bombs had made large craters to render the tarmac useless to the Migs, and generally 'coming down' after the very intense month operating behind enemy lines.

They commemorated Anzac Day in front of a huge reinforced concrete bunker with an Australian flag planted proudly on top of it, and welcomed a number of touring VIPs, including Defence Minister Robert Hill, CDF General Peter Cosgrove and Army chief Lieutenant General Peter Leahy.

Apart from the enormous relief of visiting the squadron and finding the men in fine fettle and all accounted for, Leahy was most satisfied to hear the tales about the Javelin missile.

As Chief of Army, it was not his job to fight wars, but to provide the forces with the wherewithal to do it. He had fought hard to have the regiment equipped with an anti-armour weapon. So when the SAS had encountered Russian T55 tanks in Afghanistan, he had seized the chance to cut short the lumbering bureaucratic process of Defence acquisitions.

'Word came back, "There are tanks up here. We don't like this!" Now in fairly classical special forces reporting systems, they didn't tell us that they had broken down two 55s and they were out the back of the wrecker's yard, but "there were tanks there, we need an anti-armoured weapon",' he says drily.

'Well, now it was time for a spurt of enthusiasm. I can remember calling the minister [Robert Hill] or seeing him somewhere and saying, "I want an anti-armour weapon", and he said, "What do you want? You'd better go and get it."'

The Americans provided the weapon, the troops were trained on it, and when he arrived at al Asad the general was able to hear first-hand from Trooper John the story of the first time an Australian soldier used the Javelin in anger.

'He'd obviously raided the stores on the athletics track [at al Asad] and he actually had a javelin, a field athletic javelin, and he started the demonstration by showing me the javelin,' Leahy says. 'So it was a real sense of humour going on, a sense of pride that he had a story to tell . . . for me it was a pretty special moment.

'Here you see a soldier as proud as punch saying, "The whole battlefield changed that day." And I felt great. I think that's what we should be able to do in Army headquarters — provide the guys very quickly, very smartly, [with] what they need to survive. So to me that was a real sense of completion about the whole process.'

The Chief of Army's eyes light up when he talks about his visit to al Asad.

'I was really proud. I think I was excited because it's *Boys' Own Annual* stuff, isn't it? Your soldiers there have done some pretty incredible things, they'd done some pretty astounding things, and I wanted to share it with them.'

At al Asad in late April 2003, Australia's role in the ground war in Iraq was virtually over and the men of 1 SAS Squadron were starting to relax. 'They were coming down, they were starting to relax,' says Leahy. 'I guess they had a feeling they were safe.'

But the SAS men were itching to take part in an assault on Baghdad, and Leahy had to quell their enthusiasm. 'They were still very alert and still looking pretty mean, in fact, they were looking very dirty and long-haired and dank. So I had the sense that they were coming down, that they were relieved, but that they were still [thinking], "Okay, what's next?"

For Warrant Officer Steve, part of the coming-down process was the realisation that they were finally safe. During Afghanistan the diggers had known that if they were captured by al Qaeda, death might be the most pleasant option.

'It was always tucked in the back of your mind,' he says now. 'In Iraq if we got caught we'd cop a floggin', but we hedged our bets that they were conventional forces and we might get away with a couple of fingers cut off and that was it. But we knew that in Afghanistan, if we got caught, we were fucked.'

Leahy was struck by the fact that in the early part of the twenty-first century Australian soldiers were back where they'd been fighting soon after the start of the previous century. 'I can remember from studying military history, the campaigns of Mesopotamia, that I'd a clear impression of the rivers and how difficult it was going to be and the problems with disease. Nothing had really changed. And that was that sense of the biblical nature of the place, so I guess I felt like, "Well, here are Australians tall again in the Middle East." I felt that we'd been there before, at Beersheba and about the Light Horse and the work that they'd done with [World War I General Harry] Chauvel, so there was that sense. And I know a lot of the guys were trying to look with that sense of the history. There's a definite link there, there's a grave down in Basra that's the first Australian Flying Corps officer to be killed. So there was a sense that we'd been there before.'

Peter Leahy also met with soldiers from the 4RAR Commando Regiment.

'They were right up on their tippytoes, they were so excited to have come in on the game, so excited to be there and they were really up,' he says. 'It was great talking to them, and another one of the stories I'll remember for a long time relates back to making sure they've got the right equipment and that they're properly prepared.

'There was a 4RAR commando sitting under a hoochie, he's ripped the seat out of a Toyota or something and so he's sitting pretty comfortably, 50 cal on a tripod, and I asked him, "How are you going? What's good? What's the best thing that's happened?" And this bloke said, "The best thing is that the Americans have come up here and they want to swap their kit with us, and we told them to fuck off, 'cos they ain't got nothin' we fuckin' want."'

Many of the deficiencies the SAS had identified in Afghanistan had been rectified for Iraq. Yet, despite all the modern technology and sophisticated equipment, the Army boss was left with the strong impression that the basics of soldiering did not really change. 'It was still diggers in a pair of shorts bravely doing their job.'

The Chief of the Australian Army shared his adventure to al Asad with his brother Kevin, an RAAF ground engineer who was serving with the C–130 detachment in Qatar. The two brothers had a great day at the base. They took a helicopter ride out to the cement works and along the Euphrates River, and the chief got to drive a patrol vehicle — although his brother, a qualified vehicle instructor, was less than complimentary about his driving skills. The pair even got to sit in an Iraqi Mig 29 fighter jet.

'Everyone's got a picture of the Mig 29,' Leahy says.

Travelling with Leahy was a team of RAAF engineers whose job it was to strip down a Mig 25 and box it up for the long journey back to the Australian War Memorial in Canberra. However, bureaucracy and diplomatic sensitivities intervened and the boxed-up enemy fighter remains in the Middle East.

As Leahy explains, 'I think there were local sensitivities that they might need them in the future and we'd been seen raking over the bones and dragging stuff out.'

Souvenir-hunting has always been a delicate issue for Australian troops abroad. Down the generations their booty has included all manner of military hardware, and in one famous World War I incident a young French boy, a squadron 'mascot', was smuggled back to Australia.

'We had an agreement from the War Memorial that they would want [the Mig],' says Pete Tinley, 'and they requested it, and did all the official requesting and so on. But the thing is, it was an old Mig that was never going to fly again anyway, so nobody could convey that [to the bureaucrats back home].'

Through official channels they did manage to bring into Australia some captured weapons of historical significance, including the first weapon seized in the Iraq campaign and a couple of AK47 assault rifles from Saddam's palaces. Less officially, some of the men also managed to send home some 'flying' carpets inside bulging map cylinders — but their prized Mig remained elusive.

Afghanistan was a much more productive mission, historically speaking, and the SAS Museum at Swanbourne now holds al Qaeda radios, training manuals, various weapons and other booty from the war against terrorism. And around Perth there are several homes proudly displaying some beautiful Afghan rugs.

The final days for the SAS at al Asad were spent preparing to hand over the base to the Americans, as well as using the time for rest and a re-fit for the men and their cars. Logistics staff and mechanics were flown in to do the repairs and re-equip the vehicles while the troops had a well-earnt break.

Despite this, the squadron was still conducting checkpoints on Highway One and picking up "high-value" Iraqis who were attempting to escape.

'That was pretty much the action,' says Major Paul. 'Then we were told that we were going to patrol back to FOB. We didn't really know what was going to happen from there — whether we were going to go home or go on to subsequent operations.'

Soon after Peter Leahy's visit, the SAS men packed their gear onto their freshly serviced LRPVs and set off for the drive back to their FOB. They had completed what was arguably one of the most successful missions ever undertaken by an Australian military unit overseas and they had done it without suffering even a minor injury. By the most hardened reckoning, it was an incredible feat of arms.

Task Group Commander Lieutenant Colonel Rick says that he wasn't surprised by the success of the mission or the lack of casualties: 'I was pleased, [it was an] incredibly tense time and, yeah, it was good to bring everyone home, there's absolutely no doubt about that. The responsibilities of command are enormous at that level — you're the one who has to look the guys in the eye. And it's great, it's enormously satisfying to know that [when] you've put guys in harm's way, that everyone has done their absolute best and been successful, and then to bring them all home again, having done a job very, very well.

'Furthermore, it was a smart decision to come home quickly rather than sit around over there out of the action and not be tasked. The Australian policy by that time was that we weren't going to continue to be actively engaged in combat operations, so let's get out of there. And that happened quite quickly and that was great for morale. That we obviously did it without any casualties, without even a scratch, is extraordinary. But I like to think, again, it's the quality of the guys, the training, the equipment and the plan that we were working to [that] allowed them to succeed, rather than good luck. You create your own luck, and I think in this case we certainly did that. But war's a dangerous business and will always remain so, so we can't afford to get complacent about it. Iraq was deliberately planned, you had time to rehearse it, validate your procedures, put them into practice in war. Quite unique circumstances, I would think, and I guess it worked.'

Rick has no regrets about being in the command role and not on the battlefield.

'I trusted Paul to get on and do the business on the ground. That's the way command works. That was my job and I was professionally very satisfied in seeing the blokes perform so well, and knowing that it was a team effort.'

He says that everyone involved in the operation knew and understood what the national interest was: 'I think we achieved that, and to do it and come out very quickly is a classic case study in the use of military to achieve national aims. I'm sure that staff college students will study this in some detail!'

There is an old saying that 'the plan' seldom survives the first enemy contact, but in Iraq, the plan not only survived — it endured. The one slight surprise was that Baghdad fell as quickly as it did.

The then Brigadier Mike Hindmarsh, who watched the squadron's progress on a screen at Coalition headquarters in Qatar, said that in his opinion 1 SAS Squadron in Iraq was probably the finest special forces sub-unit that the Australian SAS had ever put in the field. 'Not only because of their background in Afghanistan — they were the first in Afghanistan, so they benefited from that; they also benefited from the evolution, development of equipment from Afghanistan as well. The vehicles were modified, the weaponry was modified, we acquired the Javelins, the cold-weather gear, and ... the communications, so they had the technology.

'But what made them good — and what made the Australian soldier so good in the past and what we've really got to protect is that they still have that "poor cousin" mentality. They remember the days when they never had leading-edge equipment, when they couldn't rely on the fancy gear. Our guys still know how to function without technology. It's an Australian practical hands-on approach of doing business, to rely on your wits and ingenuity, and what you had in Iraq was an organisation which had all these highly tuned basic skills plus high-quality equipment, a potent combination.

'You had a very aggressive squadron commander and three brand-new troop commanders — it's a classic thing, these guys were all brand-spankers but bloody high quality, [plus] all great NCOs, so you had great tactical leadership, great equipment and fantastic individual soldiers — a useful combination!'

The men of 1 SAS were crestfallen that they couldn't continue with another mission, but they left Iraq on a high.

Prime Minister John Howard believes that the Iraq mission was further proof that there is always more to war than simply fighting, and that the Australian military was good at making war peacefully.

'The SAS are people who are very good at the hearts-and-minds stuff,' he says, 'seeing the value of a negotiated settlement. It's contrary to the popular view that their only interest is in vigorous hand-to-hand combat — that is not the case at all. They are small in number, they have a strong sense of comradeship and, therefore, they value the lives of each one of them and they understand the cost of combat.'

Prior to the operation, there had been a debate within the military command about whether or not Iraq was a job for special forces. Some had argued that conventional forces could have achieved the same result. The former head of Special Operations Command, Major General Duncan Lewis, disagreed; he said the main muscle group marching up from Kuwait to Baghdad and along the Tigris–Euphrates axis was a conventional force.

'Special forces, of course, were off to the flanks and the rear, peppering away at the Iraqi exposed flanks and rear areas,' he says now. 'That's historically the classic employment of special forces. We were just part of a much smaller organisation that was working around the flanks and the rear of the Iraqi forces. So the sort of work we were doing was absolutely not able to be conducted by conventional infantry forces out in the Western Desert of Iraq. That would clearly have been beyond the capacity of conventional forces.'

For Rick's 2IC, Pete Tinley, the success of the Iraq plan made the weeks and weeks of planning minutiae that a staff officer must endure worthwhile. 'That was the beauty of Iraq, because it was fantastic — you plan it, then you go and [do] it, then you [come] home and that was the end of it because it had a beginning, a middle and end.

'Timor and Afghanistan had a beginning and a whole bunch of middle.'

But Tinley says that it was also important to realise that, during the Australians' period in the field, the Coalition was never fully tested in an adverse sense.

'The system was never tested, if you like, to the point where it was absolute desperate stakes, where we were losing people or anything like that. We didn't lose anyone; there wasn't a Scud fired; there was, in fact, no WMD found — there was just a whole bunch of contacts, those guys were in contacts every day, and that was always an issue about potentially losing someone, anticipating the need for casualty evacuation and all that sort of stuff, and resupply.'

The final phase of the Iraq plan was to get the men home to Perth as quickly as possible but with an ordered process of debriefing and adjustment so that they could move back into 'normal' everyday life.

After the traumas experienced by Vietnam veterans, a great deal of work has been conducted on the psychological effects of deployments. Captain Quentin says that there is always a period of angst after an operation, but that can be mitigated by a strategy known as 'controlled release'. Instead of just arriving home and going on extended leave, crashing into family routines that have been well established in their absence, the men go back to work for a week or two from nine to five each day, so they can gradually blend back into family life. It results in less shock on both sides.

'So you don't just come home and go straight on leave and go from absolutely zero time with the family to twenty-four hours a day. They go home, they sleep at night, catch up in the morning, have breakfast and then go to work and then come home at night and you do that, so it's controlled release, which I think is a good way of doing things. Plus there's psychological debriefing done at different stages through the period, and if any guys have got any major concerns they can go through the whole process.'

Captain Quentin says that the psychological debriefing offered to SAS soldiers is cutting edge and linked into other systems around the world. 'It's not just "How do you feel?"; it's done on a number of different occasions on different specific periods of time and linked into where you're most vulnerable and when you're most likely to have upsets, and there's no stage where you feel you can't speak to anyone. You've got all the friends within the troop, your squadron, you've got guys outside of the squadron that are in the regiment, plus you've got these psychologists as well.'

A judge in a serious criminal court case in 2004 that involved two SAS veterans from Iraq and Afghanistan raised questions about the psychological effects of SAS operations. The men had conspired to assault a woman who had fallen pregnant to one of them.

'We're offered pretty top-notch psychological counselling,' says Quentin, 'but that doesn't detract from the fact that we're a cross-section of the community and you can't have a cross-section of the community without having some people that are going to be on either end of the equilibrium.'

He feels that the way the SAS was welcomed home honourably — unlike their Vietnam-era colleagues — and were widely praised for their work also contributed to the process of readjusting to normal life.

'The public's perception of what we did — even though they might not agree with the political reason why we went, [they] still agree that what we did over there was good, and we were fair and just and applied force when necessary but never stepped over the mark type of thing. That's just my perception of it.'

Mike Hindmarsh says that the period of low-intensity operations at the end of the deployment also helped. 'They did a lot of their de-psyching out there in the field. The last two weeks there were deadly quiet. They were still in harm's way to a certain extent, but I think [they] had time to chill out. They seem to have come out of it all right at the other end. I mean, they're all clamouring for more operations now!'

For the SAS padre, Dave Jackson, who was stationed at the desert FOB outside Iraq, the war was a surprisingly straightforward operation for the regiment. The good-humoured man of the cloth believes it was definitely the prayers that protected the soldiers from harm out there in the Western Desert.

'Just prior to the guys going over the line, the CO asked me to say a prayer, so I prayed a very brief prayer — the only time I was asked to pray, mind you.'

Because of the lack of casualties, Jackson's workload was kept to a minimum and revolved around a Sunday service, which usually attracted between four and six men, although he did get a record twenty for the Easter Sunday service. He also produced a message board known as 'Prattlings', which he would distribute to commanders on the secure email and ask them to forward to the men.

Padre Dave worked closely with his American spiritual colleagues and he says now that it was amazing to preach to 100 American soldiers, including many African-Americans who really got into their worshipping. According to Jackson, there was gospel singing and lots of shouts of 'Amen, brother, Amen! Preach, brother, preach!'

'They really got fired up,' says Jackson, 'and I got fired up! Their enthusiasm really drove me — it was great. It was interesting, I had a lot of the Americans come back after in the chow hall and they said, "I was moved and touched by your sermon, padre, by your message. It really made me think." I had spoken about integrity [on one occasion]. It really stirred them to a point where they were quite significantly moved. I've never moved Australians quite like that!'

Jackson recalls that there was an incredible confidence in the Australian camp in the lead-up to the war. 'I don't know whether it's our training or what it was, but people weren't focusing so much on the end result. I remember going to one officer and handing him funeral services or ministration at time of death covering Islam and also Christianity. I said, "Look, you might need this if something really bad happens." It had not even entered his mind that he might have to do something like that in the field!'

In his 'Prattlings' and in discussions before the invasion, the padre focused on courage and individual responsibility.

'We looked at personal responsibility, taking personal responsibility for yourself and the actions that you take. We looked at moral and ethical decision-making. This is all prior to going over the wire. And we looked at — because I'd been involved in a lot of trauma situations — how to deal with trauma if you experience it, the sort of first aid of looking after yourself if you're in a traumatic situation.'

Later, the focus shifted to subjects such as relationship enrichment — ways in which the soldiers could support loved ones — plus reunion and the professional consequences of the operation. 'Every soldier that was there was going to have a report written on them, and they were going to see some things in those reports that they didn't like. Dealing with negative feedback — how do you deal with that?'

Overall, the padre enjoyed working with the SAS men because of the 'special excitement' they had about life and their experiences. 'Whatever they feed them in the water, it must be good, because they are just consummate professionals in every trait. And their response to me has been really good and positive.'

Every soldier in the SAS was conscious of the lack of casualties in Iraq and the fact that in all operations since 1999 just one soldier, Andrew Russell, had made the ultimate sacrifice.

Major Neil says that the thought lingering in the back of his mind was always, '"Shit, we've been lucky, when's our luck going to run out?" So everyone's looking over their shoulder looking for the devil all the time.'

The icing on the cake for the men of 1 SAS Squadron — and indeed for the whole regiment and its 'old and bold' past members — was the Unit Citation for Gallantry parade at Swanbourne in June 2004. Not only was it the first time the citation had ever been awarded, but the Governor-General also presented streamers, to be attached to the unit colours to signify the additional citation, to 3 SAS Squadron for its Meritorious Unit Citation for its work in East Timor, and to the entire regiment for its Meritorious Unit Citation for the Afghanistan campaign.

The Unit Citation for Gallantry citation read, in part: 'Through exceptional team work, cohesiveness and military prowess that reflects their training, personal discipline and sustained focus and sacrifice over many years, the combined efforts and sustained gallantry of the 1 Special Air Service Squadron group directly contributed to a comprehensive success for Coalition forces in Iraq.'

Those same words could have been applied to virtually every operation the regiment has conducted.

'The closure to this operation was really important,' says Rick, 'and it's only in hindsight [that] you recognise how important that was. We're so busy charging ahead that we probably didn't necessarily appreciate it at the time. But you've only got to talk to the Vietnam veterans — they didn't have that — and you realise that, yep, we got this one right. For the Vietnam veterans, ex-SAS people, who turned up to that parade in June, this was closure for them as well. There was a lot of emotion. The regiment has finally been recognised for what it has done over a sustained period. Recognition is a very powerful thing. I think it was great.'

Chapter 27

A FAMILY BUSINESS

WANTED: One SAS wife. Must be completely independent, able to manage family and financial affairs alone, be very well organised, prepared to marry a surrogate husband, have nerves of steel and be able to keep secrets. A willingness to undergo SAS selection would be a distinct advantage.

These are some of the key traits that one SAS officer said he would be looking for if he were placing an advertisement seeking a wife.

Anecdotal evidence suggests that most marriages that don't survive the rough and tumble of SAS life involve wives who have come to the regiment from outside, that is, they marry a soldier who later moves into the regiment. It is far better if the soldier meets his wife when he is already in the regiment and he can therefore provide her with a better understanding of what the stresses and strains will be, so that she goes into the union with her eyes wide open.

Former commanding officer Gus Gilmore says that SAS soldiers tend not so much to take their families for granted as to overestimate their tolerance levels. 'You don't realise, until you take a step back, the pressure that it places on them. Not just the fact that you're not home, but a lot of this stuff, a lot of the other little things. You're disappearing at very short notice, with a indefinite return home. People might say, "Everyone's been busy in the ADF", and I think they have, but just the uncertainty from day to day [is hard]. You might quite literally be going to work one morning and you won't be home for some period. You need to have a pretty understanding family, and I think that burden is probably a bit great for some of the families. And always will be, I suspect.'

Captain Nick — who served in East Timor, Afghanistan and raided the *Pong Su* drug ship — says it takes an exceptional person to stand by their SAS man. 'You take your hat off to them, because they do go through a lot of hardships. And everyone has their own personal circumstances; some go through a lot harder than others. Some people might have four kids, three kids, one kid, whatever. It can't be easy.'

SAS life is almost as demanding on wives and families as it is for the men themselves. Not knowing where your husband, father, son or brother is for weeks — and, in some cases, months — on end presents special challenges, especially when there is a household to manage and children to raise.

Just how difficult it can be was shown during the 2003 Iraq war. Retired SAS veteran Major Terry O'Farrell, who was the regimental executive officer at the time, says the delay in getting the green light to deploy kept everyone on edge. There was a lot of preparation going on, but no one really knew when, or indeed if, they were going.

'That had a profound effect back here on the regimental families. There was this air of uncertainty. People just want to know — "Yep, you're going, okay." That's fine — they can get on with life — but it's being in that grey area that's really, really difficult, not only for the guys but certainly for the families.'

As soon as they received the order to deploy to Iraq, the regimental welfare system kicked into action and the families were called in for a briefing.

'The most contentious point about that was [that] there were going to be no communications back home,' says Terry. 'In Afghanistan we'd gone through that period, that initial six-week period, and then comms were established and it went from one phone call a week to, basically, we had a satellite dish and you could phone home every day.

'It becomes surreal in a way because you've got email, you can phone home — all that sort of thing. So even though you're a long way away you're keeping in touch, talk[ing] to the kids and all sorts of things. So people had become accustomed to that, and here we were going to

Iraq and we were going to have a long period — no one knew quite how long — with no contact with the families.'

When Terry stood up and briefed the regiment on the communications blackout, there were a lot of unhappy people in the room.

'And rightly so, but it's for a good reason. And so we managed that through the welfare cell [a small organisation that manages family liaison issues], through mail-outs, through interim get-togethers and all that sort of thing.'

One of the men involved with the comms blackout, Iraq mission troop commander Captain Quentin, says that the men understood the reasons for the restrictions at the time. In his view, if there was a free-for-all and everyone was allowed to speak, that would put the men and the operation at risk in terms of where they were and what they were about to do.

'The guys are pretty smart and realise it's for a reason. And to be honest, [the family's welfare] does play on your mind a fair bit, but you're so busy worrying about everything else and getting everything else squared away, and because you know they're safe, you don't have to worry about them.'

By the same token, it was hard for the blokes not to be able to check on loved ones for weeks on end and to let the families know that they were okay.

'And then the media representation of what was happening as well, that was probably the hardest. [The families] could see American soldiers being shot and wounded and getting dragged back in ambulances, and all the carnage on TV, and not knowing where we were was pretty hard. I don't think it was an enjoyable time for the families, but it was great to have that sort of support.'

Apart from information nights and CDs of photos from the FOB close to Iraq, the families were mostly kept in the dark. Many of the wives and girlfriends in the squadron support one another at such times.

'A troop goes away or a squadron goes away and all those wives and partners band together and have pretty close relationships and have a lot to do with one another,' Quentin says. 'It's pretty hard to talk about something to a stranger or a "civvy", a civilian friend who doesn't really understand the machinations of what's going on, or they can't tell them what's going on. And the unit here has a pretty good network, and all the wives come in and go up to the house and get briefs on what goes on, and that happened throughout the whole thing.'

Some wives choose to do it alone, preferring to maintain a distance between their lives and the regiment.

At about the six-week mark, Terry hosted a barbecue at the SAS Association house, which is an old residence at Campbell Barracks between the headquarters and the officers' mess. He was under considerable pressure from the families to tell them when they would be able to talk to their guys.

'I said, "I think it'll be very soon." Well, bugger me dead, it was the very next day the first phone calls started! And from that time on the pressures went off the families to a degree. But at the same time there were bits and pieces trickling out in the media of what [the SAS] were doing. And of course people were assured on one hand, but [they were saying], "Jeez, they're behind enemy lines, what are they doing?"'

Major Neil, who was Squadron Executive Officer in Iraq, believes the pressure on families is magnified in the information age, as the wives often cannot understand why their husbands have to be completely cut off from them.

'When they're back in Australia, if you were to separate someone for four weeks it wouldn't be too bad, [as] they've got the phone, they've got the email and all the rest of it. The combination of deployment on operations where your husband ... or your partner could be killed and not having that contact, the idea is, "Well, if I can't contact him he must be out doing something dangerous", and that continually wears away at people.'

Neil says that tension reaches fever pitch when there is an incident such as the death of Andrew Russell in Afghanistan.

'We used the satellite phone to ring up quite a few people ... to try to ring their wives direct to say, "It's not him, he's okay." I didn't say who it was and they'd always respond, "Well, who was it?" I'd say, "No, that's it."'

One young mother, Anne, said after Afghanistan that it was very difficult not knowing whether her husband would come home from a mission at all. 'He has just gone away now and I don't know where he is or how long he will be away.'

Anne had been married to her SAS patrol commander husband, Steve, for seven years.

'The most difficult part is the single-mother aspect of it,' she said. 'When your husband is home, it is not for long, and he wants to do the good, fun parts.'

Like many of the wives, Anne is a Perth girl. She knew what Steve did before she said 'I do' and she enjoys strong support from a close and understanding family. That helps enormously, she said, particularly when her husband is away for several Christmases in row. But would she ever pressure him to give up his job?

'Never,' she said.

SAS Captain Bob has been married for seventeen years, and he and his wife have two children. He thinks his lifestyle is hardest on the kids. 'It helps to have a wife that understands,' he says, 'I am very lucky, although the kids don't like it.'

The 'it' can mean setting off for work from his comfortable Perth suburban home in the morning and not returning for a month. During that time he might endure life-threatening situations in the service of his country and at the end not be able to talk to his family about his daring deeds.

A strong network of support organisations has been established to assist SAS families and former members: the Ladies Auxiliary, the SAS Association and the SAS Resources Trust, set up after the 1996 Black Hawk tragedy to supplement compensation for families of SAS men hurt or killed in the line of duty.

Many of the wives are professionals or have jobs of their own, as well as families to take care of without the help of their husband for long stretches. Unlike the old days, it is not simply a matter of saying, 'Let's get the wives together', because many of them either don't want to do that or don't have the time.

Everyone associated with the regiment understands the burden that SAS service places on families. That burden is never more apparent than when an SAS member is killed.

Most of those who have died have been killed in training. Often the families have no idea where the men are training, so when an accident happens there is always the initial thought, 'It could be my husband.'

In June 1996, when fifteen SAS soldiers and three Army aviators died in the Black Hawk disaster near Townsville, not only was the nation's greatest counterterrorism capability virtually wiped out in an instant, but fifteen SAS families and the broad regimental family had to grieve for their own. It was the biggest single tragedy ever to befall the regiment

According to Terry O'Farrell, the impact of the disaster on the regiment was huge. 'I'd been involved in their selection and training, so I knew them personally, and they were all a top bunch of guys, a good bunch of guys. The ripple effect on families, kids, mums and dads, everything [was enormous] ... But the place pulled together very well and it really did a fantastic job, first in reconstituting the CT response, and then in the welfare bit where the whole place got together. There were funerals all over the country, and wives looked after, and out of that came the SAS Resources Trust Fund and all sorts of things.'

The Trust provides funding to help the families of dead or injured SAS soldiers, and to top up what is universally regarded as the meagre and inadequate compensation paid by the government when tragedy strikes.

Terry's wife, Lee, who has been married to him for more than fourteen years, says that the military compensation system for death or serious injury is woefully inadequate, particularly given the hazardous nature of the training and operations undertaken by SAS soldiers.

Lee says that the amount of compensation paid to Andrew Russell's wife, Kylie, after he was killed in Afghanistan was 'atrocious' and simply served to deepen the regiment's distrust of governments of all persuasions.

Lee reckons the Resources Trust was one of the most brilliant things that has ever happened to the regiment: 'It's been a great pleasure to get to know these people. And they are so serious about what they are doing, so generous with their time and money. It is an awesome thing, it really is.'

With the support of many of Perth's political, legal, social and business movers and shakers, the Trust raises tens of thousands of dollars each year to provide educational and other support for the families of those injured or killed during SAS service.

No government has ever been able to come up with a just system for compensating military families. Despite some improvements around the edges, the core problem of how their families might cope remains a major worry for soldiers and families across the Australian Defence Force.

'It doesn't matter which government's in,' says Lee, 'they will all be the same. I really get very annoyed — the politicians keep popping up here, taking the glory. Sometimes I get really shirty, because you know the publicity is for them.'

Terry agrees, and in his book, *Behind Enemy Lines*, he describes in stark terms the plight of some his Vietnam veteran mates, who are still fighting for compensation almost forty years on: 'They have been treated shamefully by a series of uncaring governments.'

A new challenge for the SAS regiment and its family network has been the demanding tempo of operations since 1999. For some individuals it has meant six months away, a few weeks at home and then off again on another deployment or course for weeks or months.

None of the men at Campbell Barracks is complaining. For them it is a dream come true, and any suggestion that they have been too busy and should take it easy is met with howls of derision.

Married father of three Captain Nick says there has been a toll on families, but the reality is that the kind of bloke who joins the SAS loves to be busy. 'If the guys aren't busy, they're losing that professional satisfaction, so there might be more disadvantages to the family — husbands who are not happy because they're sitting around doing nothing.

'That's not to say we are all a bunch of war-mongers — it's not the case. It's just that we're competitive to get on and do the job.'

Lee O'Farrell was pregnant with her and Terry's son, Liam, when the first Gulf War broke out in 1991, and she was surprised by the level of concern for her welfare.

'I was working at the NAB [National Australia Bank] then and it was amazing — they were very protective of me because they were really concerned that I was pregnant and Terry would have to suddenly leave because that first Gulf War was on television 24/7. I think more people were concerned about it than I was, having faith in the regiment.'

As it happened, in that war the SAS only got as far as Kuwait, much to their frustration.

Lee and Terry have a blended family of four kids, and Terry has two older children as well, so life with an SAS husband and father has presented extra challenges to this very modern family. Lee says they take on slightly different roles when Terry is away on deployment. 'I always think it's easy for us at home because we tend to slip into these roles and life will be different than when Dad's here, but I think we come a little bit closer and really just try and keep everyone together so that Terry doesn't have to worry.

'Though it's the first rule of army life anywhere, that as soon as they leave, one of the children needs stitching! And that's probably the worst thing that's happened — that every time he's left, one of the kids has needed to have stitches. And I'm not good with that. Vomit, yes; stitching, no.

'I think routine is very important. Even in just having kids, because routine is a safety mechanism so that you know that if you're going to get up and this, this and this is going to happen . . .'

Another challenge for SAS families is dealing with the secrecy that usually surrounds an SAS mission. For Lee and her family, it has always been understood that if Terry couldn't talk about it, he couldn't talk about it, and that was that. 'If it can be talked about, it will be talked about, and sometimes you just say, "Look, best not say anything." It's never twenty questions or anything like that, because basically it's life — it's your life.'

And what about a stressed-out husband barging back into the household and family life after a lengthy and stressful mission such as Afghanistan?

'Timor wasn't so bad, but coming back from Afghanistan, the transition home was a lot longer and a lot more difficult,' recalls Lee. 'We had some rough times. It's never always peaches and cream.

'I felt very insecure for a while after that because that was the hardest transition back, just for Terry to fit back, even though Afghanistan was [for him] only three months, but it was a very full-on three months with very little respite.'

Lee feels there could have been a little more support for her and all the other wives at the end of that operation, because 'that was the hardest one, but we got through it because we kept talking, instead of somebody retreating to the corner and feeling hurt. The main thing is [that] you have to keep talking, and Terry is very good at that . . . and we're very good at talking.'

Warrant Officer Phil says that the transition back to 'normal' family life can be quite difficult for the men. 'It's a bit hard going into a family life where I haven't been home for six months — longer than that, actually, because I'd been on a course prior to going to Afghanistan. And Dad's suddenly come home to do his thing, and Mum's got the kids in a nice routine, and so that does have its problems. Just coming down again, just to be able to walk around and be nice and natural and normal, sometimes it's a little bit … yeah, it takes a bit to come down sometimes.'

In addition to the extensive professional counselling and psychological debriefing and support services offered to SAS troops, regimental padre Dave Jackson has an open-door policy. He is not a professional counsellor, but he acts as a sounding board for soldiers or their families who have problems or other issues. A lot of his time is taken up with grief and relationship counselling.

Because many of the men have married Perth girls who enjoy strong local family support and their own professional and personal networks, they tend to be quite settled. Jackson thinks that this is why the rate of marriage breakdown in the SAS is below the levels seen in the wider Australian Army.

'They don't need the unit to provide the home support,' he explains, 'because that's already embedded in the local community, family, extended family. So a lot of them don't need to use the sort of services that I certainly can offer or the military can offer. Many of them have young children or growing children and they tend to be a lot more settled.'

For the younger, single soldiers, however, the stresses of the job can have a negative impact on relationships.

'A lot of the single blokes might have had a girlfriend when they left, [and] when they come back they discover that she's gone, and they go and find somebody else. It's not an easy life for a guy to establish a relationship, let alone marry and then have children and do the rest of it.'

But, he says, those relationships that do break up after a deployment usually had problems before the soldier left the country. 'The absence just makes the problem come to a head, essentially.'

As far as Jackson knows, just one relationship broke down after the Iraq war deployment.

Much of the padre's work revolves around family support issues, but he uses his 'Prattlings' to canvass a wide range of topics and examine issues related to the character development of SAS soldiers by focusing on a topic that might be current in the unit or in society.

'Recently I did "Prattlings" on torture because of what was happening in Iraq at the time — in the infamous jail there [Abu Ghraib] — and had some reflection on what that might be. That was probably the topic that's created the most interest, of all the topics that I've done.

'They were obviously disgusted with what was happening. I find that the people here in the unit do have a high ethical and moral foundation. I'm fairly confident that they approach their job with that sort of concept in mind. If we're going to do what we're going to do, we're going to do it well and with integrity.'

EPILOGUE

The two young diggers lurched arm in arm from one table to the next, seeking out half-empty wine bottles. Their dinner shirts were hanging out, buttons undone, black bow ties askew.

The SAS fortieth anniversary ball, held in September 2004 in Perth, was drawing to a close and this pair was determined that no glass should be left unturned.

As they staggered to one table up near the front they noticed an unopened bottle of vintage port; one picked it up. Then they both looked around and noticed the owner of the expensive drop giving them the evil eye. It was Major Terry O'Farrell. The port was his farewell gift and had been presented to him earlier in the evening. The diggers sheepishly replaced the bottle and, with knowing smiles, staggered away. Dutch courage is one thing; stupidity is another.

On the balcony overlooking the Swan River, which looked like a dance floor for Perth's twinkling city lights, some of the men from 1 SAS Squadron were enjoying Cuban cigars and reminiscing about what had been an extraordinary four years. Major Paul, Captain Quentin, Warrant Officer Steve and Trooper John were all freshly groomed and resplendent in their dinner suits, a far cry from the stubble, stench and unwashed camouflage gear of Iraq's Western Desert. As their wives and girlfriends chatted happily and waited for the next dance, the men smoked, talked, drank and laughed. Other couples simply danced the night away.

For Australia's top soldiers and some of the 'old and bold' ex-SAS members, it was a night to savour. The regiment had come through the

Iraq campaign relatively unscathed and had been awarded the nation's first ever Unit Citation for Gallantry. Things were good, and there would be plenty of sore heads at Swanbourne the next day to prove it.

The fortieth anniversary bash marked the end of the most sustained period of operational activity for the Australian SAS since the Vietnam War. Much to the consternation of its members, the regiment's public profile was higher than ever. East Timor, the Sydney Olympics, the *Tampa*, Afghanistan and Iraq all meant media exposure and growing public awareness of what the army's most secretive unit had been up to.

The SAS had hit centre stage in the Australian production of the global war against terrorism.

The period after September 11 also marked the birth of the Special Operations Command (SOCOM) and the investment of more than half a billion taxpayer dollars, over four years, in the latest high-tech military equipment. The SOCOM motto is, after all, 'the cutting edge'.

The SAS had become the government's force of choice and SOCOM has doubled in size in five years. It had added the 4RAR Commandos, Logistics Command Support Company, the Sydney-based TAG East and the Incident Response Regiment to its ranks. Despite all of this, SOCOM accounted for just 2.1 cents in every Defence dollar spent.

By late 2004, Major General Duncan Lewis's long career in the shadowy world of special forces had drawn to a close. As he says, 'It's been quite a journey to get that organisation structured, resourced and stood up to meet this new threat, and, more importantly, to get it plugged into the whole-of-government structures that we have in Australia for protecting our community.'

Lewis himself would go on to play a key whole-of-government role, this time on the civilian side in a senior national security job.

The global security situation post-September 11 also created a high private-sector demand for ex-SAS troopers, from security firms willing to pay large sums of money to well-trained soldiers who could properly secure their clients. Other government schemes such as the sky marshal program and an expanding intelligence network also took a toll on the regiment. For young men who thrive on action, the seductive combination of dollars and danger could be difficult to resist.

That is not to say that SAS troops are not well remunerated. They are paid more than other soldiers, and operational deployments can be quite lucrative, with more allowances and tax exemptions. Many young troopers own good cars and investment properties, but it is action that they crave.

The regiment counters the big-dollar lure by offering variety, cutting-edge skills, family support and dynamic tasks in new and often exotic places all over the world.

In the lunch marquee after the Unit Citation parade in June 2004, what Prime Minister John Howard and the top brass heard over and over again was, 'When's our next job?' It was an interesting question for them to digest along with their seafood buffet.

As they chatted casually with these smart young men, all spruced up in their dress uniforms, there was a certain amount of awe on the faces of the grey-suited politicians and their officials for what these Australians had already done in those faraway war zones. And here they were, begging to go again.

Following the Iraq operation, anecdotal evidence was emerging that the gloss had worn off the high-paid security jobs and some soldiers who had left were knocking on the door to get back in. The drift back has also been assisted by the growing and more central role for special forces on the modern-day battlefield. Certainly, the SAS has shifted from being a fringe player to a central player in any Coalition operation.

General Lewis, as he now is, likens the modern military force to the carriages of a railway train: at the front, he says, are the special forces with their cutting-edge technology; behind them are the conventional forces. 'You gradually move the passengers, if you like, from the front to the back. So there's a transfer of technologies and capabilities from front to the back of the train, but the whole show's still moving along.'

The CO during the Iraq operation, Lieutenant Colonel Rick, says it was important for the SAS to tell the story of these high-profile years when, on so many operations, they had been *the* Australian contribution.

'From here on in, I don't see SAS doing what we have done necessarily over the last couple of operations. Because the rest of the Army is developing — if we had to do Iraq again in a few years' time, it would be someone else doing it, probably.' The SAS would still have a role, but the main task would be undertaken by the Commandos or some other force.

'Our future will be in less conventional operations where small forces are required to provide discreet solutions,' he continues. 'We're constantly evolving, and as new opportunities present themselves, a door opens, we'll check out what's down that hallway. That's been the nature of this place ever since it was raised. We need to recede into the shadows because the work that we will do in the future will be sensitive.'

Defence Chief General Peter Cosgrove, who has been more directly responsible than anyone else for the emergence of the SAS into the limelight, makes no apology for the part he has played in boosting the regiment's profile. 'There may be some elements of the overall SF community who say, "Unseen, unheard". Well, that's rubbish.

'These are Australians doing great things for their nation. We might say, "Please understand we don't like to put the microscope on them because it means one of the big advantages, the sophisticated nature of their tactics, remains a battlefield advantage." Apart from that, Australia needs its heroes and the SAS is often a source of our heroes.

'We do try to protect their identities, but I think we owe it to the people to say that these ordinary Aussies, trained to an extraordinary degree, are making them proud.'

INDEX